The Violence Within

THE
VIOLENCE WITHIN

PAUL TOURNIER

Published in San Francisco by
HARPER & ROW, PUBLISHERS
New York, Hagerstown, San Francisco, London

Translated by Edwin Hudson from the French *Violence et Puissance*.
Delachaux et Niestlé, Neuchâtel and Paris, 1977. © Delachaux et
Niestlé 1977.

FIRST U.S. EDITION

First published in English, 1978, under the title THE VIOLENCE INSIDE by
SCM Press Ltd.

Library of Congress Cataloging in Publication Data

Tournier, Paul
　　The violence within.

　　Bibliography
　　1. Violence—Moral and religious aspects.
　　2. Psychiatry and religion. I. Title.
BT736.15.T68　　241　　78-3139
ISBN 0-06-068293-0

78 79 80 81 82　　10 9 8 7 6 5 4 3 2 1

CONTENTS

Part I VIOLENCE

Part II POWER

PART I

VIOLENCE

1 AMBIGUITY

We are all against violence; but we are all also to some degree in favour of it. We all condemn it, and we all have a certain respect for it.

Against violence. Naturally there will be little chance of your discussing the point with the members of a guerrilla raiding-party with their hostages held at gun-point and claiming justification for their violence. The people you meet are more likely to be honest, peaceful folk, who nevertheless get worked up at the thought of violence, who are properly indignant, and condemn violence in severe – sometimes even violent – terms. They want it put down ruthlessly – violently.

In favour of violence. Those honest peaceful folk, without exception, honour their country's heroes; they admire their courage, their struggles and their victories. Our national holidays are, as often as not, celebrations of violence, homage quite properly paid to the violence of our ancestors as they founded our nation. The United States, as I write, is celebrating amid great festivity the proclamation of their independence on the Fourth of July 1776. A great day indeed, filled with the ideals of liberty, peace, and brotherhood. But no one would be celebrating it today if George Washington had not at once set about organizing the federal army and leading it to victory over the English at Saratoga Springs and later at Yorktown. La Fayette's popularity in the United States is solely due to the enthusiasm and conviction with which he threw himself into the adventure, bringing to it the reinforcement of his violence.

In the same way we Swiss commemorate on 1 August the first pact between the Confederates, sworn in 1291 on the plain of Grütli in the name of Almighty God. It was an oath of mutual assistance, a generous brotherly act *par excellence*, but one which would be quite unremembered today had not the parties to the oath shortly afterwards been involved in violent conflict with the armies of the Duke of Habsburg, and had they not defeated them at Morgarten, Sempach, and Näfels. What is really being acclaimed is the triumph of a historical revolt. All our heroes were men of violence.

In Geneva we celebrate the victory of the Escalade of 1602, and venerate Dame Royaume, who hurled her cooking-pot from her window onto the head of a Savoyard soldier. The French too have a heroine, Joan of Arc, whose infectious violence made them conscious that they were a nation. And on 14 July they celebrate the fall of the Bastille, which inaugurated the long series of acts of violence of the French Revolution. Cavour was a man of violence; as was Lenin; and Mao Tse-Tung. The examples from history are endless.

Thus violence is ambiguous, sometimes condemned, sometimes praised, depending on the camp to which the critics or admirers belong. It raises therefore for our consideration difficult problems which cannot be settled by superficial pronouncements about justifiable or unjustifiable, malignant or benign violence.

No one was ever better qualified to face these difficulties than the Californian Professor Dr Friedrich Hacker, a psychoanalyst of vast experience in the study of the human mind and its unconscious depths, and a psychiatrist who has appeared as an expert witness in several important criminal prosecutions, notably that of the murderers of the film-star Sharon Tate along with a number of other persons – a frightful slaughter perpetrated by a group of fanatics fascinated by Charles Manson.

Out of his experiences Dr Hacker has written, under the title *Agression, violence dans le monde moderne*, a remarkable book which will serve to guide us in our thoughts. It is a book which I value not only for the ideas it contains. It has for me a symbolic and emotional significance which my readers will understand when I tell them of the special circumstances in which it was lent to me by an old friend. He was a very dear friend with whom I had been closely associated over a number of years in a common spiritual experience. We had campaigned together over a long period, but then a sharp divergence of views had separated us.

We both felt the breach keenly. Of course each respected the other's point of view, but collaboration was no longer possible without one or other of us being false to his convictions. And now, twenty-five years later, on his initiative, we had resumed our old intimacy. It was a moving reunion, and it proved that violent conflicts can be resolved, not by some artificial compromise, or by the passage of time, but in the most complete and authentic fashion, and without reserve. It is perhaps because I believe that such responses to violence are possible that I dare in my turn to undertake this book.

When I told my friend about what I had in mind, he handed me Dr Hacker's book, which he had read with great interest. When we take to a book it is sometimes as much on account of the person who suggested it to us as because of who wrote it. The fact is that throughout his book Dr Hacker dwells on the many aspects of this ambiguity of violence to which I have just referred. His aim is to remove the perplexity in which those who try to sort out the difficulties find themselves. He is eager to find an objective criterion for distinguishing good violence from bad.

It is an oversimplification to use the terms good and bad, but that in fact is what is involved. We are not concerned with whether violence is legal or illegal, since it is after all the powerful who make the laws, and those who oppose them can do so only by violating their laws. We want to know in what circumstances violence is justifiable, useful, even necessary, and when it is harmful and wrong.

In order to distinguish clearly between the two kinds of violence, Dr Hacker uses two different terms: he calls it aggression when it is legitimate, and violence when it is not. And so he is able to say right from the start of his book: 'I am not against aggression, but I am against violence.' And later he declares: 'All aggression is not violence, but all violence is aggression.'

He actually uses the word aggression to designate a whole gamut of reactions, 'from simple self-affirmation to barbarity', but he reserves the term violence for one of the extremes, that of barbarity. Another comparison likens aggression to the spectrum, in which only one colour – red, of course – represents violence. This almost amounts to considering natural and normal aggressiveness as a sort of mini-violence which would merit the name of violence only beyond a certain threshold of cruelty.

That seems to me to be merely playing with words and definitions. Is it not sometimes the most atrocious acts of violence that seem to us legitimate and salutary, such as those which had to be used to crush the satanic power of Hitler, for example? They were in no sense acts of mini-violence. Similarly, velvet-glove violence, while not in the least bloody, may often be objectionable.

Might we, then, base the subtle distinction between these two terms, aggression and violence, on the intentions, the motives, of the actors in the drama? Again, we may not. Revolutionaries are always imbued with the best of intentions, such as bringing in liberty and justice. The same is true of those who resist them. We cannot condemn all violence, any more than we can condone it.

Dr Hacker himself is well aware of the fineness of the distinction he makes between the two words, violence and aggression, since at the end of his book he brings them together, whereas at the beginning he had carefully separated them: 'We always come back to the same thing,' he writes, 'to the differentiation . . . between justified and unjustified aggression, between defensive and offensive violence.' Yes, of course it is not the word, but the thing, that matters. As he says, the real problem is how to decide whether an act of violence is justified or not; and the trouble is that we have no objective criterion by which we can judge.

With him, we must acknowledge that there is in nature a force – whether we call it aggression or violence – which is normal and healthy, which introduces a relationship of rivalry between individuals, a dynamic equilibrium which can be observed in all vital phenomena. It is more than an effect of life; it is the very essence of life. And we must also acknowledge that there can be a sudden brutal amplification of this force – whether we call it aggression or violence – which no longer serves life, but acts against it, sowing the seeds of death.

2 NECESSARY AGGRESSION

Rightly, then, Dr Hacker insists on the need for a criterion: where does the frontier lie between the beneficial and the harmful forms of aggression and violence? They have too often been lumped together in the same over-simple and unrealistic condemnation of every aggressive or violent manifestation, and looked upon as necessarily brutal and inhuman. The truly human qualities, it has been naïvely thought, are sweetness, selflessness, and a complete absence of aggressiveness.

A scientific study will oblige us to differentiate between the constructive phenomena and the destructive phenomena which have thus both been equally condemned. A British psychiatrist, Dr Anthony Storr, states in the introduction to his book *Human Aggression* that the word aggression 'is used both of the competitive striving of a footballer and also of the bloody violence of a murderer'.

As we shall see, however, this distinction raises difficult problems.

Our eyes have been opened by the biologists, notably the Austrian Konrad Lorenz, Nobel prize-winner for medicine, in his work on aggression in animals. He has shown the essential role of aggression in the preservation of the life of the individual and of the species. It has a threefold function: the even distribution of the species in the territory, natural selection among rivals, and the indispensable defence of the young.

This last function is so obvious it scarcely calls for comment. I shall have more to say later about selection among rivals. As for the sharing out of territory, it leads to some very interesting observations. When a robin sings, it is displaying its aggressiveness; it is informing all other robins that it has taken possession of a territory which they must respect. This conventional ritual is so well respected that it results not in fights between robins violating it, but in their harmonious dispersal to other territories, so that each can secure an adequate share of the available food supply.

More remarkable still: as Lorenz has shown, so long as animals live in flocks, in undifferentiated bands, there is no aggressiveness among them, but also there are only anonymous relationships. It is among the territorial animals that there appears the personal differentiation which is the necessary condition for the development of personal feelings – attachment, friendship, loyalty, love – features of a superior social organization. So that aggressiveness proves to be a necessary condition for evolutionary and social progress. 'It is only when intense aggressiveness exists between two individuals that love can arise,' writes Storr (p.36).

It will be seen that all the investigators whom I quote, and many others besides, are compelling us today in some sense to rehabilitate aggressiveness. It is no longer only a calamity which must be warded off, a bad fault which must be corrected through education, a morbid state which must be treated by the doctor, a crime which must be punished by the law. It is not a perversion in a few individuals, but a force of nature present in every living thing, a gift of life which can have both beneficent and unfortunate results, depending on the use that is made of it. In the animals this use is regulated by instinct, whereas man must assume responsibility for it through free ethical choices.

Aggressiveness, then, can be seen as the very expression of life, the natural, expansive force of life, characteristic of life, with all its possible results for good or evil; but without it life would not exist. Freud, in *Civilization and its Discontents* (p.114), describes aggressiveness as an 'indestructible feature of human nature'.

'Life is the struggle against death,' as Bichat said. Life has in fact been described as the aggregate of those phenomena which struggle against death. The struggle is, therefore, a fatal one, and on every living organism it imposes inevitable conflicts with its environment, with the inorganic world whose forces it must tame, with nature upon which it depends for food, and finally with other living beings, themselves endowed with the same aggressiveness, which each must confront in an ever-changing equilibrium.

In a word, aggressiveness is an instinct. Freud asserted this. At first he recognized only the sex instinct, the importance of which was so little understood at the beginning of this century. But from 1915 onwards, doubtless under the influence of the war, which greatly affected him, he speaks also of the instinct of aggression. Nevertheless he always saw only its destructive aspect, and this soon led him, in 1920, to formulate his hypothesis of a death instinct.

Now, as the work of the biologists has shown, aggressiveness is not a death instinct, but a life instinct. It is the instinct of self-preservation which constrains every animal and every human being to constant self-defence, to 'save his skin', to inspire respect by a more or less threatening display of strength.

Life is a perpetual combat, a call to combat, an imperious duty to fight, as witness the heroes of mythology of which Paul Diel writes; a Perseus or a Bellerophon faced with the need to confront and defeat Medusa or the Chimaera. We meet with these conflicts in our own dreams and in the dreams of our patients, beset with dragons and other fearful monsters. Our unconscious proves to be more aware than our conscious minds of the harsh laws of life.

It has sometimes been disputed that aggressiveness is really an instinct. Some psychologists have attempted to interpret it as a reflex of frustration, and therefore as a movement provoked from outside, and not as an ever-present impulse proceeding from inside. The biologists deny this. Konrad Lorenz has written a foreword to Dr Hacker's book. He points out with approval that the author describes aggressiveness as an instinct and not as a reflex. And Storr writes (p.109): 'Aggression is a drive as innate, as natural, and powerful as sex, and . . . the theory that aggression is nothing but a response to frustration is no longer tenable in the light of biological research.'

The same author (p.2) shows us the considerable role played by aggressiveness in the development of the child from the very first day. 'Psychoanalysts with special experience in treating small children claim that even infants inevitably entertain destructive phantasies of terrifying intensity.' Just think of an infant in a tantrum – you would be terrified of him if he were your size! According to Melanie Klein, the infant is dominated from birth by a conflict between love and hate. Dr Charles Nodet writes: 'Aggressiveness is the necessary companion of love. This vital link between aggressiveness and love must never be forgotten. To stifle one is to stifle the other.' And Dr Guggenbühl-Craig: 'Every relationship, sexual or otherwise, contains a double potential of love and hate.'

It is not accidental, Storr remarks (p.46), that 'most of the games which children play have an obvious aggressive content'. Simply because the child is dependent and must achieve autonomy, he has no other resource than aggression against those on whom he depends if he is to differentiate himself and win his personal identity. He needs to clash with the strict authority of his parents in order to stimulate his aggressiveness. The child that is brought up too liberally, by people who give in to his every whim, will be unfitted for the struggle of life.

That struggle will remain a necessity throughout life, in order to strengthen the personality, to maintain its dynamic thrust and to stimulate its creativity. Aggression is not a necessary evil, it is good and beneficial so long as it does not degenerate into destructive violence. Competition is the source of personal progress, as all sportsmen know.

Bertrand Russell is to be admired for his struggle against war. And note that he is admired precisely because he acted courageously, because he was a fighter. But his idealistic dream of a society without aggressiveness was utopian. Perhaps we shall know it in the Beyond, in a world in which each of us will be fulfilled. But not in this world, conditioned as it is by Nature. Again it is Storr who points out (p.53) that 'Unless some biological mutation alters the whole character of man as a species, it is impossible to believe that there could ever be a society without strife and competition.' In such a society, he says, 'it is more likely that creativity would decline than that it would flourish'.

One must defend oneself, one must be strong, even threatening, not to conquer and destroy but in order to be recognized as a person and respected by others. Even in a psychiatric hospital, as Dr

Badiche remarks, 'being aggressive is sometimes the only way of escaping from the anonymity of overcrowded wards'. And nowadays the whole world is overcrowded, and I think that this explains some of the reactions of the young, who experience a feeling that was unknown to us when we were their age, the feeling of being swamped in the mass, of not counting as a person.

Dr Kurt Adler, the son of Alfred Adler, the founder of individual psychology, underlines this: 'More and more individuals are coming to feel that they are non-persons . . .' From this comes a 'feeling of insignificance'. 'Violence,' he adds, 'is a way of proving that one exists, when one believes oneself to be insignificant . . .' It should be noted that inspiring respect means inspiring fear. We talk now of the 'deterrent' in regard to the atomic bombs which the great powers are stockpiling in their underground arsenals. The word may be new, but the fact is as old and as universal as the human race. The Romans said: '*Si vis pacem, para bellum* – if you want peace, prepare for war.'

In support of this contention I can take as an example, on the modest scale of my own psychological observation, the little every-day gesture of the index finger wagged in someone's face, which means: 'Look out! Don't try my patience too far, or I shall get annoyed and turn to violence!'

Thus when a noisy child annoys the grown-ups, his father reprimands him, gently at first. But if the child does not obey, the father's voice becomes sharper – the first intimation of violence! And if the child goes on making a noise, the father's finger is raised. Even if it is done with a smile, the gesture reminds the child that his father is stronger than he is, and that he could give him a slap or a spanking and that the child could not retaliate. Such was the braggadocio of Goliath in face of David.

Often the threat has the opposite effect to that intended, because although the father is physically the stronger, the child has the moral advantage of being able to put his father on the horns of a humiliating dilemma: either the shame of giving way to someone weaker than himself, or else the shame of publicly striking this weaker person. So the child is stubborn, he shouts and screams. We see the beginning of one of those 'escalations of violence' we hear so much about nowadays.

One often gets out of the difficulty by means of some diversion or ruse, and the child willingly plays along, pleased to have got off so lightly; especially pleased at no longer having to defy the threat, since it has been removed. In any case the attitude of the father, sure of his physical superiority, was possibly a little ambiguous! Possibly he played the bogy-man without much conviction. As he scolded the child he may well have reflected with satisfaction that this was a boy who would know what he wanted in life, and would not be prepared to let anyone ride roughshod over him.

When you think about it, you realize that all social relationships follow this pattern; that between two persons, even between friends or between a loving husband and wife, there is always a certain equilibrium of forces established. Each has to establish a position, manoeuvring his pawns in the little game so as to get himself into a position of strength.

It is an unstable equilibrium, involving physical, moral, even legal factors, and factors to do with seduction and charm; an equilibrium which may be endangered by scruples or diffidence, or fortified by reputation, social esteem, or rhetorical skill. Many a wife has said to me: 'I can't argue with my husband – he always has the last word.' And many a husband: 'Discussion is impossible with my wife; she takes every remark as a personal criticism, and ends up in floods of tears.'

What, then, is the situation between two rivals, two dynamic (i.e. aggressive) business-men, between two diplomats – even between two artists or two scientists, in the elevated atmosphere of academic debate? Balance of power means balance of fear. Pupils fear the teacher who may punish them unjustly. But the teacher also fears the pupils, who may despise him unjustly, or call his competence in question by their failures.

Life is a struggle, a struggle to win and keep a place in society. It is only the very powerful who do not have to wag a minatory finger, because no one challenges them. Nothing is done without some degree of violence. If we are to believe the tragic poets, time was when people talked a lot about defending their honour and reputation. Nowadays the psychologists' watchword is simply self-affirmation. But it is the same thing. We have to have a sufficient dose of aggressiveness in order to stand up to the aggressiveness of others, and the equilibrium is always in danger of turning into a trial of strength.

The philosopher Georges Gusdorf, in his book *La vertu de force*, makes a careful distinction between strength and violence. He demonstrates that despite appearances violence is more a sign of weakness than of strength; relative weakness at least. 'Violence is the opposite of strength, for the energy it brings to bear is only the energy of despair.' Despair of 'winning the argument by argument', as he puts it; despair of being strong enough to sustain the dialogue. The stronger one is, the less one needs to show one's strength.

3   INSTINCT, ANIMAL AND MAN

You remember Dr Hacker's question from which we started. In order to win respect you have to threaten violence, and to threaten it is to take the first step in a gradation of charge and counter-charge towards violence itself. Where, he asks, is the frontier between legitimate and culpable violence? Where is the guard that patrols the frontier? Who is the policeman who authorizes and even promotes aggressive competition between brothers, but prevents them from killing each other?

In the animals it is instinct. Once again we are indebted to Konrad Lorenz for this remarkable observation. An animal kills in order to eat, without passion, without hate, one might even say peacefully. It kills what its instinct tells it is food, but not its own brother. Cats kill mice, not cats. This is order, not disorder. Meanwhile man kills man – and cats and mice as well.

On the other hand animals are extremely aggressive towards their fellows of the same species. In Lorenz's aquarium one fish attacks another of the same species in preference to any other; but this sort of aggression does not lead to murder. Most combats between animals of the same species are not aimed at the annihilation of the weaker adversary, but rather at the recognition of the supremacy of the stronger.

It is in fact very rare for one animal to kill another of the same species. The loser breaks off the combat when he no longer feels that he is strong enough to sustain it. And the victor, satisfied with his triumph, is content to let him go, without pursuing him in order to exterminate him, and without the need for a referee – as in a boxing-ring – to interpose himself between the adversaries in order to forestall a mortal blow.

In animals, then, powerful instinctive inhibitions take the place of the referee, guarding against reciprocal murder between individuals of the same species. These inhibitions clearly minister to the conservation of the species. Thus natural aggression is seen not as a destructive force, but as a constructive mechanism, building up the community by selecting leaders to organize and rule it. For if there is no longer any sufficiently aggressive authority in a society, it collapses in chaos.

This reminds one of the tourneys of the Middle Ages, which were ritualized like the combats between Lorenz's animals, and which served to establish the feudal hierarchy rather than to destroy the fabric of society: the vanquished made his submission, declaring his allegiance to the victor, whose authority was thus recognized and respected. Clearly, in this way aggression serves and organizes life, and reinforces social solidarity.

Moreover, it seems that in our own day still, among so-called primitive peoples, combat has this same constructive function. René Girard describes how the Kurelu tribes of New Guinea are perpetually at war with each other, but without there being many deaths! It is enough for one of the warriors on either of the two sides to be wounded for the battle to be broken off by common consent, and for everyone to go back home. The battle is thus a sort of ritual ensuring social cohesion on each side. It is rather like bullfighting without the killing of the bull.

Of René Girard's book I shall have more to say. Speaking of the sacrificial rites of primitive religions, he distinguishes between this 'constructive violence', constructive of the cohesion necessary to every human community, and 'reciprocal violence', violence of every individual against every other, which leads to generalized murder; it characterizes a decaying society in which there is no longer any recognized authority that could impose social order. Similarly Erich Fromm distinguishes between what he calls 'defensive aggression' and 'destructive aggression', the latter being characteristic of man.

Thus, in their instinctive behaviour there is a marked contrast between man and the animals. In animals, violence fulfils the function of selecting between rivals and of social ritualization. It does not lead to murder between brothers, since this is excluded by the instinct of conservation of the species. It is this instinctive veto which is manifestly absent in man, man who is capable of annihilating his whole race.

Ever since Cain and Abel man has been obsessed by the idea of exterminating his rival. He massacres other men just as readily as he kills bears, hares, or fish. He kills them in their millions. The same governments which today bewail the wave of violence which is sweeping over our world, unleashed that violence in two monstrously murderous world wars. As Dr Hacker writes, 'violence is as contagious as the plague'. Cats kill mice, but cats do not kill cats; whereas men kill men.

Mention of cats reminds me of a painful childhood memory. I do not know exactly how old I was – twelve, perhaps. I was staying with a friend who had an air-gun, and he had taken it into his head to try it out by shooting a cat. Not without some difficulty we had got hold of a stray cat, and had tied it to a tree. I was not enjoying the game at all, and was full of anxiety, but I did not dare to run away, for fear that my friend would think me stupidly sensitive and cowardly.

The first shot, however, was not sufficient to kill the cat, and it struggled frightfully, so that we were afraid it would break loose. We simply had to finish it off. It seemed to me an awfully long time before the animal was dead. I remember saying to myself: 'It's a lot harder than you would think to kill a cat!' But does not the fear of seeming a coward play a considerable part in the escalation of violence? What is humanity? In order to be a man worthy of the name, must one then have the courage to kill?

Of course, a Freudian might think that my friend and I were prompted, without realizing it, by our normal infantile sex instinct, sadism. But it seems to me that if we always reduce the impulse towards violence to sadism or to Oedipean hostility, we make it a by-product of the sex instinct and miss its importance and its autonomy. The biologists take this drive towards killing more seriously when they show that it is restrained in the animals by the instinct for the preservation of the species, which is lacking in man.

4 REASON?

So, if the instinct is lacking in man, what other restraint can take its place? There are a number of other dangers against which the animals are protected by a salutary instinct which is absent in man. By scent alone, for example, animals can tell with remarkable precision which foods to avoid. Try making a dog drink alcohol! Whereas a man can drink himself to death with alcohol. But then reason takes the place of instinct. It does not, of course, have the same constraining force, though it is capable of making sound judgments. While it may not be able to stop a man from drinking too much, at least it tells him that it is a mistake to do so.

Unfortunately the same is not true for aggression. If reason is to take over in default of instinct in this field, obviously it will need to be possible to establish a rational criterion for violence, and that means declaring with the logical, clear, and universal authority of reason where the precise boundary between useful aggression and harmful violence is to be found. As we have seen, this is the very criterion which Dr Hacker is at pains to discover. This is understandable, since his whole analysis rests on the distinction between beneficial aggression and harmful violence: all would be clear if it were possible objectively to determine where one ends and the other begins.

But one might also be surprised that a psychologist should wrestle with this rational problem, when he of all people understands the nature of the passions and emotions which govern men, and the way they bring in reason only afterwards to justify their actions and opinions – a point which Dr Hacker expressly makes in his book. My guess therefore is that the reason why he tries so hard to find a criterion is to make his readers realize that unfortunately there is none. If he, with all his experience, and his rigorous and clear-sighted analysis, is unable to define unjustifiable violence, it can only be that it is impossible to do so.

In fact towards the end of his book he records a fascinating conversation he had with Herbert Marcuse, the well-known Californian psychoanalyst. In it he presses Marcuse with questions, and he seems to want to compel him into formulating an objective criterion of illegitimate violence. But wisely Marcuse avoids doing so. Hacker,

however, reiterates the point: 'We always come back to the problem
of criteria.'

The whole of this discussion between our two psychoanalysts
bears upon the legitimacy of revolutionary action and the benefits
or the harm that it may bring. Then Marcuse attempts with some
care to put forward a very general criterion: 'That which promotes
life', he says, 'cannot be wrong, even if certain constraints must be
applied in order to develop favourable conditions for it.' Later he
returns to the point: 'The criterion is whether it serves to promote
life, to increase the capabilities, the happiness and the peace of
mankind.'

Elsewhere Marcuse expresses a similar thought: 'We must bring
into being a new mode of existence, in which the aggressive instinct
would be put at the service of the instincts of life, and which would
educate the rising generation with a view to life and not death.' Of
course, everyone will agree, but that is not a criterion: what life
are we talking about? Are not men frequently killed in order to
promote a better life? Do we not frequently attack the lives of
others in order to protect our own?

What life is served, for example, when Oedipus kills his father –
without knowing that he is his father – when his own life is
threatened by him? Which of them is guilty of illegitimate violence?
The one who struck the first blow? Or the one who killed in self-
defence? For Sophocles, in his tragedy *King Oedipus*, that is not
the problem. Oedipus has no intention, either conscious or unconscious, of killing his father. For the Greeks what weighs upon
men is a mysterious destiny, the *Ananke*, 'what has to be', which
directs them without their realizing it, and drives them into conflict
and even murder. The Greeks were acutely aware of this tragic
force; they believed that a gifted and inspired being, like the
Pythian priestess, could make prophecies on the subject, but
our proud modern rationalism rejects – without proof – such
beliefs.

The conclusion of the discussion between our two psychoanalysts, Hacker and Marcuse, is interesting: Marcuse realizes that
his criterion of life is a fragile one, and excuses himself by saying
that he 'does not know a better definition'. And he adds this magni-
ficent remark: 'I am just not clever enough.' Of course he is joking –
poking fun, in fact, at his colleague for trying to find a rational
criterion. His sally implies that it is not intelligence, not even the
intelligence of a Marcuse, that is going to solve the problem of

violence. It is a problem that belongs to the realm of the passions, in face of which rationality is powerless, just as reason is powerless to direct men.

I recall the epic arguments that took place in Geneva in the inter-war years, in the League of Nations: brilliant oratorical clashes between the most eminent jurists in search of a definition of the aggressor, which they never succeeded in formulating clearly and satisfactorily.

Even in criminal law, for want of a rational criterion, a whole judicial system has been constructed in the hope of determining whether an accused is guilty or not. Yet despite all the procedures, and codes whose every word has been carefully weighed by the legislator, it is never possible to make a determination with absolute certainty.

Ironically, we turn in the last resort to the quite subjective judgement of a jury from which the most intelligent and the most independent-minded are carefully excluded. And then we rely on a majority verdict, as if the greater number are more likely to see clearly than the smaller! And the eloquence of counsel turns more readily to emotional persuasion than to any other.

The ambiguity is made worse by the use of psychiatric experts. In a recent case in Switzerland two experts caused utter confusion in the courtroom because 'their respective theses differed completely, not only as to diagnosis . . . but equally on the problems of criminal responsibility'. Dr C. Miéville, whom I am quoting here, goes on to denounce 'the notion that psychiatrists have objective criteria by which they might decide upon the responsibility of an accused person, a notion which public opinion has not yet given up'. Miéville maintains that 'the psychiatrist's appreciation of res-ponsibility is as subjective and personal as that of any layman'. He contrasts the Swiss penal code with that of France, which refrains from putting to the expert the question of criminal responsibility, thus shuffling off a decision which properly belongs to the court.

Perhaps some of my readers are thinking that I am getting lost in abstract theory with this problem of the criterion; that in actual practice there are lawbreakers who must be punished or at least rendered harmless; that it is not so much a matter of finding out who is really guilty as of establishing who has broken the law – which is much easier to define; that at the cost of an occasional regrettable judicial error the system guarantees public order and the functioning of its institutions.

Of course, when only a few individuals are involved, the disproportion is so great between their strength and the joint might of Justice and Authority, that they may well curse their judges, but they cannot escape them, nor take revenge. Nevertheless we are beginning to see commando groups attempting, sometimes with success, to snatch their accomplices from the clutch of the law, by the hijacking of planes and the seizure of hostages. So it is by means of the sort of violence that society is trying to punish, that they ensure their impunity. But it is especially in the case of the more evenly balanced conflicts, as in civil or international wars, that the process of violence, once started, feeds on itself, escalating towards the most catastrophic consequences.

It is therefore a serious mistake to think that the problem of a criterion of judgment raised by Dr Hacker is merely academic. We all realize that with the advent of the atomic age the total extermination of the human race is a possibility. Furthermore, we should have to be very naïve to believe that any agreement on the banning of the most powerful weapons, however solemnly and sincerely entered into, would restrain a nation whose very existence was at stake.

I was left perplexed and worried as I came to the end of Dr Hacker's book – such a remarkable book, written by such a highly qualified scientist, who has examined great criminals with such lucidity. And yet it comes to the conclusion that reason is incapable of formulating an objective criterion of illegitimate violence. Must we then turn to a different language from that of science for help in grasping the critical point where natural, necessary, fruitful aggression degenerates into destructive violence?

5 CROSSING THE RUBICON

That other language is the language of poetry, of images and symbols. The first image that comes to mind is that of a mighty river watering a fertile plain, a symbol of life, of its power and its fecundity. Suddenly the river rises and there is a flood as the waters reach a certain height, spreading destruction and death. This is the result of meteorological factors – and how closely the moods of the human mind resemble those of the weather, with its tempestuous winds, its sunlit calms, its freezing frosts and its burning heats!

Another more human image will lead us towards more profound reflections – the crossing of the Rubicon. In the year 49 BC, Julius Caesar was at Ravenna in northern Italy, the capital of Cisalpine Gaul, of which he was proconsul. He had come fresh from his glorious victories in the conquest of Transalpine Gaul – modern France, Switzerland, and Belgium. But he was at loggerheads with Rome and the Senate, and especially with Pompey, then at the height of his power.

Pompey had triumphed over the Scythians, conquered Jerusalem, won more than forty brilliant victories, firmly establishing the Roman peace from Spain and Africa to distant Armenia. He had adroitly manoeuvred Rome, playing off the aristocrats of the Senate against the people and their tribunes in order to establish his own absolute power.

He had recently been ill, and the delirious acclaim which greeted his return to health had confirmed his enormous popularity. As the eighteenth-century historian Charles Rollin writes, 'his renown at that time reached up to the heavens'. But in the north the fame of Caesar, the conqueror of the Gauls, was growing. He could not but be offended at it. He distrusted Caesar, and credited him with the most ambitious of intentions – that of supplanting him in Rome itself. With the complicity of the Senate he hatched murky plots to prevent his advance, and while negotiations with him dragged slowly on, the consul Marcellus, a friend of Pompey, proposed to remove Caesar from his command in Gaul.

Julius Caesar then secretly moved one of his legions up to the bank of the Rubicon, which marked the frontier between the north and the south, between the Gauls, now subject to him, and Pompey's Italy. He spent one more evening in Ravenna, attended a banquet, but withdrew on the pretence of being indisposed. Commandeering some mules from a near-by mill, he rejoined his troops overnight, and with them crossed the Rubicon. He pushed on at once as far as Rimini, of which he took possession without striking a blow.

During a seaside holiday in Rimini, when our children were small, we went as a family to see the Rubicon: a diminutive stream, then almost dry, which one could easily miss in a broad featureless plain were it not for a notice on the bridge that crossed it, bearing the name *Rubico*. A famous name, for it was at that spot that Julius

Caesar unleashed the civil war which tore the Roman Republic apart and contributed to the collapse of its institutions. And so to 'cross the Rubicon' has become a proverbial expression meaning to take a final or decisive step – often with the idea of achieving a solution by force.

And so Julius Caesar attacked his rival while negotiations were still in progress. From the formal, legal, rational point of view he was incontestably the aggressor. Perhaps he felt a little ashamed of the fact, for he makes no mention of it in his *Commentaries*. Note that as yet no battle had taken place. But what counts is the inner decision to precipitate matters, to appeal to the arbitrament of arms, even if no violence has yet been perpetrated. And so the Rubicon aptly symbolizes the turning-point of which Dr Hacker spoke, where the equilibrium between the aggressive forces is upset. It means that there comes a point in time when a chain of violent consequences is set in motion, which no one has the power to stop.

Caesar realized this, for on the bank of the Rubicon he said to his friends: 'If we cross this little bridge, we must carry through our enterprise to the end by force of arms.' Pompey too realized the significance of the act. Such was the consternation caused in Rome by the news that Caesar had captured Rimini that immediately Pompey, the Senate, the patricians, and all the influential notabilities hurriedly left the city for Brindisi, ready to flee to Greece.

So the inexorable process of violence had begun, even if Caesar was able to conquer the whole of Italy and Rome almost without resistance. Similarly, nineteen centuries later, Napoleon, having disembarked from the island of Elba, was to be able to descend in triumph upon Paris, from which King Louis XVIII had fled. Caesar, however, did come up against a few of Pompey's adherents, like Lentulus and Domitius, who attempted to bar his passage. With the complicity of their demoralized troops and of the local populations, he soon had them at his mercy. But with astonishing generosity he showed them clemency.

The better to understand our problem of violence we must listen to what he says to them as he grants them their lives and liberty. Rollin (p.251) tells us that he declared to Lentulus 'that he was not come out of the bounds of his province with an intent to injure any body; but to repel the injuries done him by his enemies, to revenge the wrongs of the Tribunes, and to restore to the Roman People, who were opposed by a small faction of the Nobles, their liberty and privileges'. Even before crossing the Rubicon he had made Pompey a generous peace offer, proposing 'that all the armies should be disbanded; that throughout Italy arms should be laid down; that a ban should be put on everything that smacked of terror and violence'.

Thus Caesar, who behaved like an aggressor when he crossed the Rubicon, and who was legally and formally the aggressor, looked upon himself as the champion of liberty and the rule of law. He solemnly declares that it is he who is moving against violence, against Pompey's unjust and unlawful tyranny. Who is right? Who is wrong? Where does equity lie? Cicero, the lawyer, lets his heart rule his head, and declares: 'I would rather be defeated with Pompey than win with Caesar.' In the eyes of the Senate, devoted as it is to Pompey, and of those whose privileges Pompey's power protects, Caesar is no more than a rebel, a conspirator, who has set out to overthrow by violence the established order in Rome. But in the eyes of those many who were proscribed, of the weak and the malcontents, he appears as the champion of democracy. Who is misusing his strength? they ask – Pompey the powerful. Who is the conciliator? – Caesar, who is defending them but has no other course open to him than to march against Pompey in order to re-establish liberty. This is why the numbers of those who were on Caesar's side increased to the point where Pompey had to flee, and his lieutenants to surrender.

There are plenty of arguments in favour of Caesar. Has not Pompey already been in conflict with all his rivals on the road to power, long before the conflict arose with Caesar? With Crassus, with Lucullus, whom he dismissed during the war with Mithridates in order to take his place as leader and victor; with Piso, whom he perhaps had assassinated? Was it not in order to reconcile Pompey with Crassus and bring peace to the Republic that Caesar proposed that both should join him in the triumvirate? Did he not give to Pompey in marriage his only daughter, Julia?

Had not Pompey contrived to get himself nominated as consul, illegally, it being less than ten years since his previous consulate? Had he not taken advantage of this in order to annul the principal social reform carried out by Caesar at the time of his own consulate, withdrawing from the peasants of Capua the state lands which Caesar had distributed among them? Had he not then withdrawn two legions from Caesar on the pretext of sending them to fight the Parthians, but in fact kept them in Rome to swell his own army?

And in the negotiations had not Caesar offered in vain, in order to restore peace, to renounce his own command in Gaul, and to content himself with a single legion in Illyria? Finally, had not the people's representatives, Caesar's friends, the tribunes Antony and Cassius, had to flee from Rome by night in disguise in order to save their lives and rejoin Caesar at Ravenna? It was this last incident which decided Caesar to take the offensive and cross the Rubicon.

I have gone into some detail in recounting these ancient events in order to show the reader how difficult it is to determine objectively who is the aggressor, who is guilty of using improper force. If it was Caesar crossing the Rubicon, it certainly seems that it was no less Pompey and the Senate who were responsible for the Civil War which ensued. Being in power in Rome, Pompey's faction had plenty of apparently less violent means of combating Caesar, whereas the latter's only trump card was surprise attack. And yet it was the crossing of the Rubicon which marked that fatal point of no return from which an inevitable escalation of violence proceeds.

In referring to this far-off and celebrated example, I am in a sense referring to all the conflicts of history, both public and private, both social and military, as well as cultural: the eternal struggle between those who are in power and the rest. My readers will no doubt have been reminded of plenty of contemporary events that have taken place in our own lifetime. If I were a journalist or a polemicist I could have analysed them. But my aim is quite different. I am seeking to state a more general law which will throw light on the problem of violence, which is such a live issue for all of us today.

6 THE MORAL CONSCIENCE

All conflicts have broadly the same pattern. There is always a privileged party, standing by an established order which benefits its members, the reigning party in power. These privileged people do not need to have recourse to naked violence, because they have law and power on their side. Caesar, on the other hand, symbolizes all those who contest their right and challenge them, and whom they can justly accuse of fomenting trouble and discord by unlawful and immoral means.

In Pompey and Caesar we have, face to face, two equally aggressive and equally ambitious men. 'Caesar could not suffer a superior, nor Pompey an equal,' writes the Roman poet Lucan (Book I, lines 125f.). There are always two aggressive powers, one balanced against the other. But one is invisible and legal, the other visible and illegal. The one who crosses the Rubicon, thus designating himself as the violent aggressor, is the one who does not have the forces of law and order on his side, whether it be the actual force of army or police, or the force of public opinion. It was Caesar who crossed the Rubicon, not Pompey, for the simple reason that the latter was in power in Rome.

In the same way, when a wife explodes in an outburst of hysteria – an act of violence which puts an end to a dialogue with her husband – it is a sign that the dialogue has already failed, that she feels powerless to make herself understood. It is she who is crossing the Rubicon, but it is her husband who has made her cross it by his refusal to understand her. The husband can flatter himself that he has remained calm and apparently conciliatory; he has kept control of himself and can blame his wife for her outburst.

Violent challengers of the established order always appeal to a more profound, immanent, ideal justice, against legal and formal justice. The Romans themselves, the inventors of our formal law, had a saying, *Summum jus, summa injuria*: the most perfect law may constitute the worst injustice!

The Roman writer Seneca, in one of his *Moral Epistles* (CIV.31), describes the war between Caesar and Pompey as the conflict between the revolutionaries and the conservatives: 'On the one hand the people, and the whole multitude of those whom the bad state of their fortune rendered avid for change; on the other, the great ones, the order of knights, all that was illustrious and respectable in the city . . .' The establishment, we might call it today! And he adds: 'In the middle, Cato and the Republic, alone and abandoned by all.' Indeed, Cato, the man with the incorruptible conscience, remained for a long time unable to decide between Pompey and Caesar, and consequently isolated and impotent. And the Republic of which Seneca speaks means society – the general interest that is being sacrificed.

In fact each side is right in a conflict, or at least has good reasons for its point of view, and it is impossible to arbitrate justly. I have seen this often enough in the individual conflicts of which I have been the confidant all through my life as a doctor. I see the good reasons on each side, and remain alone and impotent like Cato. One can denounce the more visible violence of the one – usually the weaker of the two – but there is also a less obvious violence in the other, which was the first to be brought into play. Alas! There is no criterion of improper violence.

We have seen, then, so far, that it is not possible to condemn all aggressiveness *en bloc*. That it represents a positive aspect, the instinct of life itself, which impels every individual to assert himself, to take his place in society and to defend it; that it plays an essential part in the development of the child, and then through competition in personal progress and the structure of society. But that beyond a certain threshold it can turn to fratricidal violence. And finally that this threshold is defended in the animals by an instinct which is lacking in man.

We then asked ourselves whether reason might take the place of this missing instinct and provide an objective criterion for the definition of the fatal threshold. We have seen that that is not possible, that those most lucid observers of the human mind, the psychoanalysts, have had no success in this search. And so, leaving aside theoretical argument, we have made a pragmatic and pheno-menological examination of violent conflicts, both on the vast scale of war, and on that of individual quarrels. And we have seen how hard it is to distinguish who is responsible for the degeneration of fruitful competition into murderous violence.

Then, in the absence of an instinctive barrier and of a rational criterion, what can mount guard on the threshold of this doorway between beneficent aggression and harmful violence? You will naturally reply, the moral conscience. Alas, it is not only reason which is rudderless in this matter, but also the moral conscience. Neither says, with proper caution, 'So far as I can see, I am right.' Each is absolutely convinced of it.

Thus President Truman was able seriously and with a good conscience, it seems to me, to take the decision to bomb Hiroshima. He was putting an end to a horrific war and saving a great number of human lives. It was his duty, his responsibility as President. I am not saying that he was wrong, simply that there is no moral criterion any more than there is a rational one for deciding whether or not it was right. In an armed conflict the government recognizes no imperative save that of victory, and it can legitimately throw the responsibility for its actions on those who started the war.

Though there may occasionally be some hesitation before the conflict begins, it is quickly swept aside as soon as the struggle is on. There is never any unanimity so great or so sure of being right in a nation as when it is caught up in a serious conflict. If some independent spirit utters the least doubt, he is at once accused of the worst of crimes – treason. And the most pitiless of wars are wars of religion, in which each of the belligerents is convinced that he is obeying not only his own conscious but the commands of God himself. Remember the Crusaders' cry: 'God wills it!'

Of course, war defies all human wisdom, that of the combatants as well as that of the conscientious objectors, and even that of the historians who will judge it afterwards only in accordance with their subjective opinions. You will perhaps object that there is a sort of mob psychology involved, which eclipses the essentially personal moral conscience. But it is definitely the individual conscience to which Professor Henri Baruk, of Paris, is referring in his *Psychiatrie morale expérimentale.*

In this book he details the researches he has carried out aimed at an understanding of the most deep-rooted and strongest feelings of hate that are known – those of certain mentally ill people. He demonstrates very clearly that they are related to the moral conscience, to the repression of a bad conscience. The subject, repressing a feeling of guilt instead of recognizing it, projects it onto someone else, and so fixes his own guilt on another person, who becomes the object of his hate. With this repression and projection we are dealing with a typical psychoanalytical mechanism. There is a certain piquancy in the fact that this is so clearly stated by an opponent of psychoanalysis such as Henri Baruk.

But I have found it easy to verify, even in myself. Since reading Henri Baruk I have often asked myself when annoyed with my wife in what way I had wronged her. And I always found that I had. What a paradox! So it is because he is endowed with a moral conscience, which the animals lack, that man is capable of hating in a way that animals never do. Thus, on both the national scale and the individual, the moral conscience is liable to the gravest aberrations.

7 DIVINE INSPIRATION

Let us proceed further. There are believers, of whom I am one, who take care not to confuse the two domains of morality and religion. The moral conscience is an immanent, philosophical notion, dependent on man, on his intuition of good and evil, as Kant has shown. It elaborates principles, and then from them deduces all sorts of everyday moralities. It is a formal and legalistic system. Religious conduct is not as concerned with principles, however sublime they may be, as with following the will of God, who may very well upset all our noblest principles. It is always disconcerting to people with high moral principles.

The conflict between these two attitudes – the legalism of the Pharisees, who were so authentically moral, and the prodigious moral liberty of Jesus – runs right through the Christian gospel. The Pharisees constantly accuse him of violating the law. Thus when Jesus heals a man born blind, on the sabbath, they are scandalized (John 9). The evangelists deal at length with arguments of this kind. This is understandable, since the violation of the law of the sabbath, instituted by Moses, was sacrilege in the eye of Jesus's pious opponents: to violate is to use violence.

Even the unbeliever recognizes Jesus as one who always knew when he must use violence and when he must not. He was quite capable of being violent. Not only did he use a whip of cords to drive the money-changers from the temple (John 2.14–16), but he inveighed against the Pharisees themselves with unheard-of violence! He described them as rotten, as 'whited sepulchres' (Matt. 23.27), as murderers of the prophets, as a 'brood of vipers'.

He always knew when to resist and when not. 'I say this to you: offer the wicked man no resistance . . . And if anyone orders you to go one mile, go two miles with him' (Matt. 5.39). But when certain ill-disposed men came and asked him for a miracle in order to test him, he refused, accusing them in violent terms of being 'an evil and unfaithful generation' (Matt. 12.39).

Even towards his own mother he was capable of adopting an attitude which any other mother would consider offensive: read again the story of how his mother approaches him in an attempt to dissuade him from entering further into violent conflict with the authorities, a conflict which she perhaps foresees will lead to his death. He will not even see her, and while she stands outside he exclaims: 'Who are my mother and my brothers?' And answering his own question he points to his disciples sitting round him, saying, 'Here are my mother and my brothers' (Mark 3.31-35).

He is no less hard on his disciple Peter when the latter tries to dissuade him from following the road to Jerusalem and the cross. He says to him: 'Get behind me, Satan! You are an obstacle in my path, because the way you think is not God's way but man's' (Matt. 16.23). It is quite clear that it is to those who want to deflect him from the path of obedience to his heavenly Father, even when they are those dearest to him, that he shows himself implacable and violent.

It is this very submission to his Father that leads him to non-violence: at his arrest, when this same apostle Peter draws his sword and cuts off the ear of one of the high priest's servants, Jesus says to him: 'Put your sword back in its scabbard; am I not to drink the cup that the Father has given me?' (John 18.11). Throughout his Passion he was to maintain this non-violent attitude, even refusing to defend himself before Pilate, who pressed him with questions in an attempt to save him. His secret, the secret of his liberty, was that he allowed himself to be led by God. He himself said so: 'My food is to do the will of the one who sent me' (John 4.34).

Frequently he goes off into the desert to meditate alone with God, seeking guidance – especially when the enthusiastic crowds want to drag him into a violent political adventure! It seems to me that Jesus is here giving us his answer to the problem of violence. He was able to be violent or non-violent in each circumstance, in accordance with God's will. It is not difficult to understand that God should prevent a man from committing a violent act. But that he should sometimes call a man to violence – that is what is so upsetting to pious and moral minds. Nevertheless, it is what an honest reading of the Bible reveals. There can be holy acts of violence.

So you see, we started with Dr Hacker from the distinction he makes between aggression and violence, which furnished a very useful starting-point for our analysis. But we saw that he himself was seeking in vain a criterion for defining the frontier between them. And now we see this frontier itself being shifted: it no longer seems to us to separate necessary aggressiveness from reprehensible violence, but to be situated in the field of violence itself, between that which may sometimes be ordained by God and that which he forbids.

I point this out not in order to oppose Dr Hacker, but in order to clarify our analysis. From the start I have shown that all the terms we employ – aggression or violence – are too imprecise really to come to grips with the problem in hand. What Dr Hacker was really seeking was the frontier between the permitted and the forbidden. On this fundamental point we agree. But I do not think it possible – in the light of the Bible any more than by a logical process of thought – to condemn outright all violence and to say, 'I am against violence.'

Everyone recognizes, it seems to me, that there is a violence which is necessary to resist culpable violence, a violence organized by society, with its police, its courts and its prisons, in order to stop brutal violence triumphing with impunity and destroying the fabric of the community. Quite rightly Dr Hacker himself writes: 'Criminal violence is outlawed; punitive violence is within the law: change the name of violence, and you legitimize it.' Rightly too he maintains that this legal violence brings no real solution to a conflict, since it invites retaliation. Violence, he says, comes from a lazy mind giving up the patient search for a true solution through thought and negotiation: 'What we must do is to recast in a new form the problems to which the only solution we know is violence.' But we must recognize that negotiation is hardly ever possible except when the two parties are obviously equal in strength, otherwise violence remains the only way of making oneself heard.

Everything is further complicated when deeply held convictions are involved. A person who throws himself heart and soul into an enterprise he believes to be just and holy is not inclined to negotiate, but rather to use violence, for fear of betraying his ideal. Even if he is an unbeliever his attitude is a religious one, in the sense that he looks upon the demands of his conscience as being absolute. I can understand him, since I feel myself to be in an analogous position when I echo St Peter's words: 'Obedience to God comes before obedience to men' (Acts 5.29). This bring us back to the question of God's guidance, which it seems to me only Jesus was always able to distinguish, and which made him sometimes violent, sometimes non-violent.

We are often left perplexed because we do not have his intimate communion with the Father. I am not saying that it is easy to see what God expects of us in every circumstance of life. But I am convinced that this search for God's guidance is our most important task. I have practised it for more than forty years, and I can see clearly that that has been the source of my most fruitful experiences. I have been even more faithful to it since my wife's death, as if dialogue with God had to take the place of the marital dialogue which I can no longer have; and feeling, too, that this rendezvous with God is a sort of spiritual tryst with my wife who is with him. Yet I know that we are very often mistaken in our search for divine inspiration, and that we are prone to take our thoughts as those of God.

It is important to say, however, that the worst thing is not being wrong, but being sure one is not wrong. Nothing is more dangerous for us than to believe ourselves to be the authentic interpreters of the divine will. This is the source of all illuminism, of all brutal intolerance, of all proselytism and fanaticism.

See how delicate a problem it is: objective criteria tend towards overbearing moralism, towards the infantile morality of permissions and prohibitions like that of the Pharisees, which psychologists have to contend with in their efforts to turn people into autonomous and responsible adults. On the other hand a morality of personal inspiration leads to the arrogant bigotry denounced by psychiatrists who see the paranoiac aberrations it can lead to.

If I am asked what I think about the search for God's guidance, after so many years' reflection, I may make three points. First, that the use of the word 'search' leads to misunderstanding. In the most striking examples, those recorded in the Bible and in history as well as those that I have myself been able to observe, God's call most often comes upon a man totally unexpectedly, and not in response to his search. His first reaction is generally astonishment, and he does not at once grasp the significance of the call.

Thus when St Francis of Assisi felt a call to rebuild the church, he took a mason's trowel and set about repairing the church of S. Damiano. It was much later that he realized that what he had to be about was the spiritual life of the church, corrupted by its wealth and power. So, when we are obsessed by a question that we are putting to God – 'Ought I to use violence or not, stand fast or give way?' – it is very rarely that we receive an answer. Our preoccupation with the need for an answer may prevent us from hearing a quite different question that God is putting to us: 'Why are you so critical and aggressive towards this or that person?' Or we may be missing a completely unusual command that God is giving us.

Next, God's guidance is strictly personal. It is for each of us to receive for himself and for no one else. I can never know what God is expecting of someone else. That would be to put myself in God's place, to claim the right to judge, and to fail to respect another person and his spiritual autonomy. Finally I think that we must seek God's guidance, wait for it, hope for it, believe in it – and yet question it, so that we remain open to a fresh search, attentive to further calls. 'Let us seek', writes St Augustine in his treatise *On Order*, 'as they seek who must find, and find as they find who must go on seeking.'

What other way could there be for us, indeed, even to discover our mistakes, but that of deeper prayer and ever closer intimacy with Jesus, so as to see his will more clearly, and come to a better understanding of ourselves – to see more clearly the obstacles within ourselves which too often delude us: our prejudices, fears, passions and complexes? It is in the course of my meditation that I can see that I have been aggressive where I ought not to have been, or that sometimes I am not as aggressive as I ought to be, that I lack the courage to express my aggressiveness, that the gentleness which I have looked upon as a virtue is really pretence and cowardice.

8 VIOLENCE IN OTHERS AND IN OURSELVES

For all that, we must become aware of our own aggressiveness, an awareness which is much rarer than one might think. Here meditation can play a decisive part. Once more I must let Dr Hacker's analysis enlighten us. He notes that in the absence of any rational criterion, all men in practice adopt a very simple criterion which none dares to profess openly, namely that their own aggressiveness always seems to them to be legitimate, while that of others is to be condemned. How true that is! It is humiliating for human reason; it is humiliating for the moral conscience, but that's the way it is. The culpable violence of others we see as colossal and scandalous; ours we see as insignificant – even when the truth is quite the reverse. Is not this exactly what Jesus meant with his image of 'the mote in my brother's eye' and 'the beam in my own' (Matt. 7.3)?

Let us once again take the example of the foundation of my country, the Swiss Confederation, or, making due allowance, the very similar foundation of the United States. When the leaders of the first three Swiss Cantons met on the plain of Grütli they invoked no principle of the right of a nation to self-government – no one had thought of it at that time – they simply concluded a pact of mutual assistance 'in the name of Almighty God', that is to say under God's guidance.

It is quite clear that in the eyes of that powerful Pompey, the Duke of Habsburg, they were no more than a gang of conspirators, guilty of sedition, just as were the representatives of the first thirteen states who met in Philadelphia in 1776 to vote for the Declaration of Independence of the United States, in the face of that powerful Pompey, Great Britain. To the Swiss or American fighters engaged in their wars of independence, their own violence was legitimate and even sacred, whereas that of Austria or England they looked upon as culpable. Like Caesar they justified their rebellion in the name of liberty. On the other hand, to their enemies it was they who were at fault.

It is always like that. When we denounce and condemn violence, when we complain about the wave of violence which is breaking upon us today, we always mean other people's violence. The violence of which we read indignant accounts in the papers is that of the enemies of society, the gangsters, the criminals, the gunmen, the militants – never our own. What I discover in the course of meditation and in reading my Bible is my own violence, which I had been calling legitimate indignation. Yes, indeed, what the Bible reveals is that it is not a case of the righteous on one side and the sinners on the other, peacemakers on one side and men of violence on the other, with a clear line of demarcation between them, but that violence is in the heart of all men.

I do not write for gunmen. It is pretty unlikely that any of them will read my book. I write for decent people – like you and me – of whom it is often said that we 'wouldn't hurt a fly'. Flattering, is it not? It permits us to discuss the problem of violence at our ease, as if it did not personally concern us. We all have an inbuilt resistance to recognizing it as a thing that concerns us. No doubt you are actually feeling that resistance as you read what I have to say. You protest within yourself more or less violently. You think I am exaggerating when I say that all men are violent.

There are, then, on the subject of violence, two opposite views. One is optimistic, and thinks that on the whole things are not so bad; that the vast majority are decent, peace-loving people who abhor violence; that violence appertains only to a handful of antisocial militants on the fringe of society, who need to be treated because they are sick, or to be kept under control. This commonly held and reassuring view is natural enough in those who find that the present order of society suits them well enough, who know how to play along with it and take advantage of it.

The other view is pessimistic and realist. It maintains that all men are violent, without exception; that the differences are only in the appearances, not in the nature, of mankind. It denies that violence is a trait only of an ill-disposed minority, and maintains that the optimists are blinkered and naïve and that they are refusing to see man as he really is.

The truth is that violence reigns. Everywhere there reigns either the silent, cold, respectable violence of Pompey, or the burning, brutal violence of Caesar – the violence of the policeman or the violence of the bandit. You need only to open a history-book to see that it is full of violence: war, murder, outrage, slaughter, revolution, tyranny, sedition, and treachery. Why then do we always affect to regard as exceptional something which is the most ordinary thing in the world? How do we sort out from it all what is healthy and proper enterprise, and what is culpable folly? We all judge always in accordance with our personal inclinations and prejudices.

'Violence is father and king of everything,' said the Greek philosopher Heracleitus, as long ago as five centuries before Christ. H. G. Wells said: 'Life is born of violence. On the head of each of us weighs the ancestral curse of fifty million murders.' And our author, Hacker: 'Everywhere and always, the strong has triumphed over the weak; the law of the jungle is the fundamental law of life.' He adds a statistic: 'One murder every twenty seconds during the last fifty years.'

If you are unwilling to accept a book of secular history, open the Bible. It is the same picture. I always admire the realism of the Bible. It describes man not as we might like him to be, but as he is. The story begins with the murder of Abel by Cain from no other motive than jealousy, the subtlest of jealousies – the feeling of being less loved by God. And then there is Abraham who lies because he is afraid of being put to death. There is the sombre story of Hagar, banished with her baby because she is only a servant and a foreigner. Then Abraham preparing to kill his son Isaac; and the childlike astonishment of the boy that they had forgotten to bring a lamb for the sacrifice.

There is the long quarrel between the two brothers Jacob and Esau, in search of the divine blessing; the sinister deception contrived by the mother; and also the quarrel between Jacob and his father-in-law, riddled with trickery, with the abuse of power, and revenge. There is Joseph, sold into slavery by his brothers. Moses was a man of violence. Not only did he, when still a young man, kill an Egyptian, but also later when he was unchallenged leader of his people, he was seized with such holy wrath at the sight of the golden calf that he smashed the tablets of stone on which was inscribed the law that God had revealed to him on Mount Sinai.

And then there is the tragic story of Samson. And the wars, with all their many battles – the conquest of Canaan by a people convinced that it was fighting the war at God's command. Again, the interminable civil war between Saul and David; the recreant kings; the disruption of the kingdom; and much more besides.

A scripture teacher was having her pupils act out biblical scenes one Christmas. She thought that the story of David would be a good one to do, but she soon saw that the children, to imitate David, had made for themselves out of strong elastic quite lethal slings – the Molotov cocktails of antiquity, one might say! And she saw that there were many other incidents in David's life into which it would be preferable not to initiate the children, and so she gave up the idea.

The prophets of Yahweh are no less violent than the kings. Read the denunciations uttered by Amos, Isaiah, and all the others. There is much more to be found than the soft words and the promises of distant idyllic times when 'the wolf and the young lamb will feed together' (Isa. 65.25). There are the most brutal curses. That most timid of prophets, Jeremiah, sees the hand of God arming the violence of Nebuchadnezzar, his servant, who will conquer Egypt, capture Jerusalem the holy city, and take away the chosen people into exile. The most zealous of the prophets, Elijah, massacred four hundred and fifty priests of Baal, their only crime being that they served the god whom they had been taught to serve (I Kings 18.40). Good people, all of them, full of good intentions; not criminals.

The New Testament is no less harsh. The epic story of the redemption begins in a bloodbath, the massacre of the Innocents. And the three years of Christ's ministry are marked by the increasingly dramatic trial of strength between him and the religious leaders. He inveighs against them with unrelenting violence. Long before they unmask their real intentions, he hurls at them the accusation: 'You want to kill me' (John 8.37). And the Prince of Peace says to his disciples: 'Do not suppose that I have come to bring peace to the earth: it is not peace that I have come to bring, but a sword' (Matt. 10.34). He announces to them 'the abomination of desolation' (Matt. 24.15), foretold by the prophet Daniel. He weeps over Jerusalem, at the thought of its imminent destruction.

Then there is Judas' betrayal, Peter's denial, the connivance between the three powers, Herod, the high priest, and Pilate, and the crowd yelling 'Crucify him! Crucify him!' And there is the most revealing crime in all history, that of Golgotha. Even this is not the end. Very soon the stoning of Stephen (Acts 7.55–60) opens the long procession of the army of martyrs that is to continue in the games in the Roman arena and the persecution of the church. St Paul already has a long tale to tell of all his hardships, and how he has only narrowly escaped death (II Cor. 11.22–27).

For his own part St Paul was not lacking in aggressiveness. He had used it on the Christians until his conversion, and thereafter he transferred it into his apostolic mission to win the ancient world over to the new faith, even standing out inflexibly against St Peter at the Council of Jerusalem (Gal. 2.11), which was itself a foretaste of many conflicts which were to tear the fabric of the Christian church – certainly not out of malice, but from a noble desire to defend the truth against error.

The Bible concludes with the vision of the cosmic violence of the Apocalypse, which goes as far as to speak of the wrath of the Lamb before the appearance of the New Jerusalem, which is no longer of this world.

We are a long way from the sickly-sweet image that we have often been given of Christianity! A long way from the picture of the 'gentle Jesus' of which Paul Diel speaks in his book on biblical symbolism, in which he describes the destiny of man as a hard struggle. I was talking about it the other day with one of my friends, who said to me, 'You astonish me! I was always taught that Christianity meant turning the other cheek' (Matt. 5.39). Of course I am not forgetting the biblical texts which call us to love, forgiveness, self-sacrifice, and non-resistance. But it would be just as tendentious to thrust aside all the others.

The Bible is complex. Some find it even too contradictory. Precisely because it is not a detailed moral code, but because it calls us to reflection, to meditation, and to responsible personal choices – sometimes to gentleness, sometimes to unyielding firmness. We are a long way too from a certain idealist philosophy which professes a fine optimism about man and his capacity to raise himself to the highest virtues. Man is violence. Sometimes it is from sordid and selfish motives, but it can sometimes also be in the holiest of causes. The Prior of Taizé, Brother Roger Schutz, has written a book entitled *Violent for Peace.*

Man must indeed have been violent for him to attribute even to his God the most murderous of intentions in a cataclysm such as the Flood, for example, or in the ten plagues of Egypt, or again in sending disease among men! We may well recall Voltaire's words: 'If God made us in his image, we have certainly returned the compliment.'

The Greeks did precisely the same with the divinities of their mythology, who never ceased committing the most brutal atrocities, always fighting among themselves. It is most touching to see the pious Socrates, in the *Symposium*, imagining, in order to excuse the gods, that these instances of violence occurred in some far-off era, before the birth of Eros, the god of love. The trouble is that it is a long time since the birth of Eros, and the thing still goes on – Eros himself being the instigator of many a murder.

9 DEPTH PSYCHOLOGY

So our everyday observation, the study of history and of the Bible, and even mythology, will not allow us to look upon violence as an accident, a sort of bungle by Nature which might be put right by means of some judicious technical measure. We might as well recognize that it is an indestructible part of human nature. Psychology also demonstrates that this is so.

I interview a shy, meek man who sits on the very edge of the chair as if he had no right to a whole place in life, and is afraid of looking me in the eye. He apologizes for taking up the time of a person as busy as I am, especially as he does not even regard himself as ill, but of no importance. It was not he who asked for the appointment; he has not got sufficient initiative, and in particular he has no hope whatever that he will be able to escape from the mediocrity and anxiety of his life. His friends have had to make him come, or else it is his beloved mother who is worried about his not getting married, and his lack of any ambition to get on in his work.

He is a most conscientious and devoted workman. His fellow employees at the office can unload on to him all the unpleasant and uninteresting jobs, so that they can show themselves off in the more pleasing tasks. They never thank him for it; instead they laugh at him. As a child he was a darling, the apple of his mother's eye – so sweet and obedient! She tells me that she has never heard him utter a cheeky word.

Not only did he keep out of every sort of conflict with his parents and with his brothers and sisters, but he was also terribly afraid of the conflicts that often broke out between them. Fighting and shouting terrified him, and he took care always to regulate his own behaviour so as to avoid any argument. He would even admit to some stupidity that his little brother had committed in order to save him being punished; for he found it easier to bear being unjustly punished himself than to see his little brother being thrashed.

It is difficult to establish a dialogue with him. He answers all my questions politely, but volunteers nothing spontaneously. Gradually he may come round to telling me of instances of unjust treatment he has received, but he speaks of them without any feeling, as if he were talking of someone else's experiences, and he does not omit to point out all the extenuating circumstances that might excuse those at whose hands he has suffered. Here is a man who really does seem to be devoid of all aggressiveness.

It will take him a long time to reveal himself in a different light. It will need an exceptional confidence to be established between us before he will dare to express openly the bitterness that has been ceaselessly gnawing at his heart since childhood. And once the floodgates are opened I realize that it is not a little stream but a mighty river of complaints that will come gushing out! What has happened is that he has put up with everything, but forgotten nothing. Then, all at once, while he is talking to me of a friend whom he has not previously mentioned, and who had shamefully betrayed his ardent friendship, I see a flash like lightning in his eyes. The word aggressiveness is far too weak to express what I read in that glance; it is violence, rage, hate.

And I say to myself, what enormous, dynamic psychic force there is in there, blocked and sterile! It ought to have been used to build and defend the person – but it could not be, because he did not dare to give it any external expression or let it face the conflicts of life. It was turned inwards, to paralyse and destroy the person. Dr Alphonse Maeder has admirably described this turning-in of violence against the self in those who have not dared to give it expression. It can happen that such people are frightened at the discovery of their own violence in the course of treatment. This was the case with a girl who writes to me today: 'I have always been afraid of being violent.'

I am always glad when a patient is able at least to say aloud what he has so often thought to himself. Of course you cannot say what you think to everyone; but when the discrepancy is too great it arouses anxiety. Yesterday, after a patient had revealed to me with some feeling the bitter criticisms he had been harbouring against his parents, without letting it ever be seen, I had a dream during the night. I am always glad when I have a dream like that, relating to an interview of the day before. It demonstrates to me that the consultation has not just been a matter of professional routine, but that I have committed myself personally to the dialogue, and that it has aroused as much emotion in me as in my patient. In my dream, I thought I was speaking one language, but was actually speaking another, and I was surprised at this double speech.

We all have a double language – an internal language and an external one – one language for other people, as decorous and objective as possible, often too friendly, in order to put them off; and a language in our minds, often indecorous, offensive, and crude. So the fact that my patient was harbouring these complaints without ever daring to voice them openly to those they concerned, had reminded me that that happens to me as well, despite my great desire always to be absolutely sincere. And so true sincerity involves acknowledging that we are insincere.

Carl R. Rogers points out how rare is this 'congruence', as he calls it, of self with self, between our two languages, between the feelings we experience and those we express. It is the fundamental theme of his book, *On Becoming a Person*. He analyses what it is that prevents us from achieving it. It is always fear: of a conflict, of being rejected, of breaking up a harmonious relationship. But he shows that it is this very lack of congruence which stands in the way of the establishment of true relationships between persons. And he goes on to say (p.318) that his client 'discovers, often to his great surprise, that a relationship can be lived on the basis of real feelings, rather than on the basis of a defensive pretense'.

A young woman is talking to me. She is her mother's slave, exaggeratedly devoted to her, but inwardly discontented. She says to me: 'I'd do anything to avoid my mother getting upset with me.' It is this terror of a scene that is preventing her from giving vent to her aggressiveness, which, because it is being repressed, grows in her subconscious, and poisons her mind.

My dream about the two languages has reminded me also of the slang words which genteel people are careful not to employ, but which they readily use in their inner language. You need something stronger than genteel refinement if you really want to insult some-body. Slang is the language of the passions – of aggressiveness as well as love. There are some people who are using mental swear-words all day long.

But when the gulf is widened between the internal and the external languages, like the two banks of a river becoming further apart, it becomes impossible eventually to bridge the gap, and the result is a state of anxiety, a sign of rupture in the unity of the person. The psychotherapist's consulting-room, with its exceptional climate of truth, is the place where a bridge can be built joining the two sides together again, so that the patient may at least become his real self.

This is particularly so when he dares to voice his complaints not only against others, but also against the doctor himself, who can never fully come up to his patient's expectations of him. It is a sort of return to the normalcy of life with its inevitable struggle to assert oneself and one's desires in face of the assertion of others – not only of those who are aggressive and domineering, but also those who are gentle, whom we admire, and who can crush us with the strength of their personality without our realizing it.

No one can develop his own personality except at the expense of other people. Even the most saintly and humble man – the revered and much loved leader of a devoted congregation, for example – inevitably makes his followers dependent upon him, like little children. It is not his faults, but his virtues, his fame and his richness of spirit, which hold them back and prevent them from growing up themselves. He will plead in vain for them to show more initiative. They will only do so when he has gone. Little trees do not thrive when they are too close to a big one.

Imagine then what will happen in the case of the active, enterprising, dynamic businessman. Everyone submits to him – his family as well as his business associates – eagerly and happily, for it is an exciting adventure to follow in his wake. But that is the point: it is his wake they follow, and no one can set sail on any other course in his vicinity.

Or think of the woman who has such a high conception of her vocation as wife and mother that she has become the conscience of the family. Nobody would dream of making any decision at all without first seeking her advice. It is not that she is dictatorial, but simply because her judgments are so sound, so upright, and so loving.

Some people, because they are shy and over-conscientious, and sometimes out of love, efface and defraud themselves, and allow themselves to be trampled upon. Others, less sensitive, trample on those who get in their way, even those they love, without realizing that they are doing so. The former are repressing their natural aggressiveness, while the latter are giving it free play. They may agree very well together. I used to think when I saw a henpecked husband that it was the fault of an overbearing wife. But I have come to realize that often the wife has had to assert herself because her husband has not asserted himself enough. People who suffer from repressions can live happily on the dynamism of others until one day they realize that they are no longer themselves. And the others can be sweet and charming until one day they come up against a personality that is as strong as their own, and they find themselves thwarted.

At times of crisis one can suddenly become aware that hidden behind an apparently peaceful and harmonious scene there are powerful forces of nature which can burst out all at once into the light of day. A husband and wife, or two friends, who had thought that they had established an ideal relationship find themselves, to their own astonishment, exchanging an incredible volley of mutual accusations. Violence has come like a bolt from the blue, in the form of long-repressed aggressiveness, unconscious, unsuspected, and no one feels himself responsible for it. So a great river can flow for a long time smoothly, without a ripple; the frightening energy it contains is revealed only when its peaceful waters cascade with a deafening roar over a precipice.

That is the truth about human life. Well-brought-up, reasonable, kindly people, gentle as lambs, can suddenly break out into brutal violence, in words, thoughts, or deeds – and it happens more often than you would imagine. The sheep suddenly turns into a wolf. I have on occasion slapped my wife, and have often spoken to her in the most wounding terms. I might try to reassure myself with the thought that it was only a passing accident, a mental aberration, when I was no longer myself in the heat of the moment – something soon put right! It would be more honest to say to myself that it was I who did it, and to see that it reveals an aspect of myself that I find it hard to recognize; that I am much more violent than I care to acknowledge.

I am sincere when I say that my wife and I achieved an exceptional degree of unity in our marriage. But the same sincerity obliges me to admit that that did not preserve us from storms that remain like ugly blots on the carefully-written pages of a schoolboy's copy-book. It is worse when our offence is against someone weaker than ourselves. I do not forget the cold sweat that broke out on me once when I realized that I had tweaked the ears of one of my sons more roughly and more angrily than I ought.

When am I myself? When I am expressing my best feelings and my noblest aspirations? Or when I am behaving like a brute? The chances are that it is when the brakes of my moral and social con-ditioning fail. Thus it is that our mental patients often seem to be more ready to show us a truth about humanity which our up-bringing in society has taught us to hide. Professor Ajuriaguerra pointed this out in a recent interview: 'We are afraid of mad people, we hate them, because we are afraid of our own aggressiveness. Those who are mad hold up a mirror to us – the shameless mirror of our own conflicts.'

Perhaps the reader thought just now as he read my admission, 'Fortunately that has never happened to me!' Can he however be sure that it is his virtue that stopped him, or was it merely that he did not dare? I do not deny the virtues, the sincerity of love, or right feelings. On the contrary, I am aware that brigands have them too. The real truth is that we are all contradictory beings. And we all find it hard to admit that that is so. Our rationalism rebels against the reality of our contradictions. If we are caught out in some contradiction we launch into the most tortuous excuses in order to deny it.

People have often said to me: 'I do not know what I am; tell me what I am. I do not know if I am cowardly or brave, violent or gentle, aggressive or inoffensive. When am I being myself, and when am I not?' Unfortunately, we are always ourselves! Even when we are acting a part in society, we are ourselves. As Socrates showed, one can never know oneself. But we can get nearer to self-knowledge by being ready to accept that we are contradictory. For it is our revulsion against our contradictoriness that prevents us from becoming aware of that part of ourselves which C. G. Jung calls the shadow, and in which is concealed the violence which we denounce in others.

When psychotherapy brings about progressive self-knowledge, the patient sometimes experiences a kind of vertigo. Perhaps he discovers that he is harbouring feelings of resentment against the very person he loves most. The simple image he has built up of himself becomes blurred. The very thing he has thought most solid is shaken. He cries out in anguish: 'Am I a monster?' No, he is not a monster. He is normal, like you and me. The most contradictory feelings can coexist in each and every one of us. Perhaps some reader will think: 'That is the same as saying that we are all monsters!' Well, no; I do not go along with this word 'monster'. It is better to recognize the truth, namely that this tension between our contradictory drives is normal.

10   HIDDEN VIOLENCE

I think we ought now to do for violence a 'truth operation' analogous to the one Freud once did in connection with the sex instinct. I say violence, not only legitimate aggression. The good bourgeois of the year 1900, in the hypocritical society of Vienna which Freud was observing, affected to be free of those sexual lusts which he condemned severely in other people; he claimed that only a few immoral deviants were obsessed by them. Who is lecherous? Other people, he thought, not I.

Freud came and hurled at him the accusation made by the prophet Nathan against King David: 'You are the man' (II Sam. 12.7). You put on a fine front, but behind it, in the secrecy of your heart, you hide the very vices you condemn. Your desires are the same, even if you won't admit it. Sex is not shameful, as you claim; it is a universal reality of Nature; it is neither good nor bad in itself. It depends how it is used. And as far as its use is concerned, it is the same problem for all men.

There was a fine outcry! But Freud won the battle. No one claims any more nowadays that unbridled lust is not equally widespread among all human beings. What the good bourgeois of our own day claims to be free of is brutality. Who is guilty of violence? Other people, he thinks, not he! When he bemoans the escalation of violence, it is always other people's violence he is thinking of. Freud revealed the subterranean sexual urges that fester in the dark layers of the mind, and we must recognize that our urges towards violence are just as real. We need to see that violence is already present in the child, just as Freud proved that sexuality is.

The thing that upset decent people at the beginning of the century was that Freud showed man to be sexually more immoral than was then thought. Freud once remarked that the normal man is not only more immoral than he thinks, but also more moral than he suspects. You will see that this is precisely the contradictory man of whom we were thinking just now. In the same way, with regard to violence, while we must now recognize that man is more violent than is generally thought, we also see that most of the violence that is unleashed in our world – apart from sordid and vicious crimes which are the exception, and which often have their origin in pathological states – arises from a holy exasperation with the unjust violence of those who wield power.

Note that Jesus, in the Sermon on the Mount (Matt. 5.21, 27), set sex and violence side by side. To the moralistic bourgeois who condemned the adulterer, he says: 'You yourself are one, for in your heart you lust after the woman who is not yours.' A moment before, he has said to the same man, proud of never having killed anyone: 'Whoever is angry with his brother will answer for it before the court,' like a murderer.

Ah, anger! It is convenient to refer to anger in ourselves, and to violence in other people. For us, anger is an excuse, an extenuating circumstance: I was angry; don't take what I said seriously. When the gunman fires his tommy-gun, is it not because he is angry?

Jesus will not countenance these subtle distinctions that we make in order to divide men into two camps, putting ourselves among the righteous and condemning the others. He asserts that all men are alike. This certainly not in order to condemn them all, but to bring his grace to all.

Jesus accepts men not on account of their virtues, but on account of their weakness. In my book *Guilt and Grace* I pointed out that the gospel speaks of forgiveness for those who acknowledge their guilt, while it arouses the consciousness of guilt in those who flatter themselves that they are innocent. In the same way we can see Jesus forgiving the violent men who are nailing him to the cross – 'Father, forgive them; they do not know what they are doing' (Luke 23.24) – but we are aware also that he awakens in us the realization of our own violence when we think we are not tainted with it at all.

Indeed, aggressiveness, anger, and violence are very often unconscious. Carl Rogers (p.340) tells the following story: 'When a friend says [to a man who has allowed anger to get the better of him in the course of a group discussion], "Well, let's not get angry about this," he replies, with evident sincerity and surprise, "I'm not angry! I don't have any *feeling* about this at all! I was just pointing out the logical facts." '

We have all witnessed similar scenes, even in high-level academic debate. A speaker is carried away by the vehemence of his feelings. His opponent asks him, mildly, 'Why are you being so aggressive all of a sudden?' Then the other exclaims, even more violently, 'Me, aggressive? You must be joking! You're just trying to avoid having to justify your argument. I am not in the least aggressive; I assure you that I am in complete control of myself. I am just being objective, that's all, and I refute your thesis because it is untenable. I'm sorry if you don't like it and so have to accuse me of being aggressive instead of answering my arguments.'

I once gave a lecture on aggression in a small town in Switzerland. I had told them of Rogers' amusing remark in order to show that aggressiveness is often unconscious. Some friends of mine, a husband and wife who lived in a neighbouring town, had pleased me by taking the trouble to come over to hear my lecture. A few days later I received a letter from the wife. She told me that they had talked a lot together in the car on the way home. Her husband, she said, had realized that he was much more aggressive than he had thought; and as for her, she went on, she had been able to appreciate much more keenly the rare privilege she enjoyed of not being aggressive towards anyone.

That was the first paragraph. All the rest of her long letter was full of complaints about her husband! Her complaints were certainly justified, but they were expressed in a markedly aggressive manner. She was of course sincere, and we can understand her: most people reserve the word violence for violence which seems to them to be unjustifiable, i.e., other people's violence. But since we all have at all times the absolute conviction that we are right in all conflicts, our own violence, since in our eyes it is justified, we do not see as violence at all, but as indignation.

This explains the fact that seemed to us earlier to be rather naïve, namely that people look upon their own violence as legitimate, and that of others inadmissible. The truth is that they do not see their own violence as violence at all. It is thus a problem of awareness. See how psychology and the Bible agree on this point: in the moving dialogue between God and Cain before the murder, look how God tries to awaken in Cain the realization of what is going on in his mind (Gen. 4).

No nation is conscious of its own spirit of violence when it is setting out to fight a war. I happened to be travelling in Italy just when that country was starting the foolish and shameful war with Ethiopia. At every station men were joining the train, having been called up for the armed forces. At every station the crowds who had come to see them off displayed delirious enthusiasm, with flags flying and the singing of the Fascist song *Giovinezza*. No one could have stood out against that universal exaltation. If I had been able to ask, 'Why are you so violent?', they would have answered, 'But we aren't in the least violent, just enthusiastic.'

Look at the photographs of other convoys of troops setting off for other wars that have quickly ended in disaster. The scene is the same! Is it just the universal love of adventure, or the considered resolve to fulfil a patriotic duty? Is there not also a certain pleasure at being authorized, even urged, to commit what up to then has been forbidden? I do not mean expressly to kill, the thought of which is hardly conscious, but to be violent. Is there anyone who has never been tempted to do the very thing that is forbidden?

Consider, too, how irrational it all is: the thing that has been severely proscribed becomes suddenly obligatory; one is punished if one refuses to do it. This is perhaps what sometimes gives a nation the feeling afterwards that it has been manipulated – it has been given an enemy to hate so that its soldiers will march to the war with enthusiasm, only to find that it is given the same foreign nation a few years later to love as an ally! That there is in the human heart a need to love, everyone admits. What I am maintaining here is that there is also, and at the same time, in the same heart, a need to hate and to kill. It would be impossible to manipulate people if there were not already in their minds the feelings that are being played upon.

The cinema and the television are accused of portraying too much violence, and rightly, since the constant spectacle of violence is a dangerous invitation to crime. But there is just as much in the Bible, which is piously read to children. And think of literature, the theatre with its tragedies and its horror plays, bullfights, crime novels, even children's comics, and the police brutality which is increasing in all countries. Everybody knows that it is happening, and yet no one seems able to curb it. Has not man always been fascinated by violence? Would violent shows be put on if they were not popular? And how could they be popular if there were not in the human heart an extreme thirst for violence, which in default of real violence which the law forbids, is satisfied to some extent by proxy, by identification with the criminals of stage and screen and the fighters in the arena?

A mother may suddenly be assailed by an absurd and terrifying thought: what if she were to commit some terrible crime against her child whom she loves so tenderly? The thought worries her so that she cannot put it out of her mind. Is she then a monster? How is it possible that such a horrific thought should have entered her mind? It becomes a veritable obsession. The doctor tries to reassure her. He knows that a mother who is obsessed by such a thought is never the one who will put it into practice. We are not responsible for the thoughts that spring into our minds as the result of a spontaneous association of ideas. It is clear that the idea of love may give rise to that of hate, the idea of making alive that of causing to die, just as the thought of white evokes that of black.

But these reassurances are ineffective. The woman remains obsessed not only by the thought itself, but by her shame at being an unnatural mother. It may be necessary to undertake a long process of analysis in order to track down the unconscious factors which have provoked this unfortunate association of ideas. For as Freud has shown, there is always a modicum of truth even in the most absurd of obsessions. I do not at all deny, of course, that these unconscious mechanisms exist, and I have been able, as every psycho-therapist has, to verify their presence in my patients.

But what I see is that psychic mechanisms do not explain every-thing. They tell us why it is this mother who has fallen ill and not another; in other words, they explain the personal circumstances, the personal occasion of the disease, but not why it is possible for such a disease to exist. In the same way the inquiry after an accident explains the circumstances which brought about the death of the victim, but it does not explain the mystery of death, and after all every living being must die, whatever the circumstances of his death.

There is therefore a level that lies deeper than that of analytical psychology – an ontological, existential level. It does not con-tradict psychology, it goes beyond it. The modicum of truth that Freud speaks of is not only about the repressed drives which reveal themselves in a disguised form, it is a more general truth, inherent in man's nature, which we find it very hard to accept. It is that in the depth of the human personality, alongside a life force which aspires to self-realization and the increase of life, there is also a destructive force which tends to promote death, and which is the source of all violence, both real and imaginary, even the most absurd and the most revolting violence – our own as well as that of the violent criminal.

Freud himself admitted it, acknowledging at the time how hard he had found it to give up the simpler view of man that he had had up to then, namely that there was but one motive force in the mind – Eros, the life impulse, the sexual drive. And so he came back to a dualism which admitted also the existence of a death impulse, Thanatos. Man is torn not only between his life impulse and the external moral and social obstacles it comes up against, but also within himself between his life impulse and his death instinct. As Dr Rudolf Affemann pointed out in a paper on aggression read at the Twenty-Second Session on the Medicine of the Person, at Stuttgart in 1970, this dualistic concept of the mind is that des-cribed by St Paul in his epistle to the Romans.

We may well come to the conclusion that our patient suffering from obsessional neurosis has a more penetrating intuition than we have of the nature of his inner impulses. He may be unaware of the psychological mechanisms at work within him (which psycho-analysis may reveal to him) but he probably understands better than we do that there is a potential murderer in every man, and any of us – even the most virtuous – could become that murderer according to circumstances. Moreover there are people who, without being ill, suddenly experience a sort of flash of consciousness reaching into the depths, and feel the overwhelming power of the tumultuous destructive forces at work in the mind, a sort of craving to smash everything, which is fortunately restrained by solid moral and social barriers.

Thus, in contrast with my illustrious fellow-citizen Jean-Jacques Rousseau, who thought that man was by nature good, and perverted only by society, I think that he is violent by nature and that he is preserved from the worst effects of his violence by society, though at times it stirs up and exploits his cruel instincts. As Denis de Rougemont has remarked, 'The atom bomb is not in the least dangerous. It is a thing. What is fearfully dangerous is man.' To that I add these three quotations from Dr Anthony Storr: 'We are the cruellest and most ruthless species that has ever walked the earth' (p.ix). 'It is a mistake to believe that the ordinary man is not capable of the extremes of cruelty' (p.99). 'Each one of us harbours within himself those same savage impulses which lead to murder, to torture and to war' (p.ix). Really to understand that is to stop passing judgment on our fellows.

Shortly after the second world war C. G. Jung published some reflections along these lines, entitled 'After the Catastrophe'. He addressed himself in particular to us, his Swiss compatriots, scandalized as we were by the atrocities committed by the Nazis and inclined hypocritically to think that such abominations could never have happened in our country. In his oracular style, as one familiar with occult powers, Jung warned us that such pretensions were as absurd as they were arrogant. He recalled the saying in the gospels that when a devil is cast out, he has to go somewhere, and there is always the fear that he will return with seven other devils. Was this not prophetic of the present wave of violence?

11 A CONGENITAL DISABILITY

Dr Hacker, in his book to which I have already referred at length, tells of a conversation he had with Dr Menninger, the well-known American psychiatrist. Menninger was telling him of a visit he had made to the Nazi extermination camp at Buchenwald, immediately after the war, with a group of doctors from the United States. 'My colleagues', he said, 'were horrified at what they saw. They could not believe their eyes, and found it hard to accept that human beings were capable of such horrors. I was astonished at their astonishment, and I put the same question to several of my colleagues: "What did you expect? Why did we join the war? Why are we here, if it was not in order to destroy a régime which puts human beings in concentration camps, and tortures and annihilates them?" '

Why then was Dr Menninger not astonished, although he was as moved as were his colleagues at what they saw? Without any doubt it is because as a Christian he sees man as he is and as the Bible shows him to be. He says so himself. After reminding Dr Hacker that throughout history awful atrocities have been committed, he goes on: 'Man is in fact a violent and also a sinful being.' Those who reject the biblical concept of sin always tend – logically enough – to minimize the problem of violence, looking upon it as a kind of anomaly, an exceptional deviation, confined to a few sick persons, and a few ill-disposed persons; and this is reassuring to the others. But they are astonished when events give the lie to this easy optimism.

Sin is a word which psychiatrists do not often use. I understand them, nevertheless sin is what is involved. I understand them because the biblical idea of sin has been radically distorted by moralism, and because psychiatrists see, as I do, far too many pious souls weighed down by it. And not only religious people: there is a secular moralism which is quite as pathogenic as that of our churches. But we must recognize that it is particularly religious people who, far from being joyously liberated by the good news of grace, are so obsessed by the fear of committing sin that all their spontaneity, their growth and their development is stifled.

This explains the mistrust on the part of large numbers of

psychiatrists of all religious influence. And yet it is they who could most readily recognize how far removed from the faith of the gospel this moralism is. Moralism forbids this, forbids that, and ends up forbidding everything that is most worth while. It sets up a casuistry of the permitted and the forbidden which is just like that of the Pharisees, against which Jesus fought a battle to the death; for that is what it was, since he died on the cross as a result of it.

The point is so important, and misunderstandings are so common, that I must return to it. Let us take up again Jesus' words on violence which I have already quoted: 'You have learnt how it was said to our ancestors: You must not kill; and if anyone does kill he must answer for it before the court. But I say this to you: anyone who is angry with his brother will answer for it before the court' (Matt. 5.21–22). Think how busy the courts would be! It must not be therefore taken literally. We are not to think that because Jesus speaks of courts that he is setting himself up as a judge who condemns. His attitude is just the opposite of that of the judge, since he extends a wide-open welcome to all sinners.

The intention of Jesus in this text is clear: he is addressing himself to decent people who are certain that they themselves are free of the taint of violence, because they have not obviously killed anyone, and who are willing to hale the rest – the murderers – before the court. What he is saying to them is that they deserve just as much to be brought before the court themselves, because they too are violent: even so much as to be angry with one's brother is to reveal one's violence. Which of us could boast that he has never been angry with anyone?

Jesus is here combating the clever distinctions that men make between different degrees of violence in order to flatter themselves that they are innocent, and in order to judge others to be guilty. We are all violent. We cannot live without getting angry with others, without giving offence to others, without experiencing feelings of aggressiveness and hostility against those who stand in our way. Just as we cannot live without being arrogant, jealous, and selfish, without often telling lies, without having impure desires, without failing in love – in short, without sinning. So this pretension of moralism to live without sin is mere self-deception, a vain utopianism which only serves to implant in the hearts of the faithful a morbid and obsessive fear of committing sin.

That is the biblical message: 'There is not a good man left, no, not one' (Rom. 3.10). It is not a case of there being two camps, the camp of the violent and that of the non-violent, however hard the latter try to hide their violence. But though Jesus puts all men in the same camp, it is not in order to condemn them all, but on the contrary to accord to all the divine grace. As the scripture says: 'God sent his son into the world not to condemn the world, but so that through him the world might be saved' (John 3.17).

He himself used a medical analogy: 'It is not the healthy who need the doctor, but the sick. . . I did not come to call the virtuous, but sinners' (Matt. 9.12–13). Jesus acts like a doctor: he makes a diagnosis, a diagnosis of inordinate violence. All men are infected by it. He has nothing for those who claim not to be violent. But to those who recognize that they are sick with violence, he brings grace. He does not make a diagnosis in order to condemn, but in order to heal. His attitude is not that of the judge, but that of the doctor. Who could deny that Jesus was at home among people whom society condemned, whereas he was in conflict with religious people proud of their virtue, and denounced their hidden sin.

Well! The biblical view of sin is this diagnosis pronounced on man. To say that he is a sinner is to say that he suffers from a certain distortion, that there are unhealthy impulses in him which contrast with the health of Nature, with the harmony of Nature. He has fratricidal violence in his heart, without also having the instinctive curb which contains it in the case of the animals; and he has no power in himself to contain it. Sometimes he may be quite aware of it, and will feel the need to confess his guilty acts and thoughts of violence. But he is never capable of drawing up a complete inventory of it. All he can do is to recognize that he is ill, and turn to the great Doctor.

This analogy with sickness comes home particularly to us doctors. We see the inexorable determinism to which man is subject, how much he depends on his body, on his hormones! It only needs a little adrenalin to run, for him to display anger. As soon as we fall ill we see that it is our bodies that rule us, when we thought the opposite was the case.

Then there is psychological determinism, psychic traumas which bring interminable reactions in their train. What is the meaning of praise and blame, but that men are always ready to set themselves up as judges and arbiters in order to exalt themselves? What is the meaning of exhortation, of appeals to our will, and criticism of our conduct? Dr Jean de Rougemont expounded all this with some humour in a lecture at the Protestant Medico-Social

Congress at Cannes: 'Had I not been taught from my earliest youth that man must govern himself by his strength of character and his will-power?' How is this possible, when the doctor is compelled 'to accept that man, despite his conviction to the contrary, possesses no authority over himself, no power he could use to control himself'? 'For this reason,' he goes on, 'man ought to be considered as disabled.' Later he spells it out: '. . . born irresponsible, congenitally disabled, really sick.'

The notion of a congenital disability reminds us of the idea of original sin, which is even less popular today than the notion of ordinary sin. It means that this sickness of excessive violence is a congenital disease which man does not contract by accident, but that he receives it as he receives his life. We owe the expression 'original sin' to St Augustine. There was someone who really knew human nature! And without being in the slightest degree moralistic. Consider his words: 'It is through love that one asks, seeks, and knows.' 'Love, and do what you will' (*Homily* VII.8 on I John).

There was plenty of violence in St Augustine's day. Greco-Roman civilization, nearly a thousand years old, was crumbling under the hammer-blows of the barbarians. Alaric had invaded Italy and sacked Rome itself. To say nothing of the internal violence that marked the decadence of the empire. Then the Vandals passed over into Africa, and St Augustine, Bishop of Hippo, was to die in that town while it was under siege from the Vandal King Genseric. From where did all these misfortunes, this wave of violence, come?

Around St Augustine the Christians were accused of having brought down these catastrophes on the people by banning the worship of the ancient divinities which for so many centuries had protected Rome. The gods were taking their revenge! St Augustine replies that unjust violence has always existed, because man has always turned away from his Creator; because he has misused the liberty his Creator has given him; because he has taken it upon himself to judge between good and evil, to do without God instead of letting himself be guided by him. The essence of the problem does not lie in events, but in the heart of man, who remains in distress so long as he does not come back to God. Thus St Augustine gave to the West what was to be its philosophy for ten centuries.

The reader will see that St Augustine's thought, nurtured on the Bible and his own fundamental experience of conversion, accords exactly with the analysis we have made so far of violence. At bottom it is one aspect of the great problem of evil raised by the Bible from the third chapter of Genesis onwards. That is no doubt why Lorenz gave his book on aggression the subtitle *A Natural History of Evil*. The sickness of which I have spoken is not the aggression which is inherent in life, nor even a certain violence necessary for the achievement of the noblest human aspirations, and ordained by God. It is the loss of limits. It is a deficiency disease, like the diseases due to lack of vitamins.

An instinct is inherited. So is the deficiency or absence of an instinct. The instinct which prevents an animal from killing its fellow is the constraint which man lacks. So I think we may say that this is one aspect of the original sin of which St Augustine spoke. Its instinct submits the animal automatically to God's order. It sets the necessary limit to violence. God has granted man a measure of liberty in respect of instinct. But man has presumed to judge for himself what is good and what is bad, in other words to decide where lies the notorious frontier between good aggression and evil violence. To do so we have sought in vain for a criterion. Instinct needed no criterion: it arrested without fail the guilty arm.

Is it not this which distresses man, especially now? This realization that the barrier is missing, that part of our human make-up is a violence which is indeed useful, but which is boundless, so that it could well end up destroying the human race. The knowledge that there is a fire smouldering in the human heart, which may at any moment break out and cause disaster even before we have become aware that the boundary between permissible and impermissible violence has been crossed. It is this awareness of the presence of subterranean forces of which we were speaking in connection with the destructive power of obsessional neurosis.

Ah! if only we could find criteria, make a clear separation between good and evil, put mankind into two distinct camps – the good and the wicked – as we believed we could when we were children and as the Pharisees still claimed! But as we grow older we perceive that there is good in evil and evil in good; that we are capable of perpetrating in good faith the most unjust acts of violence, with the best of intentions; and that the most violent hates derive, as Baruk says, from that excellent thing, the moral conscience.

We desire to bring liberty to a people, and we bring war, destruction, and death. We see that there is a great deal of selfishness in the purest love, a great deal of vanity in the deepest devotion. A married couple wish to maintain peace in their home, and so have avoided violent confrontations, and have as a result become strangers to one another, ruining the marriage they wanted to save. Others are ruined by the excessive demands of a too impatient love. The most disinterested of loves, that of the mother for her child, can without her realizing it at all become possessive and stifle the child, preventing him from becoming himself, free and responsible. A father's selfless desire to bring up his child properly can be what makes him beat him quite improperly.

Worse still, it is often a high-minded desire to be faithful to God and to defend the truth that has set men against one another. I have already made mention of Cain, the archetype of fratricidal violence, and remarked that what moved him to attack Abel was spiritual jealousy, the anguish of believing himself to be less loved by God.

And then we are beginning to realize that all the technical progress, of which the industrialized nations are rightly proud, is having harmful effects against which hardly any precautions have been taken. We see that man, intoxicated with the excitement of his great techno-scientific adventure, has massacred Nature and is suddenly realizing, to his surprise, that it cannot be done with impunity. The first command that God gave to man was to cultivate and keep the garden of Eden – to protect Nature (Gen. 2.15). Carelessly to massacre Nature means in the end to massacre the people who die, for example, poisoned by the mercury discharged by prosperous chemical factories into the neighbouring streams.

It seems that the systematic massacre of Nature, of which the overwhelming scale of the threat it constitutes for the survival of the whole of humanity is only now being understood, is nothing but a titanic manifestation of the aggressive instinct of man. Proof of this is that we speak of man's 'conquests' and his 'victories' over Nature. The destruction of Nature has no doubt served as an outlet for human violence and protected men from exercising their violence on each other. Thus, when two boys are fighting over an apple, one can put an end to the quarrel by giving them a second apple so that they can work out their violence by devouring an apple each, instead of hitting each other.

Similarly, instead of fighting over an oil well, we can agree to drill a second one, so that Great Britain, for example, in exploiting the North Sea oil deposits, can be less aggressive than other nations towards producer countries and their demands. So men have agreed together at the expense of Nature, which could not defend itself against increasing exploitation due to technical progress. But when it appears that the resources of Nature are not inexhaustible,

aggressive tension grows among men. The vicious circle is com-
pleted: strategic imperatives have stimulated research into a source
of energy that is apparently inexhaustible: the atom.

12   LIMITING THE DAMAGE

And so the threat of the atomic bomb hangs over our age. No
powerful government can renounce the ceaseless effort to improve
it, or to go on adding to its stockpile of bombs, without betraying
its trust, however sincerely it might wish to do so. What a wonderful
adventure is atomic physics, into which disinterested scientists
have enthusiastically thrown themselves with a clear conscience!
Their interest has been pure scientific research, but the vicissitudes
of history have complled governments to take it over – with consciences equally clear.

And so the potential of violence is increased ten times, a hundred
times over and more, without anyone being responsible. We have
seen atomic scientists giving up important research in face of the
awful possibilities of disaster that are opened up. How hard it is then
for the great powers, however sincerely they desire peace, to come
to an understanding on the limitation of nuclear arms. Once again
they are up against the problem of the impossibility of defining
limits.

An impossibility at any rate, as Pope Paul says in his encyclical,
so long as there is no world authority in a position to act effectively
on the legal and political plane. There are various movements
striving to achieve this, such as the Humanist Club of 'world
citizens' in Paris, to which my friend Dr Armand Vincent has
contributed, writing an excellent article on violence in the Club's
magazine *Somme Mondialiste*. I am afraid, however, that world
government is still a long way off, not only because of obstruction
by the great powers, but also because of hesitation by the weak,
which I know well, since I belong to one of the smallest countries
in the world. And that is why I am not really persuaded that a world
government would result in less violence. It seems that nations are
intuitively aware that the concentration of power is a double-edged

weapon – that it puts an end to minor iniquities among the weak, but that it allows greater ones among the powerful. One can imagine the terrifying political rivalries that could break out among those who would like to seize this world-wide power. Remember Caesar and Pompey! Indeed it was the attraction of the world power of their day that set them against one another.

One is reminded of the time when Hitler promised Europe a thousand years of peace under his jack-boot. We in Switzerland, his neighbours, apart from a few who were purblind, and a few traitors, were unanimous in thinking that liberty was worth more than such a peace. The weak are always a little suspicious of the strong.

When I was a medical student an English writer, Lord Bryce, had asked a professor of law at Geneva, Charles Borgeaud, to get one of his students to make a collection of important documents on the working of democracy in Switzerland. And since the professor had been unable to find a law student willing to undertake the task, he had suggested that I should do it.

I threw myself into the work with the enthusiasm that has always fired me when delving into a discipline other than my own. I soon discovered that one of the smallest of the Swiss cantons, actually a 'half-canton', that of Inner-Rhoden of Appenzell, had until then – apart from one unimportant poll – always voted 'No' to all the bills submitted to it by the federal government. One can minimize this fact, and see in it nothing but an example of a quaint old custom; but I see it myself as an illustration of the fact that when small nations are truly free to express their opinion, they speak up against the concentration of power at the centre.

It took my little Swiss homeland several centuries, the agency of foreign invasion and the scourge of civil war, to evolve from a simple alliance between sovereign cantons to a federal state. Less than a century and a half ago each canton had its own army, the symbol of political independence. It was only after several majority votes that my own Republic of Geneva was incorporated into the Swiss Confederation, in 1814, despite the exhortations of far-sighted statesmen. What does this mean, if not that the concentration of power hardly ever appeals to free people as being their best protection against the threat of violence?

I am old enough to have known the last years of the 'Belle Époque', which my English readers know as the 'Edwardian Era', with its naïve euphoric belief that humanity was progressing towards universal peace. I was sixteen on the outbreak of the first world war – that great historical turning-point that put an end to several centuries of easy humanist optimism. A deep feeling of anxiety filled men's minds, a sense of fate which the Greeks knew well, of being in the grip of a cruel and tragic destiny, so that every effort to do the right thing only brought down fresh ills – an intuitive feeling that the whole fabric of our civilization was warped.

A brief wind of optimism blew again over the West between 1950 and 1970, helped by the belief that prosperity must result from a continuous growth in the level of economic production. The West paid little heed to the fact that its prosperity rested on its flagrantly unjust exploitation of the natural resources of non-industrialized countries. It needed only a few violent incidents arising out of this injustice, and warnings from the scientists of the Club of Rome, for people to fall back into a 'period of disenchantment', in the words of Michel Albert and Jean Ferniot, of whom I shall have more to say in Part Two. Some limits must be set, but no one knows how to define them or where to put them. And if it is man that sets them, man can also remove them. It will always be those who are most violent who will remove them. What other authority than that of God could guarantee their inviolability?

St Augustine spoke of original sin only in order to announce redemption. The word seems rather old-fashioned today. 'Redemption?' writes M. Henri Fresquet, 'Modern man finds the idea of Christ as Saviour repugnant to him because he does not feel the need to be saved... The idea of salvation could with advantage be replaced by that of liberation, which is in any case biblical.' Is it not somewhat odd that that is written at the very moment when there is a growing feeling that some curse hangs over humanity?

There is no doubt in my mind that the idea of salvation has been devalued by its restriction in pietistic circles to the individual meaning implied in the question 'Are you saved?' which well-meaning and zealous believers used to throw at passers-by in the street. I have had to reply to many pious people tormented by the question 'Am I saved?' or else, 'Is this or that person whom I love saved?' Though the Bible calls on each of us for a personal decision, for personal dedication to Jesus Christ, it actually announces the collective salvation of the whole human race, and not only that of Christian believers. I believe that Jesus came for the salvation of all men, and it seems to me rather uncharitable to doubt it. It is our privilege as believers to know our Liberator.

Let us then adopt M. Fresquet's suggestion and speak of liberation, in face of this feeling of a tragic fate which man himself is powerless to alter, since his efforts only bring him new trials and a new servitude. This feeling of being subject to an implacable fate is due to our consciousness of being caught in a web of vicious circles, the evidence for which is a matter of everyday experience. Everything is a vicious circle in biology, and even more so in psychology and also in economics.

Examples? The master who lacks authority is played up by his pupils, and the resultant chaos puts the finishing touches to the ruin of his authority. The pupil who is afraid of failing his examinations get confused and does not even manage to say what he does know; he is so mesmerized by the spectre of his failure that he does not even understand the question that he has to answer, and he fails. After that he will be even more afraid of his next examination. The candidate who has confidence in his lucky star comes to the examination as he would to a game; he finds ways of hiding his ignorance and making the most of the things he does know. He passes, and his confidence for the future is reinforced.

The young woman who suffers from being unmarried and lonely has such an intense longing for any sort of real relationship with someone else that she is paralysed with shyness when the chance presents itself. She has no idea what to say; her stiffness is mistaken for indifference, and she withdraws into the bitterness of her frustration. You have to be rich to make more money, and through making it the rich man is enabled to invest more and so go on making more. The poor man, on the other hand, lacks the indispensable means to raise himself from his poverty. Jesus pointed this out: 'To everyone who has will be given more, and he will have more than enough; but from the man who has not, even what he has will be taken away' (Matt. 25.29).

It is the same with violence. It carries within itself a dynamic of growth which condemns it to increase. Violence always sets going a chain reaction. This is true on the individual level. A woman was saying to me recently, 'I blame my husband not so much for his aggressiveness, as for making me aggressive myself.' All the more in social conflicts. Revolutions often begin quietly under the inspiration of idealists, proud of achieving an orderly revolution, without too much blood-letting. But there are areas of resistance which must be broken if the revolution is not to be betrayed, and the tough measures required only exacerbate the resistance. A fatal vicious circle is initiated, and no one can stop it. Soon the idealists run foul of their more violent partisans, and the end is a reign of terror.

The same law applies to dictatorships, which may seem beneficent to begin with, for in re-establishing order they put an end to much violence. I always remember the conversations I had with Bishop Wurm, one of the leaders of the German Confessional Church, which was among Hitler's most tenacious opponents. I met him just after the war, when he was sick and exhausted by the struggle he had had to maintain.

He told me how hard it had been to see clearly at the start. Had not Hitler solved problems which seemed insoluble under the Weimar Republic, such as the question of the Saar, and the rapid rise in unemployment? Had he not come to power by legal means on a great wave of popular enthusiasm? Was there ever a political movement entirely free of violence? What government did not make mistakes? Was it not all the more necessary to collaborate in order to exert some influence on it?

It was through a dream that God had opened Bishop Wurm's eyes, and impelled him into the resistance movement – a fine example of divine direction, reminiscent of the dream the wise men had, which warned them not to go back to Herod (Matt. 2.12), and the dream in which Joseph was told to take refuge in Egypt (Matt. 2.13). But however a dictatorship begins, it is subject to an inexorable evolution through ever harsher measures and increasing violence, towards the worst kind of disaster. It is easy enough to start a dictatorship, impossible to stop it.

Clearly this law of the vicious circle explains our feeling of helplessness in the face of violence. We cannot let it go unchecked, and yet to fight it is to engage in a deadly auction with no limit to the violent bidding. One is reminded of the physical law governing falling bodies, whose speed accelerates proportionately to the square of the distance. At the same time the phenomenon of the vicious circle once again calls in question the idea of limits which was engaging our attention just now, and on which the law depends. Can there be a limit to a movement which, once started, can only grow inexorably? Is not the seed of evil and destructive violence already present in benign and innocent violence?

Journalists are fond of using the term 'brinkmanship' to describe a situation of political or economic blackmail in which each side is trying to see how far it can go with a threat of violence. But it is already going over the brink to use the threat of violence to hold violence in check – even if it is still done with impunity. The notion of limits rests on the idea that there is continuity between useful violence and harmful violence, a progressive continuity like a chromatic scale, as if a little violence were beneficial, and a little more, harmful – like a drug that will heal in the right dose, whereas an overdose will kill.

Is it not evident that large-scale violence may be legitimate and necessary? I remember the astonishment of many of those present at the 'Church and Society' conference of the World Council of Churches at Geneva in 1966, when Richard Shaull maintained that 'Christians might be called upon to participate in acts of revolutionary violence'. Conversely, may not actions whose violence is so slight as to be imperceptible already be sinful? Since the law of the vicious circle teaches us that the most disastrous violence evolves from tiny acts of violence, automatically and ineluctably, ought we not at the very start to be sorting out the beneficial from the harmful acts of violence? In other words, ought we not to be making a qualitative rather than a quantitative distinction? That, however, is more utopian than ever.

Of course we cannot shut our eyes to the importance of degrees of violence. We cannot, on the pretext that they all have to do with violence, say that the threat of a spanking is the same as a spanking itself, nor that a spanking is no different from grievous bodily harm or murder, despite the fact that there is an obvious progression from the one to the other. There are degrees of violence, and it is on this fact that the law is based. The law allows all sorts of minor acts of violence – threats, coercion, unfairness, constraints by society upon the individual (which it may well itself originate) and by the strong upon the weak. But the law sets limits which must not be crossed, and which are symbolized by the presence of the forces of law and order. It defines a Rubicon, to take up again the image which occupied our attention at length earlier on.

These legal limits, however, are entirely conventional and change with changing moral climates, as is proved by the need constantly to modify legislation. Thus the authority of the father was once that of an absolute monarch. His wife had no remedy against the abuse of his power, and his daughter could not marry against his will. The case was the same with the rights of the employer over his workpeople before the rise of the trades union movement. And as we have seen, in wartime the law may prescribe the killing which it forbids in time of peace. Lastly, anyone who thinks himself strong enough may defy the law. Thus on the day that Hitler broke with the League of Nations, the road lay open before him to every sort of aggression.

In principle, the law takes account only of the degree of violence, though nowadays, under the influence of the psychologists, it tempers its rigour by taking motivation into account. The law shows some indulgence where crimes of passion are concerned, as if it had an intuition of the truth proclaimed by the biologists: 'I am . . . inclined to believe,' writes Lorenz (p.184), 'that in every case of genuine love there is . . . a high measure of latent aggression . . . There is no love without aggression, but there is no hate without love!' As motivation is always subjective, and as the law has a rather naïve pretension to objectivity, the argument goes on without coming to any definite conclusions. Only revolutionary tribunals seem to have no difficulty in assessing guilty motives.

Alongside conscious motives are unconscious ones, much more powerful and universal; those which are connected with the Oedipus complex or with the sadistic element in the sex instinct, or else the 'existential void' of which Viktor Frankl speaks, the feeling that life has no meaning, which, he claims, plays an important role in juvenile delinquency. But whatever the value of such interpretations, they are dependent upon the personal doctrines of the individual psychologist. We must not forget how people can deceive themselves as to their real motives – as Dr Hacker says, it is always other people's violence that seems to us to be wrong; our own is always legitimate.

It is clear that neither the degree of violence nor the personal motivation behind it will help to settle the question. The law does not solve the problem of violence. It confines itself to preserving us from its worst effects, to limiting the damage, from a pragmatic point of view. It confines itself to checking excesses, to protecting life and property, as we say, despite the fact that a man and his property can be destroyed without a blow being struck, by means of psychological manipulation. Nevertheless it does ensure a degree of protection for the weak. This is stated by Plato in his *Gorgias*, where Callicles contrasts law with Nature. In the state of nature, he says, the strong trample upon the weak. So law was instituted by the weak as a defence against the violence of the strong.

This is also the purport of many of the prescriptions of the law of Moses: the protection of widows, orphans, and strangers (Ex.

22.20), of labourers, who must be paid their daily wage (Lev. 19.13), of the slave who must be set free if his master has injured him (Ex. 21.26), or of the poor, through the restitution of their land in the year of jubilee (Lev. 25.28). And the notorious *lex talionis*, 'a life for a life, an eye for an eye, a tooth for a tooth', by legalizing the right to return blow for blow, establishes the limitation of retaliation. It is a measure taken against the escalation of violence. The law aims only at avoiding the worst consequences, which is a great thing. That is its function, a limited but an indispensable one. Disorder soon appears where power is lacking; a wave of violence submerges a country as soon as there is no governmental authority capable of imposing respect for law. Men and nations revert to the law of the jungle as soon as the restraining influence of the forces of law and order is removed.

This factor of social stabilization is not peculiar to man. Besides the well-known inhibition against murder between individuals of the same species of which I have spoken, Lorenz observes that in animals the hierarchical relationship between generations still subsists. He refers (p.37) to the example of baboons in the wild state, who are 'led . . . by a "senate" of several old males'.

There is, however, another side to the coin of repression of violence by the law. When it uses imprisonment it sets up yet another vicious circle. Dr Hacker writes: 'Prisons, especially those that are camouflaged under the name of Borstals, are training centres for crime.' Well known too is the role of emergency courts in legalizing the violence of totalitarian regimes, but even under the most liberal of regimes the law is never anything more than a recourse to violence to combat violence – the very essence of a vicious circle. Necessary though the judicial system may be, it can only ever be a palliative.

13 TWO KINDS OF VIOLENCE

So we come back again to the fundamental problem of a differential diagnosis, as the doctors say, between good and bad violence. A difference not of degree, but in kind; a difference of nature, of quality, not of quantity. We are well aware that the slightest constraint can itself be wrong, in that it implies a lack of respect for another person, to whom it does violence; and that at the other end of the scale the most brutal violence may be justified, legal, and even legitimate.

I am writing these lines at the beginning of August. It is, as the newspapers are pointing out, the thirtieth anniversary of the dropping of the atomic bomb on Hiroshima. I read that neither the commander of the plane, General Paul Tibberts, nor his subordinates, Thomas Ferebee and George Caron, have any regrets. 'You only fight to win a war,' says the first. Indeed! And the second: 'I'm not proud of having killed so many people, but I am proud of all the lives we saved.' Indeed!

We had been told that the pilot had committed suicide, and that one of his comrades had gone into a psychiatric hospital. White lies, all of it, to set decent folks' minds at rest! The truth is that the most violent act of all history was perpetrated without arousing the least sense of guilt.

But we have seen how difficult it is to make a differential diagnosis between benign and malignant violence. Could we then try to tackle the problem from the other end – that is to say, not the source of the violence, its motivation or its degree, but its results and its fruits? A saying of Jesus suggests this proceeding: 'A sound tree produces good fruit but a rotten tree bad fruit' (Matt. 7.17). Thus we judge as doctors the value of a medicine by its favourable results, even if it does have some awkward side-effects. Jesus was talking of how to distinguish between true and false prophets. But it must be admitted that the distinction is not always an easy one to make, and depends upon one's individual idea of what are good results.

Is this not what Marcuse meant in his conversation with Dr Hacker, which I have already referred to? 'That which promotes life,' he said, 'cannot be wrong, even if certain constraints must be applied in order to develop favourable conditions for it.' All revolutionaries and protesters think this. They justify their recourse to violence as the price of the better world which they promise. They are like Caesar crossing the Rubicon. The trouble is that they always honestly believe this – that, at least, is my opinion. The same is true of those who stand in their way, who may be compared with Pompey, invoking the defence of the traditional order to excuse their violence: the end justifies the means.

This line of thought is liable to be quite immoral if it is only a pretence aimed at excusing the recourse to violence; if the intention is to win a propaganda victory by putting the adversary in the wrong, whether it be Caesar or Pompey, the revolution or the counter-revolution. This is not at all the line that Jesus was taking. He was speaking as a naturalist, as a biologist, if I may put it so, as a simple observer pointing out that there are true prophets and false prophets, trees with good fruit and others with bad fruit – quite different trees, of different kinds.

There is therefore no longer any question of laying down an invisible and hypothetical frontier somewhere along the continuous line of aggression and violence, but rather of seeing that there are in fact two kinds of violence, essentially different and even opposite to each other. In reality the violence of Caesar and that of Pompey are of the same kind – the ambition for power which brings men into collision with each other. There is another kind of violence which unites men! Put like that, such an assertion may well surprise my readers after all I have just written. At least it merits a careful examination in depth.

That is what I am going to try to do, following as I understand it the thought of a fascinating writer, René Girard, a Frenchman who teaches in the USA. His book on 'Violence and the Sacred' is one of those which have made the greatest impression on me in recent years. In the first place – if I may begin with a digression – it is because it was written not by a professional psychologist, but by a man of letters, a literary critic. Never before had I realized how good it would be for us to be more familiar with the literature of all periods and all outlooks, that literature whose sole task has been to describe the thousand and one facets, the many ups and downs, of the human personality. Having read Girard, I set about re-reading Sophocles and Plato, and I have enough to keep me occupied for the rest of my retirement if I am to complete my education – not forgetting the latest publications, since it is the leaders in the field of economics who, as we shall see later, are today asking questions about the meaning of life!

We tend to be dazzled by the rise of the so-called science of modern psychology, and are apt to forget the numberless treasures of literary psychology, which preceded it by several thousands of years. The distinction is not as great as we think, for Plato already saw in dreams, like Freud, the realization of repressed desires. Take, for instance, what he writes in the *Republic* (IX, 572b): 'My point is this – that even in the most respectable of us there is a terribly bestial and immoral type of desire, which manifests itself particularly in dreams.'

What tremendous lessons in psychology we can draw from the great legends of antiquity, from epic poets like Homer, from the Greek tragic and comic theatre, and from mythology, which is nothing but a compendium of human passions. Add to them the long line of the great philosophers, the French classical theatre, Goethe, Shakespeare, right down to the modern novel and the private diary.

Freud was not mistaken in turning to Sophocles for the myth of Oedipus. Nevertheless a literary critic like Girard puts a quite different interpretation upon it; and it is quite possible that he knows Sophocles better than Freud did. Freud used the idea of mythological divinities with his Eros and Thanatos. In Jung there are even more borrowings from the Bible, from other sacred books, from legends, from literature, from various cultures, and even from astrology and the medieval alchemists.

So I am careful not to make too great a distinction between the two psychologies, the literary and the scientific, and I recognize the importance of our great modern masters. But the reader will understand that after so many years spent trying to assimilate them I felt a certain sense of shock on reading Girard with his intimate knowledge of world literature. It was like a breath of fresh air; as if a window long closed had suddenly been opened on the infinite variety of the world.

The characteristic of the schools of scientific psychology is that they all set up a doctrinaire model into which they attempt to fit the whole of human behaviour in terms of a few relatively simple mechanisms – projection and introjection, identification and differentiation, unconscious repression and liberation of complexes, drives and resistances, and the rest. It is this systematization which confers upon these mechanisms their prestige and attraction. They can be learnt and taught, whereupon the adept becomes a member of a 'school' which has its own peculiar explanation of everything. You can easily recognize the followers of each 'school' because they have a sort of catechism which they faithfully and tirelessly trot out like good pupils. It all sounds like the old schoolmen. They invoke Freud, Jung, Adler, Rogers, and one or two others, in the way people used to invoke Hippocrates or Galen, who had said everything there was to be said.

Not that there is not very much that is true and valuable in these models. But I have always felt that it is in the very fact of their being elevated into systems that there is a great risk of the sense of the infinite diversity of life and of the mind being lost; and even a risk of losing sight of the fact that the essential problems are not about mechanisms, but about values, not about functions but about the person, problems which cannot ever be reduced to an inventory of functions. Literary psychology cannot be learnt – it is too rich, too varied, too subtle, because it never allows itself to be reduced to any sort of model. It may be looked at as one might contemplate a big bunch of wild flowers, with its medley of colours, its lively freshness and its rustic charm. It is quite possible to describe each flower, admire its simplicity, its vividness and its distinctive quality, but the bouquet as a whole does not deliver up the secret of its harmonious unity.

Then, reading Girard, I thought how concerned universal literature is with violence, how it takes a central place, especially in the tragic theatre. It is a veritable obsession, showing that violence has fascinated and obsessed mankind throughout the ages. And so my reading of Girard encouraged me to tackle this formidable problem of violence. Before reading his book I had already been convinced that man's nature is much more violent than he realizes, and that he has some intuitive recognition of the threat that hangs over his destiny: it is not only the violence of others that he fears, but also the violence within himself; for it is always there, underneath, and it might break out at any moment to ravage all he holds dear. Perhaps, even, it is the man who is apparently the mildest who is really the most violent, and it is because his own violence frightens him that he has thrust it into some obscure recess of his mind and bolted and barred the door upon it. What I found in René Girard was the confirmation of that view. Like Freud and Jung he refers constantly to ethnology, which teaches us that primitive peoples have the same obsession with the need to cope with their own violence.

The author's starting-point is ritual sacrifice, the first and most universal manifestation of the sense of the sacred in humanity. The etymological connection between these two words 'sacred' and 'sacrifice' bears witness to this fact. However far we go back, we always find religion first expressed in ritual sacrifice. That this is a sort of magical attempt to conciliate the supernatural forces to which primitive people attribute the benefits they enjoy and the misfortunes they suffer seems so obvious that everyone readily accepts it.

Our own clinical observations show that this kind of reasoning is still very widespread today. All kinds of people impose sacrifices upon themselves, sometimes quite naïve ones, like giving up cigarettes or chocolate, but sometimes very severe ones, in the hope that they will thus earn some sort of merit, some chance of success in their enterprises. The idea lies behind all kinds of asceticism including the hope of winning heaven by eschewing earthly pleasures.

But René Girard sees a much deeper significance in sacrifice. All sacrifice is violence. This has not been sufficiently realized up to now. It is of course obvious in primitive human sacrifice; and it is equally true of the sacrifice of animals, which has much the same meaning: blood must flow. The expression of violence is further emphasized by the ritual in which the priests, and often the whole people, eat the victim. Devouring is the archetype of violence.

The Christian religion still has its supreme rite in the eucharist, a symbolic manifestation of violence, commemorating and renewing the sacrifice of Christ, and ensuring the mystic communion of the faithful who together eat his body and drink his blood. Perhaps some of my fellow-Christians will be surprised that I write of it in such terms. But it is the actual words of Jesus that they hear in the liturgy: 'Take and eat, this is my body,' he said as he gave the bread; then, giving the cup of wine: 'Drink all of you from this, for this is my blood' (Matt. 26.26f.).

Freud had already pointed out the similarity between the eucharist and the totemic meal in his last book, *Moses and Monotheism*. Faced with such a striking analogy between the most primitive rites and the most highly-evolved of religions, one understands that violence is the essence of the sacred, as René Girard maintains. When an anarchist stabs a king, he has in him something of the priest performing a solemn and sacred rite.

We shall now turn our thoughts to the link which our author sees between the two kinds of violence which he calls respectively 'reciprocal violence' and 'inaugural violence'. Reciprocal violence is that of Caesar and Pompey, the violence that divides men, bringing them into mutual conflict. Indeed, they cannot live in a community without some clash of interests, desires, and ambitions. Every wrong done, every insult, fires hostility in the heart of the one who is its victim. Rancour and grievances mount up; through the phenomenon of the vicious circle which I have described, the whole of this charge of violence increases inexorably from one act of revenge to another. For want of an instinctive brake on murder between warring brothers, it tends towards mutual extermination and the destruction of the community.

In the case of sacrifice, however, it is as if all men found themselves united together as they direct and discharge this potential of violence from their hearts upon a single object, the victim of the solemn sacrifice, which cannot take its revenge. Now at last the community is saved, and that is why René Girard calls this violence 'inaugural', because it inaugurates society. 'Sacrifice restores the harmony of the community,' he writes.

Freud, writing about war, had already sorrowfully remarked that it took a common hate to unite the community. Girard's analysis, however, is more penetrating, because it brings out the sacred meaning of violence. Dürkheim had rightly seen, he says, that in early man the social community and religion make their appearance at the same time, and seem bound up together, but he had never been able to give an explanation for this fact. René Girard's book furnishes the explanation. He holds that there is a connection between the two kinds of violence, the violence which divides and the violence which unites – 'religion' means 'binding, uniting'. This link is to be seen in the mutual compensation or annulment effected by the explosion of ritual violence as it extinguishes the reciprocal violence which threatens the community.

It is as if there were a system of communicating vessels so arranged that the destructive violence can flow away into another receptacle where it becomes beneficent. Or as if a powder-barrel were to be poured out just as it was about to explode, and as it pours out it turns into cement which is used to make firm the foundations of the community.

14 INVESTMENT

Another comparison occurs to me: it is impossible to read René Girard's book without noticing that he describes violence in the way Freud describes the libido. Girard's violence, like Freud's libido, appears as an indestructible force, a natural life-force, which can be repressed but never destroyed, and which is turned upon another object when its way is barred by psychological censorship. It is a force which will always seek and find an object. One thinks at once of a term familiar to psychoanalysts: investment. A financier sells stock in order to buy a house. In doing so he is transferring from company shares into bricks and mortar a sum which in itself has nothing of the nature of either shares or houses. The psychoanalyst speaks in similar terms of successive 'investments' of libido. Libido, a spontaneous force, seeks an object, chooses an object of love. First it is the maternal breast; then the person of the mother; then comes a narcissistic stage in which the object is himself; and finally the sexual partner.

In the same way violence, in Girard's view, is a spontaneous indestructible force which chooses an object. It may be invested in a rival and lead to a brawl with him. But it may also unite two rivals if together they invest it in an expiatory victim. They experience an intense, almost divine enjoyment in this reconciliation which will cement their community life. For at bottom they loved each other without knowing it even when they were quarrelling. So lovers have all the greater pleasure in their sexual rediscovery of each other after a quarrel. They invest in their amorous embraces the same violence with which they fought each other, a fact which clearly illustrates the ambivalence of violence and love. Paraphrasing Marivaux, we might speak of the 'games of violence and love'.

Just as there is the transference of love studied by psychoanalysis, so there is transference of violence. It may be observed in everyday life, notable in those embittered people who are always grumbling about somebody. They are quite convinced that it is the behaviour of that particular individual that rouses their feelings of aggressiveness; but one knows that if that person were not there to act as a target for their criticisms, they would find someone else at once. They are the Don Juans of violence.

I think I agree with Freud when he admits rather unwillingly to a dualistic view of the psychical dynamic with his Eros and Thanatos. My reading of Girard has led me to look upon the life-force as fundamentally dualistic and ambivalent. It is at once both creative and destructive. Not solely because the living organism grows only at the expense of its environment since it must kill to nourish itself (which is true even of the vegetarian), but because it is also self-destructive, in the sense that it derives the energy necessary to life from katabolic processes.

Freud was careful not to identify the libido with the life-force. Nor am I here identifying violence with it. What I am suggesting is that both are expressions of the vital energy which is always manifested in drives towards both love and violence: they are two aspects of one and the same reality, distinct and even opposed, but interdependent like the two faces of one coin. This would explain how it is that love can so easily turn into violence, and violence into love; that there is violence in love, and love in violence. This fits in with what we are told by Hacker and Lorenz, that violence is not a mere reflex to the frustration of love, but that it is already there as an autonomous force seeking an outlet.

Psychoanalysis has of course observed the link between them, but it has tended to subordinate violence to Eros, calling it sadism or Oedipean aggression, thus making it a secondary and not a primary phenomenon. In the discussion I have referred to, between Hacker and Marcuse, the latter expresses his surprise that sexual liberation has not brought with it a diminution of aggressiveness, as the Freudian theory would lead one to expect. This is, however, precisely what one would expect if violence is recognized as a primary force on a par with libido.

Freud's virtue lies in the fact that he turned psychology from a descriptive, static attitude towards a dynamic view; and dynamism means violence. When I was a student the psychology course consisted of the enumeration of the 'faculties of the mind': memory, intelligence, will, imagination, and so on. Everything was explained in terms of deficiencies – lack of will, lack of intelligence, and so on. Freud substituted for these shadowy 'lacks' positive forces in conflict, the vicissitudes of the mind being explained by the successive 'investments' of these forces.

I think therefore that we may extend to the problems of violence the notion of investment which we owe to Freud. Violence is there, and must be invested in some object. It cannot be eliminated. To combat it only results in stimulating it, and making it grow. All that can be done is to direct it onto another object, like the lightning-conductor which attracts the lightning as it strikes and so averts the conflagration it would cause elsewhere. Similarly, many people have told me of how as children they drew down upon themselves the violence of their father in order to protect their brothers and sisters or even their mother.

René Girard refers to another ancient institution which, like sacrifice, provided a transference of the investment of violence. This

was the festival. We all understand the religious function of the
festival and the considerable social function which festivals per-
formed in antiquity, a function which they still have today among
primitive peoples. When routine had blunted the magical effect of
sacrifice, and especially when political and legal organization had
succeeded in repressing individual vengeance, festivals came to
provide a periodic opportunity for discharging at need the violence
that had been built up in people's hearts by social constraints,
conflicts, and injustices.

The analogy with ritual sacrifice is striking. Festivals were
violent to the point of frenzy. Like sacrifice, the festival had its
rites, a sure sign of its sacred meaning. And just as the ritual of
the sacrifice prescribed a murder – of all things the most strictly
forbidden – so the rites of the festival authorized and prescribed
everything that in normal times was forbidden: extravagances,
improprieties, orgies of eating, drinking, and sex, even incest. The
effect was the same: the restoration of the unity of the community
as it was caught up in a common enthusiasm. All at once grudges
and rebellions were forgotten. Something of this still survives.
Roger Caillois writes: 'Everything suggests that we should look
upon the modern carnival as a dying echo of ancient festivals of the
Saturnalia type.' There is still the sacred victim, the king of the
carnival, who is paraded in triumph to be burnt afterwards. Caillois
notes further that the thing that gave the events of May 1968 in
France their enormous public importance was that they were in
many respects a festival in the ancient sense.

Nevertheless the ancient festivals attained an extravagance which
their counterparts do not have today, and Roger Caillois wonders
what has taken their place in the modern world. He thought at first
of holidays, which do indeed have a character of rebellion against
the constraints and contrarieties of normal life. But our holidays are
a private matter, whereas the festival was supremely social. Perhaps
the bank-holiday slaughter on the roads, however, ought to be seen
as an explosion of repressed violence. But our author has no
hesitation in saying that it is wars which correspond to the festivals
of ancient times, as 'paroxysms of existence' and 'periods of strong
socialization'. Denis de Rougemont in his 'Letters on the Atomic
Bomb' has maintained the same view. Caillois notes that war, like
the ancient festival, is the time when everything that one has
previously saved is spent all at once. The comparison seems to be
valid, but it is paradoxical, since Girard speaks of the sacrifices and

the festivals of antiquity as examples *par excellence* of the peaceful use of violence.

The phenomenon of the investment of violence and its transference from one object to another is to be found in many everyday situations. When an argument becomes heated, one of the participants will suddenly break off, saying, 'I'm going for a walk to clear my mind!' He is investing in the effort of walking the violence he felt mounting within himself and which might have made him resort to blows. The investment may be symbolic: the man lights a cigarette. It is a sacrifice by fire. Yes. Indeed! He invests his violence in the immolation of the cigarette. Proof of this is that if the smoker is too angry he does not have the patience to wait while it is peacefully consumed: almost as soon as the cigarette is lit he crushes it in the ash-tray.

And if, in my anger, I seize a porcelain vase and smash it on the ground, I am investing my anger in the vase. One psychologist – I forget which – has remarked that in such cases one tends to choose a vase which is not too precious. But not always. I remember hurling my Bible into the far corner of the room in the course of an argument with my wife.

We often noticed that we had an argument every time that I had reconciled another couple. The couple had invested their violence in me, and I was investing it in my wife. I have always been aware that my workshop provided a place where I could discharge my violence. Working on wood, steel, or gold, with hammer, saw, or file, I could invest the violence which my patients had poured out on me in the consulting-room. That is possibly why there are fewer neurotics among manual workers than among intellectuals. The material one is working with serves as an expiatory victim, whereas one cannot raise one's hand against one's office manager without losing one's job.

In my consulting-room I had a large leather armchair with big buttons disposed in the form of a quincunx. One by one all the buttons were destroyed, the victims of the violence my patients had invested in them. Psychotherapeutic catharsis is a substitution investment, and we may well be right in saying that the primitive blood-sacrifice, as described by Girard, with its miraculous reconciliation, constitutes a catharsis of violence. This is also true of the motor agitation which betrays our exasperation, when we tug at our jacket buttons or turn a penknife over and over in our pockets. The mind unloads its charge upon the body. It is true even of disease, as Dr Heinrich Huebschmann of Heidelberg has pointed out: 'When the mind is silent, the body cries out.'

Investment in sport is too obvious and too well-known for it to be necessary for me to describe it at length. Let us merely note that it is considerable: think of the enormous, systematic, even relentless efforts that athletes make to achieve the glory of victory. Far more worth while than fighting with one's neighbour! But there are those who gate-crash on this activity and discharge their violence on the cheap, by watching a match on television. True sport metamorphoses contention into competition. But you know how vigilant sports associations or the Olympic Committee have to be to avoid the reverse process – the metamorphosis of competition into brutal violence.

Rules have to be multiplied with the detailed sophistication of a penal code, in order to curb the violence that can be unleashed by exasperation. Even that does not suffice. Rulings are challenged. Then referees must be appointed, and they in their turn may be the victims of players or spectators. How can one be surprised, then, at the resistance put up by the great powers to the institution of obligatory international arbitration, advocated for so long by my own country? In the same way the Olympic Committee has sought hard to preserve the chivalrous spirit in sport. And so we are reminded of the tourneys of the Middle Ages, of which I spoke at the beginning of this book, and which are a good example of the beneficent investment of violence.

What of art, science, civilization, culture? Freud saw them as investments of the libido. It is just as possible to see in them investments of violence, for do we not talk of the victories of science and the triumphs of art? No work of science or art is possible if one does not set about it with all one's vigour. Even at this moment I am investing my violence in this book that I am writing, which I hope will manage to make its way through the dense jungle of the publishing world. At this moment too, actually as I write these lines, Russian and American cosmonauts are meeting 200 kilometres above the earth, shaking hands in the sight of all the spectators, exchanging gifts and eating together. What finer example of the transference of an investment of violence could there be than that? The two super-powers, condemned by their very size to being rivals, instead of hurling atomic bombs at each other have hurled rockets into space (with what violence!) in order to fraternize.

At first they did it separately, still investing a little violence in their rivalry. But now they have wisely decided to make their investment in common, with its tremendous cost in money, intelligence, and courage, which makes it possible to smile and applaud both Washington and Moscow at the same time, instead of first one and then the other, as each competitor wins some victory. It is well worth the cost of the operation. The common investment of violence, creating or restoring brotherhood among men, is precisely what René Girard describes as pertaining to primitive ritual sacrifices.

How then are we to explain the fact that this successful rendezvous in space does not quite arouse in us the feeling of awe which characterizes our reaction to the sacred? We admire it as a feat, a great feat, an intelligent and beneficent feat, likely to encourage *détente* between the two great powers and to avert fatal outbreaks of violence; but we do not, it seems to me, experience that sense of the sacred which used to grip our ancestors in the presence of a sacrifice. How is this? No doubt it is because there is no victim.

What I have just written will surprise you less if I remind you that the sacrificial victim is the object of a murder, and that murder is forbidden except . . . except when it is sacred, prescribed by an authority superior to man – a god, fate, or justice. The contrast is striking. All of a sudden that which was forbidden and shameful becomes obligatory and praiseworthy. This is what marks the boundary between the profane, the human sphere, and the sacred, the superhuman sphere. This is why to kill in war, or to kill a criminal in the name of justice, can seem even to an unbeliever to be a sacred duty.

So Russians and Americans have accepted great sacrifices, including that of their rivalry, but there is no victim. In order to arouse the emotion of the sacred, there must be blood. That is what limits this event in space to the category of artifice – a valid, grandiose artifice indeed, but lacking magical power. The quality of sacredness cannot be manufactured by an artifice, however good an imitation it may be. Sacredness is recognized by man as a presence that is beyond him and imposes itself upon him. Watch the diffidence with which an unbeliever enters a church, a mosque, or the sanctuary of any other religion, unless he is entering as a triumphant conqueror. He looks about him with a certain anxiety to ascertain how he ought to behave, how far he can go in, whether he may sit down, take off his shoes, take off or put on his hat. The sacred is there, for unbelievers as well as believers, and it is manifested in the performance of rites. Nowadays only court protocol reminds us of it – a last vestige of the divine right of kings.

If then we confine ourselves to the limits of the profane, without the intervention of the sense of the sacred or of religious awe, today's rendezvous in space appears as an exemplary model solution to the universal problem of violence. A relative solution, but a valid one. To the extent to which men can devote themselves together to social and cultural enterprises worthy of their enthusiasm; to the extent, in fact, to which they can enthuse violently together over such enterprises, and so together invest their violence, the danger of reciprocal violence, which destroys the community, will be dispelled.

15   THE SCAPEGOAT

One cannot but feel the distance, however, that there is between these relative solutions, which we might call mini-solutions, and the maxi-solution provided by the primitive ritual sacrifices that Girard describes. It is here that the sacred intervenes; and the thing that confers its sacred character upon the event is the fact that there is a victim. It is the blood which is endowed with magical virtue, the blood of a victim in which the whole tribe has invested its store of reciprocal violence, and which takes it away with it in its death. In other words, the blood poured out which puts an end to the shedding of blood, a bloodshed that will not be avenged. 'Sacrifice', Girard writes, 'is an act of violence without risk of vengeance.'

Indeed, the key to the vicious circle of reciprocal violence, which grows diabolically, is in the reaction of vengeance. Each act of vengeance calls for another. Each awakens a thirst for further vengeance, and so on until there is a state of complete social chaos in which no one knows any longer who is avenging whom, nor on whom, nor for what. General panic ensues, no one knows who is the victim and who is guilty, what vengeance is legitimate and what is corrupt. This is what Girard calls the loss of distinctions, the effacement of the frontier between the sacred and the profane, between good and evil. It is this powerful chain-reaction of violence which creates the feeling of tragic fate. Sacrifice breaks the chain, because the victim assumes the violence of the community without paying it back. At last one knows who must die.

René Girard gives examples less remote than those of primitive tribes. 'In fifth-century Greece,' he writes, 'in the Athens of the great tragic poets, human sacrifice, it seems, had not completely disappeared. It was perpetuated in the form of the *pharmakos*.' The *pharmakos* was a person under suspended sentence of death; a miserable outcast of society, whose death no one would trouble to avenge. He was entertained at the state's expense, as a remedy against social crises, rather as you might keep in a cupboard medicines to which you could turn in case of need. He could be executed in order to stave off the threat of some popular sedition that was lusting for blood.

Later, the games in the Roman arena, the Christian martyrs thrown to the wild beasts, fulfilled this same psychological function of catharsis of popular violence, as bullfighting does in our own day. We may go all sentimental over the fate of the victims of the primitive sacrifices, or over the fate of the *pharmakos*; we may even be revolted by such cruelties. But we must see that though the fate of these victims was tragic and unjust, it was also a glorious one, since they saved the community from the threat of civil violence. Society senses this, and repays them afterwards with real veneration. Through their deaths the victims come to be honoured, like war heroes, as saviours of their country.

Thus in Sophocles' masterpiece *Oedipus at Colonus*, Oedipus – cursed, driven out, execrated for the crimes he has committed and for which he is not responsible – already appears, in the light of his approaching death, as possessing supernatural efficacy. Athens and Thebes are already arguing over who shall have his body, for his tomb will be a holy place, a source of blessing for the nation that possesses it. Girard writes: 'The hero appears as a kind of redeemer as soon as he is eliminated.' This fundamental ambivalence of execration and veneration, blessing and curse, is to be found in every tragic situation. All honour to him who delivers humanity from its murderous violence by taking it upon himself and not repaying it in kind!

All these reflections provoked by René Girard's book point to the sacred verities of Christianity. One cannot avoid being reminded

of the prophecies of Isaiah about the Suffering Servant, in which
one sees the figure of Christ himself:

> . . . a thing despised and rejected by men,
> a man of sorrows and familiar with suffering,
> a man to make people screen their faces;
> he was despised and we took no account of him.
> And yet ours were the sufferings he bore,
> ours the sorrows he carried.
> But we, we thought of him as someone punished,
> struck by God, and brought low.
> Yet he was pierced through for our faults,
> crushed for our sins.
> On him lies a punishment that brings us peace,
> and through his wounds we are healed.
>
> (Isa. 53.3–5)

Christ broke into the vicious circle of violence by taking upon
himself the violence of men, and then refusing – though he knew
how to be violent! – to pay back violence for violence. He is literally
a saviour, as we still call him without really understanding the
significance of the word: a sacred saviour from human violence,
breaking its fatal determinism. Girard's study restores its full
meaning to the word. The martyrs in the Roman arena, in common
with Christian martyrs throughout the ages, were conscious of being
identified with him, of uniting their fate with his in death, trans-
figuring death into victory over violence.

Another figure comes to mind: that of Socrates. He too accepted
the verdict of the court, though he was ironic about the meagre
majority by which he was being condemned. In his defence, the
Apology, he confines himself to saying little more than that they are
wronging themselves more than him in sending him to die. But
he goes on (29d): 'Athenians, I honour and love you, but I shall
obey God rather than you.' He refused to escape from Athens when
he was given the chance, despite his disciples' pleas. It is to this
glorious death that his undying fame is due. One could quote
many other examples of men, both humble and illustrious, who were
able heroically to resist the temptation to violence.

The striking thing about Jesus and Socrates is that both explain
their conduct as being obedience to God, so that they are conscious
of a supernatural, transcendental factor intervening in the interplay
of instinctive drives and directing them in accordance with its

sovereign will. My resolutely determinist colleagues – the organicists, who believe only in the psychochemical determinism of the body and the interior environmental situation, or the psychoanalysts, who disagree with the organicists but also believe in the determinism of the instinctive drives – even these colleagues feel in general terms a certain admiration for personalities such as Jesus and Socrates. Is not this because they feel them to be freer than other men in regard to these determining factors in nature? What ground would there be for admiring any particular behaviour if it was the inevitable result of blind determinism?

I am not denying the fact of scientific determinism. There can be no question of denying the view of man which science has revealed, the Pavlovian reflexes, the Freudian drives which act from behind, the Jungian archetypes which pull from in front, or Adler's compensation mechanisms. All these combine to make up a machine that is highly wrought, rigorously programmed (to use the modern jargon), whose intricate workings are endless, about which there will always be more to discover, but whose reality is undeniable.

Now, there is no contradiction whatsoever between this reality and that of the sovereignty of God. It is not that the Holy Spirit is one more drive alongside those of nature, either holding them in check or cancelling them out, as it is sometimes imagined to be. The drives are immanent, they come from within, whereas the divine action is transcendent, it comes from without, causing no dislocation of nature: '*Gratia non tollit naturam*,' said St Thomas Aquinas, 'Grace does not eliminate nature.' It uses and directs it. Was it not God who invented all the mechanisms studied by science? If it was he who laid down their laws, why should he break them?

I see this complicated human machine as a great organ, with all its registers, its stops, and its pipes. But according to whom you put at the manuals to play it, you will get a frightful cacophony, or marvellous heavenly music! And to get this heavenly music the organist does not have to spoil the instrument, to dislocate its mechanisms, but rather to press all its resources into service.

Observe that in this pair of instinctive forces that I have described, love and violence, we are describing very precisely the two things that most fascinate our contemporaries, like twin headlights attracting the moths. Sex and violence draw the crowds. The really successful producer is the one who knows how to combine them in one – to put violence into his sexy scenes and to lace his violent scenes with sex. What does that mean, if not that our age is truer and more genuine than many others, that man is revealing himself more freely now as he really is, passionately interested in sex and violence?

A civilization which has dismissed the organist, which believes only in nature, only in the virtue of the machine, has invited the rising generation to make it work at random amid deafening noise; to satisfy their instincts as they like, their sex instinct in pornography and their instinct for violence in hitting hard to get everything they want. The noticeable thing, however, is that these young people do not seem to be any happier than we were in the days of the sombre moralism of our childhood. Just listen to how sad their songs are!

Are they any less sick than we? I am not sure. Their instincts are more satisfied (when could they ever be fully satisfied, and at what cost?) but they suffer from something else, as Viktor Frankl says, from the 'existential void', from no longer being able to find any meaning in their lives, for only God gives a meaning. The organ is meant for the organist, and without him it has no meaning. The view of man that so many of our psychologists have, reduced to his instincts, his drives, his mechanisms, to what is inside him, detached from what is outside him – from what gave meaning to the beautiful machine – is a dour view with no poetry in it.

So what is to be done? Shall we return to repressive moralism with its threats of eternal damnation? We all know that that would no longer work. What I think we must do is to help men and women to discover that there are other joys, other ways of finding happiness than by giving free rein to their instincts, and perhaps to show them that giving free rein to their instincts was not at all what Freud had in mind, for he was a man of the highest moral scruples. This would mean giving a different interpretation to his pleasure principle from the one that most of our contemporaries have of it.

16 THE PLEASURE PRINCIPLE

I do indeed believe, with Freud, that men are ruled by the desire for pleasure; and I think that it is possible to build a morality on his pleasure principle. Not saying to people, 'This or that is forbidden', so much as 'Choose your pleasures well. Love God as a pleasure and not as a duty. Live through pleasure as honest and fruitful a life as possible.' For the more man is free to manifest his desires, the more responsible is he for his choices. Yes! A morality built upon the best-chosen pleasures, and on the joy that results from them.

When a visitor comes for the first time upon a religious movement that is founded on personal encounter with God rather than on traditional teaching, the thing that strikes him most is how joyful its members are. Such are the modern pentecostal and charismatic movements, or formerly, the Oxford Groups, which had such an influence on me, and many others.

The visitor suddenly realizes that he does not have that joy. He sees that the members do not achieve it through tradition or through obedience to a law, but because they are experiencing something personal and find in their experiences the liveliest joy imaginable. One is not asked to be a hypocrite and to deny that there is pleasure to be had in looking at pornographic pictures; or in taking advantage of another's weakness in order to humiliate him and to shine at his expense, or in order to do him violence, to exploit him for one's own personal profit. One aspires rather to other, greater pleasures.

There are many pleasures. None of them is obligatory – they are to be chosen as freely and as seriously as possible; not in the fear of violating some prohibition, for it is that sort of anxiety which has crushed so many of our patients and which is so contrary to the spirit of the gospel. 'For me there are no forbidden things,' boldly writes St Paul, adding at once, 'but not everything does good' (I Cor. 6.12). What is that if it is not a call to reflection and to a choice based upon a scale of values?

We need the personal autonomy so dear to all the schools of psychology. We must lead our own lives, assume responsibility for them, instead of being blindly led by any and every desire. See how most people use their leisure time, and later on their time in retirement. It rarely happens that one's professional occupation is chosen and carried on for pleasure, as mine has been. So that leisure, and the interminable leisure of retirement, ought to be the occasion for the pleasure principle to come into its own. But that is rarely what happens.

It ought above all to be the occasion for becoming more personal, for choosing leisure pursuits that accord with personal preferences, and thinking them out carefully. If this were in fact what generally happened, should we be witnessing the present growth in mass entertainment and the commercial exploitation of leisure with all its attendant publicity? People are being turned into robots by their leisure pursuits as much as by their work. If that is what they choose and take pleasure in, I see nothing wrong with it; but I fear that it is happening through laziness and lack of imagination and personal initiative. That young people throw themselves un-thinkingly into the first pleasures that come to hand is under-standable enough. But how many of the less young are just as naïve, and come to see us, burdened with insuperable problems, because they have chosen their pleasures badly, or even have not chosen them at all!

Freud himself had chosen the pleasure of understanding men and women, especially those who were hard to understand, the neurotics, who it was thought until then talked only nonsense and acted absurdly. He took pleasure in easing their suffering. He took pleasure in the discovery of certain truths about the human mind. He took pleasure in living a life of exemplary devotion and rectitude, and finally in accepting with the utmost courage the most atrocious physical suffering. That, it seems to me, is his lesson in the pleasure principle.

On that score I can very well declare myself his disciple, even if I do not share all his views, even though I am not a psychoanalyst, not having undergone the training which is indispensable for that. And I realize that the pleasure he took – and which later I myself took also – in trying to help people to become more honest with themselves, led him, as he says, to be more morally strict with himself: 'Perhaps . . . my being scarcely able to tell lies any more is a consequence of my occupation with psychoanalysis.'

He says 'scarcely', because he has just confessed that he had lied to one of his patients. In order not to distort anything, I copy here this moving account from Freud's book, *The Psychopathology of Everyday Life* (p.221):

One day . . . a patient reminded me to give him the two books on
Venice that I had promised him, as he needed them in preparing
for a journey at Easter. 'I have them ready,' I replied, and went
to the library to fetch them. The truth, however, was that I had
forgotten to look them out, for I did not entirely approve of my
patient's journey, which I saw as an unnecessary interruption of
the treatment and a material loss to the physician. I therefore
took a hasty look round the library for two books I had had my
eye on. One was *Venice, City of Art*; but besides this I thought I
must own a historical work in a similar series. Quite right, there
it was: *The Medici*. I took it and brought it to my waiting patient,
only ashamedly to acknowledge the error. In reality I of course
knew that the Medici have nothing to do with Venice, but for a
short time it did not strike me as in any way incorrect. I now
had to be fair; as I had so frequently confronted my patient with
his own symptomatic acts I could only vindicate my authority
in his eyes by being honest and showing him the motives (which I
had kept secret) for my disapproval of his journey.

You see, a mistake, a 'bungled action', as he calls it, makes him
realize that he has lied to his patient in saying that he had got the
books ready. He has the courage to admit it, and the still rarer and
greater courage to admit to him the selfish motive for the lie. Do
not let anybody tell me again that Freud forbids the psychoanalyst
to talk about his own personal problems to his patient! What can
be more personal than to confess to someone that you have told
him a lie? And if Freud had the courage to do so, was that not
because he recognized the value of frankness, and took pleasure in it?
At the same time he actually obeyed the 'pleasure principle', if
one bears in mind the definition he gave of pleasure: a lowering of
the psychological tension between a need and its satisfaction. Freud
needed frankness, he took pleasure in this relationship of truth. In
this passage he also speaks of his authority: he took pleasure in
being respected and even admired by his patient, and needed to
safeguard that pleasure. Furthermore he admitted his lie and the
motive for it not only to the patient, but also to his many disciples
and the thousands of readers of his book, because he took pleasure
in opening their eyes to that honesty which comes from being
attentive to the hidden significance of our bungled actions.
Last year I was preparing a lecture when I thought of these confessions of Freud's, a note of which I had preserved in my big

card-index. But I needed to get the actual passage, and I could not find the book on my shelves, nor in the public library, as it was out on loan. And so I went out and bought a copy. As I was coming out of the bookshop I met a Genevan industrialist whom I knew well, having lectured in his factory. He greeted me with great cordiality. 'Ah, doctor, always the same – a book in your hand!' 'Well now, you see: it's one of Freud's books – the one in which he tells how he lied to one of his patients and then admitted it to him. It's not often that a doctor's as frank as that, is it?' 'But doctor, you know quite well that we all have to tell lies every day, even if they are only white ones!' 'Yes, of course, but sometimes one can be more honest and admit that one has lied. And that at once creates a new climate.' 'Oh, doctor, you always have the last word!' And he went off with a laugh and a friendly wave of the hand.

There it is – it would be absurd and idealistic to try to prove Freud's moral stature by trying to show that he never told a lie. The proof is the fact that he confesses a lie to his patient and to all his readers instead of concealing it. The honourable man is the one who recognizes and confesses his lapses from honour. It is not, for instance, that he never covets other men's wives, but that he realizes that he does covet them. He does not claim to be without violence, and free from injustice; rather is he aware of his own violence.

So we are back to our problem. But we have not digressed. The root of the problem of violence is indeed the problem of evil and its great paradox, namely that we are called to perfection, and that is impossible. That we are so called is not only written in the Bible; it is in the hearts of all men, since they pitilessly criticize every imperfection in others. Consider the reaction of any wife when she discovers that her husband has lied to her; or *vice versa*, of course.

We expect perfection from others, and we aspire to it ourselves even though we know well that it is inaccessible; and we can never resign ourselves to that fact. It is most disagreeable, but that is human nature. What we ought to resign ourselves to is not evil, but our human nature. To resign oneself to evil is to try and minimize it. I imagine, for instance, that some of my readers may have thought that Freud's lie was no very serious matter. Why attach such importance to that story when it concerned what after all was such an unimportant, ordinary little lie? Is that not what my industrialist friend meant?

Those readers will have decided that the plain fact was that

Freud was too fussy. Yes, Freud was fussy about truth, and that is just what I admire. I am too; at least I hope that I am as fussy as he was. I hold as dishonest all that is not absolutely honest. Why do we use such a scornful term about people who are scrupulous? Would you not rather do business with a scrupulous man than an unscrupulous one? I think that it is because scrupulous people tend to embarrass us with their demand for perfection, because it makes us aware of our imperfection.

See how eager people are to reassure a scrupulous person: 'It's nothing! You're only making things more difficult, splitting hairs!' Are they not trying to convince themselves that you don't need to try to be too honest? But such remonstrations never reassure the scrupulous person. There *is* a pathology of scrupulousness, but it has nothing to do with taking evil too seriously, but rather with not being able to forgive oneself nor to accept God's forgiveness, which is granted in particular to those who feel their own imperfection.

I think therefore that Freud was showing normal, not pathological scrupulousness. It is quite noticeable that the people who minimize evil – the little everyday lies and the little daily acts of violence – are the very ones who show the liveliest indignation at the spectacular deceit and violence that hits the newspaper headlines. It is still the same problem: where do they draw the line? Is not all excessive constraint itself an improper act of violence? Whereas the most scrupulous people are usually also the most indulgent towards others. Freud was at once both very severe with himself and very understanding of others. In this he was an instrument of God's grace.

This anecdote about Freud helps to clarify the role of psychology. Psychology studies only the automatic mechanisms of the mind, and takes nothing from either our responsibility or the need to make value judgments. The latter are concerned with means as well as ends, and that involves the right and wrong use of violence. As we have seen, there is no rational criterion to help us at this point, nor does our moral conscience suffice, because it is so easily mistaken, and because our violence is often unconscious. The function of psychology, then, is to supplement, enlighten, and deepen both reason and the moral conscience. This will be clear as we go on to the problem of vengeance.

17 VENGEANCE

A woman has confided in me at length. I risk a question: 'Would it be fair to say, madame, that you are taking revenge on a number of men, one after another, for the injuries inflicted on you in the past by your husband?' After some thought she says with a smile: 'Let's say I'm getting my own back.' A charming way of putting it, don't you think?

What is the difference between getting one's own back and taking one's revenge? Vengeance is getting one's own back on someone who has done us a wrong. If I play a game of chess and lose, I certainly hope to get my own back in the next game. That is not vengeance, because my partner has done me no wrong. We agreed to play, and we have observed the rules of the game. If I say, 'I'll have my revenge', I do so with a laugh in order to underline the fact that the word is not justified.

Now all social relationships are like so many games of chess. We might even say we are like those champions who have to play twenty or thirty games at once; and we are more affected by the games we lose than by those we win; and our wins never console us for our losses! Especially since in this case it is no longer a game: we did not choose it and we are too concerned about what is at stake. So our failures in this social game seem to us like wrongs done to us, and we try to get our own back. This time it really is vengeance we seek, if not against a person, at least against fate.

So when our mind is aroused by such thoughts, we realize that a considerable number of our acts and words are unconsciously determined by this mechanism of getting our own back or taking vengeance. This is the explanation of the pleasure that honest people derive from cheating the tax-man or the customs. It is a way of getting one's own back on society or the state for the constraints they put upon us. It is a reaction which is especially common among eminent people – artists, politicians, doctors, churchmen.

It was following upon a painful conflict in my own life that I wrote my book *The Strong and the Weak*, a sort of plea in favour of the weak, whom it is unfair to despise, for they are the victims of their nature or their upbringing. It was only several years later that I understood that I had really written the book to justify myself for being weak, and to avenge myself for having capitulated to friends who were surer of themselves than I was.

This mechanism is universal. An infernal round of revenge is danced ceaselessly around the earth. The blow received from one is paid back on another. And just as all the little streams flow into and swell one river, so all these chains of revenge come at last to one scapegoat which is incapable of defending itself, and upon which is unloaded the violence of all, which it cannot pay back. A timid person whose normal aggressiveness, necessary to life, has been stifled by his upbringing or his psychological complexes, is a ready-made target that can be attacked without risk of retaliation. In a school class, a family, an office, in any group, such a victim always contributes to a better understanding among all the other members.

Everything that since Alfred Adler has been called psychological overcompensation is a way of getting one's own back for some inferiority. Of course it also has its favourable side. Adler never denied this. But he tried to make people more aware of the springs of their behaviour and to help them to accept themselves as they are. Emulation, rivalry, competition, are valuable factors working for progress in the arts, science, sport, the economy and even in religion.

Nevertheless, even at the level of beneficial competition it is important to know oneself. I hope that I shall be understood when I say that the need to compete introduces into the noblest and most generous action a certain anxious tension: to act spontaneously, for fun, from life's natural need, like a tree producing its flowers and fruit, is one thing; it is quite another to obey a cold and compelling need to get even. It is something like what we mean when we say that the first is being a good sport and the second being a bad sport.

We have here once more the distinction we made with Dr Hacker at the beginning of this book between the spontaneous, innocent aggressiveness which is a necessary part of life, and that which leads to a violent brawl. What gives the action its acute tension, its impatient character, when it is provoked by the reflex of vengeance, is its compelling need to be satisfied. Here we have a further analogy between libido and violence: Libido does not subside until it has found satisfaction. Vengeance likewise. The bad sport is the player who cannot bear to lose.

So, if it is necessary at all costs to avoid losing, the temptation grows to hit harder. And if both adversaries are possessed by the same passion to win, an escalation of violence is inevitable. This brings us back from the minor retaliations of daily life right up to the most tragic acts of violence. The one leads without a break into the other. Even the peaceful game of chess is in danger of being brutally interrupted by a fist banged down on the chess-board if one of the two players cannot bear to lose.

Without a break, because when the need for vengeance invades man's heart he never lets it go, he holds it prisoner until it is satisfied. 'Penitents', writes Dr Jacques Sarano in *Christus*, 'are often more truly liberated than those who refuse to conform.' It is true – all avengers are fighting for liberty, but they are not themselves free. They are the slaves of their struggle. There is something uncontrollable about the impulse to vengeance. An American colleague, Dr Harold W. Glidden, has sent me an article he has published about the Arab world. The key to the attitude of the Arabs, he explains, is to be found in these two words: 'The defeat inflicted by Israel was a *disgrace* which can only be eliminated by *revenge*.' But as I read it I wondered about what other nation one ought to say the same.

It is the major theme of every patriotic speech in every national festival in every country. In my own country we have the exchange between William Tell and Gessler, the Habsburg governor. The latter questions William Tell about the second arrow which he has stuck into his belt, and the Swiss hero proudly replies: 'It would have been for you had I killed my son, and I would not have missed!' Soon afterwards came the ambush on the Sunken Road, in which William Tell did not miss, and the despot was killed.

No one has ever gainsaid such noble sentiments. The subject is so exalting that it has attracted the attention of many foreign artists. Schiller put it into verse and took it into the theatre, Rossini put it into music and took it into the opera. Although the story of William Tell has nothing to do with me, although serious historians have even informed me that he did not exist, he plays his part in making me proud to be Swiss. Naturally we took our children to the plain of Grütli, to the Tellenplatte, and to the Sunken Road. They must be initiated into the national traditions.

The same legend is found in Norway, which goes to show that it can serve to inflame the ardour of any nation. It is doubtless due to the influence of these glorious traditions that shooting is a national sport in Switzerland. Every little village has its rifle range. It is for more serious reasons that every citizen remains a soldier to an advanced age. He must keep his rifle at home, well looked after, with its ammunition, and take part in a practice shoot every year, a regulation which fits in well with this mystique of shooting. And in all good conscience I am writing a book on the dangers of violence.

If there is one state of mind in which the moral conscience does not direct, but on the contrary obeys, it is that of vengeance. The avenger does not ask himself whether his violence is permitted or forbidden. He feels it to be obligatory, on pain of dishonour. It imposes itself upon him as a sacred duty with the intransigence of the 'categorical imperative' in which Kant saw the basis of morality. Violence lies at the heart of some of the most edifying of stories: I have been shown in Beirut the spot where St George slew the dragon. It is always in the name of the highest moral values – honour, justice, liberty – that vengeance is taken.

There are two senses in which the process of vengeance is continuous. First there is the sense to which I have just referred, in that when the impulse to vengeance enters a man's heart, it does not subside until it is satisfied. The other kind of continuity lies in the fact that when the thirst for vengeance is slaked in the victor through his victory, it is at once aroused in the heart of the victim. That is why the dance of violence goes round endlessly. It even tends to grow more and more vigorously as a result of this continual transplanting.

As the prophet Joel says, revenge recoils on the heads of the violent (Joel 4.4). A vicious circle; a chain reaction. 'Vengeance,' writes Girard, 'an infinite process . . . the feed-back of violence . . . the nonsense of violence . . . which obsessed Shakespeare.' He refers of course also to Electra and her cry for vengeance – and indeed to the whole of the classical theatre. But above all he makes it clear that it is not just Shakespeare and his fellow dramatists who are obsessed by this theme, but the peoples of every age, and especially our distant ancestors in the dawn of civilization, and in our own day those races whom we call primitive.

18 AN ORIGINAL MURDER?

When there is as yet no political power, and no well-established system of law, when individual vengeance is prompt and implacable, it can easily be imagined with what terror a tribe sees it grow rapidly into a devastating tornado. At all costs the vicious circle must be broken, the growing flood of private settlements of accounts must be stemmed, a scapegoat must be found on to which the flood may be turned in order to assuage all this rancour without arousing new conflicts of retaliatory vengeance.

For the purpose a victim must be chosen who will neither avenge himself nor be avenged by others. René Girard demonstrates the process clearly. In the tribe, he speaks of the 'violence turned aside on to an innocent victim so that it will not strike its own members'. And so we have the institution of the ritual sacrifice, and the birth of the sacred, for it is at once realized that this event, at once both cruel and pacificatory, has a solemn and supernatural character. The effect is magical, in the proper sense of the word. Girard points out that this is the explanation of many facts that ethnology has brought to light but which have hitherto remained inexplicable. For example, the fact that, among the Chukchis, when a crime has been committed it is not the criminal but an innocent person who is sacrificed.

To our modern rational minds that seems absurd. You must get back to the magical way of thinking. The overriding need is to avoid the diabolical chain reaction of vengeance; and in particular to put an end to individual vengeance. Ritual sacrifice is not an individual but a collective act. And to perform this social function sacrificers or priests are solemnly instituted, clothed with divine authority.

It was also in order to break the tragic chain of individual vengeance that Moses, in the great song whose words he recited on the eve of his death, attributed to Yahweh this stern reminder: 'Vengeance is mine, and requital' (Deut. 32.35). To take away from men the right of vengeance means reserving it to God, and is the means whereby the sacred put an end to the nightmare of un-limited reciprocal violence. Unfortunately God's vengeance is not as swift as men would wish, and the book of Psalms is full of the voices of believers crying to heaven:

Yahweh, God of revenge,
God of revenge, appear! . . .
Yahweh, how much longer are the wicked,
how much longer are the wicked to triumph?

(Ps. 94.1, 3)

The Greeks had the same thought, and consoled themselves with their doctrine of the deferment of divine justice, in reality not a very comforting doctrine, since the deferment was always impossible to understand.

Girard then asks what has replaced sacrifice, the 'violence without risk of vengeance'. His answer is that it is the judicial system. This is what 'removes the threat of vengeance'. Proof of this is that historically sacrifice 'dies out where a judicial system is installed'. The right to individual vengeance was suppressed, and, in Moses' words, vengeance and requital belonged to God. Now we obtain the same suppression by reserving vengeance to the state. It is as if the state were now saying, 'Vengeance is mine, and requital.' We have already seen the limits of this repression of violence by the law and the courts. But it is at least a way of avoiding the vicious circle of individual vengeance.

As for the biblical rite of the scapegoat (Lev. 16.10), it seems to be a compromise between the solution of sacrifice and that of the law. It is not a true sacrifice, because the scapegoat is not killed. It is banished into the desert, taking with it all the sins of the people magically placed upon it; that is to say, all the accumulated grudges of social life which would call for revenge. Professor Henri Baruk has emphasized the psychological value of this ritual institution. He even tells of how he studied Hebrew in order to be able to read the Bible.

Thus far what Girard has to say concerning the appearance of the sacred in history, the institution of ritual sacrifice, and the preservation of the primitive community by the diverting of reciprocal violence on to a sacrificial victim, seems to me to be well founded. It is all most striking. He then proceeds to a further step which is purely hypothetical. He supposes that this collapse of the community into the chaos of unlimited individual vengeance was not merely an alarmingly possible eventuality, but an actual historical event which had really taken place, leaving behind it a fearful memory. This is precisely the step that Freud took in *Totem and Taboo*, the same jump backwards into a distant past.

Thus, despite the quite severe criticisms which he makes of Freud, Girard follows him on this point, and praises him warmly: Freud here made, he writes, 'an important discovery; he is the first to claim that all ritual practice, all mythical meaning has its origin in a real murder'. This is quite piquant, for it is precisely in this audacious hypothesis that Freud's disciples have generally refused to follow their master! Of course, I am not competent to enter into discussion of such conjectures. I must say, however, that the experience of the human mind which my long career has given me might well prompt me to think that deep down it is still haunted by a faint forgotten memory of some terrible catastrophe.

In any case it is quite interesting to see two eminent thinkers such as Freud and Girard converging by different paths upon this idea of an original murder, despite everything that divides them. Where they differ is that for Freud this primitive assassination was parricide, the murder of a father, whereas in Girard's view it was the result of a fratricidal struggle. The divergence is profound, for the theme of rivalry between hostile brothers is as dear to Girard as was that of the rivalry between father and son to Freud. Freud sees the source of the father–son conflict in their amorous rivalry in relation to the wife and mother. Girard does not deny this rivalry, but sees it as part of a more general rivalry over possessions.

This divergence is to be seen again in their respective theories of desire. For both, it is desire that rules men. But for Freud desire is bound up with libido, while for Girard desire is *mimesis*, i.e., imitation: one desires what the other desires or possesses. He points out that Freud himself gave this mimetic explanation of the father–son relationship the first time he described it, before referring to their amorous rivalry and the Oedipus complex. It is a fascinating discussion, but really somewhat academic, since what the libido desires is indeed possession, and also because if desire is imitation, then love is also imitation. Girard quotes a remark by Proust to the effect that one loves a woman all the more if she is desired by other suitors.

However that may be, Girard's mimetic theory of desire is extremely interesting. If you express your admiration even of a child who does a good somersault, his brother or a friend will try to imitate him with a 'Me too!' And if you give him a piece of chocolate, the others will expect the same. 'Me too!' is the cry of mimetic desire. From imitation to imitation desire spreads and grows throughout the world into the most terrible conflicts and acts of violence. Girard's mimesis corresponds to Hacker's contagion of violence. Girard quotes a nice remark made by Charles V to Francis I: 'My royal brother and I wanted exactly the same thing, namely the city of Milan.'

This mimesis of possession dominates the whole of history, right down to oil wells and uranium mines. It also dominates daily life, and Girard points out that the art of publicity does not consist so much in vaunting the excellence of the article it is bringing to our notice as in persuading us that other people desire it. He demonstrates also in connection with violence that the theme of the warring brothers and their conflicts recurs constantly in mythology, in the Bible and throughout literature. He believes therefore that the first catastrophic experience of mankind was the unleashing of fratricidal hate, and that sacred rites were instituted to ward off any repetition of it.

It should however be noted that Freud, in his last book, *Moses and Monotheism*, speaks also of disputes between brothers, though he sees them as 'following upon the murder of the father', and concerning the succession. For Girard, on the other hand, the great reality is the rivalry which hurls men into conflict with each other until the time comes when they all pour out their violence together upon one of their number who is too weak to defend himself. He thinks that it was this 'first spontaneous lynching which restored order in the community because it reinstated, against and around the scapegoat victim, the unity lost in reciprocal violence'. Thereafter the sacrificial rite would be only the commemorative re-enactment of the primitive event.

The reader has no doubt been reminded of the story of Cain and Abel (Gen. 4), in which the Bible too records an original murder, not a parricide as Freud imagined it, nor a collective lynching as described by Girard, but a drama of personal rivalry between two brothers. At all events when one considers all the legends, the mythologies, and the literatures of mankind, as well as the dreams of our patients (and our own), the human mind is indeed haunted by death – not just death to come, but death in the past; not just apocalyptic catastrophes in the future, but murderous cataclysms in the distant past. However it is all rather vague; and Caillois remarks that there are in the collective unconscious two contradictory pictures of our remote origins: that of chaos, and that of a Golden Age!

They can perhaps be reconciled in the hypotheses of Freud and

Girard, of a sort of Apocalypse, not at the end of time but at the beginning, and its miraculous solution in a reconciliation which has never again been fully realized in history. It is perhaps to this kind of unconscious memory, still alive in the human mind, that one ought to attribute the endless fascination that violence and horror have for people, a fascination that is very evident in our own day. You might compare it to a pruritus: it irritates, but one cannot help coming back to the place and making matters worse by scratching it. Even our most respectable and tender-hearted citizens enjoy the occasional horror film.

Nevertheless, all of us dream of a Golden Age, a state of perfect happiness, a peaceful and harmonious understanding, whereas our noblest and most generous efforts only set us against each other to the extent even of killing each other. It seems that man has paid too dearly for his privileges: he has lost the instinct which protects the animal against murder of its own kind. Next he has lost the sense of the sacred which restored the unanimity of society around the ritual sacrifice. What he has gained in intelligence he has lost in tutelary instinct. What he has gained in rational critical power he has lost in protective magical belief.

The two authors whom I have abundantly quoted, Friedrich Hacker and René Girard, have helped us to make explicit these two tragic realities, the loss of the instinctive answer and the loss of the sacred answer. If I dared to express such serious truths in familiar and rather sacrilegious terms, I should say that in man his bump of instinct does not work, and in modern man his bump of sacrifice does not work either. And so man is condemned to living dangerously. He can protect himself to some extent from the threats that come from Nature, but much less well against those that come from his fellows. Man's worst enemy is man.

I cannot omit to mention here a certain fear of others that I detect, either conscious or unconscious, in the minds of all those who open their hearts to me. In our well-ordered society it is not so much the fear of being physically killed, as that of being spiritually killed. It is a fear of losing one's personal identity, one's originality, one's autonomy, one's own personality, under the influence of some other person; the fear of a kind of break-in, an invasion by suggestion. And that sets up a defensive attitude, even (and especially) in those who most long for affection.

19 THE SACRED AND THE PROFANE

I have said enough about the missing instinct. What Girard has to say shows that the magical or sacred solution to the problem of violence, which may have been valid for our remote ancestors, and may still be so for primitive tribes, is not available to our civilized society, because we have lost our respect for the sacred. Even if we do not agree with the whole of Girard's analysis, each of us feels that the idea of the sacred has played an important part in the building and cementing of human society. It has for thousands of years been the foundation of social order.

That time has finally passed. Not that the sense of the sacred has disappeared, as many people say. It is too much a part of the human make-up for that. Depth psychology leaves no doubt on that score. But the sacred has crumbled, so to speak, it has been broken up and diversified. Instead of a unanimous recognition of what is sacred, there are as many things held sacred as there are different people. Each has his own little thing that he sees as sacred. I myself am no exception: the thing that is sacred for me is the human person, and I sometimes imagine that it could form the unifying principle of a civilization different from our own, for which it is impersonal technology that is sacred. A fine utopian dream, but very naïve, is it not?

If it is true that every man has his own private little thing that he holds sacred, then far from uniting men, as in the idyllic picture that Girard paints, their sense of the sacred divides them. One sacred thing against another, violence against violence! For Pompey, it is traditional order and the authority he has acquired that is sacred. For Caesar as he crosses the Rubicon what is sacred is the liberty he claims to be bringing to Rome. It comes to this, that when you take away from men the God in whom they were united, they soon find another, and thereafter fight each other in the name of their respective gods. Roger Caillois has written:

That being, thing, or idea is sacred, which governs all a person's actions, about which he will permit no discussion, no mockery or pleasantry, which he would not deny or betray at any price. For the passionate lover it is the woman he adores; for the artist or the scholar it is the work he is engaged upon; for the miser, the gold he hoards; for the patriot, the good of the state, the health of the nation, the defence of its territory; for the revolutionary, the revolution.

Nevertheless, the same author at the beginning of his book *L'homme et le sacré*, tries to find a definition of the sacred, and finds none but this: 'It is the opposite of the profane.' One can understand, then, the mental confusion one ends up with when one makes sacred a thing as profane as the gold of the miser. Yet it is quite true that people do confer a certain sanctity upon profane things, which then take on the unifying virtue of the sacred as described by Girard. This was true, as we saw, of the space rendezvous of the cosmonauts. It is true of sport, of art, and of scientific research.

Proof of this is that all these unifying enthusiasms rapidly become ritualized. It is particularly obvious with sport – the Olympic torch, the solemn ceremonies, the long list of traditional practices. Every music or film festival has its rites; it consecrates its stars, soon to be dethroned to give place to others. Lorenz has shown the important role of ritual in the animal world, where he points out (p.63) that it fulfils two functions: 'The first of these is the channelling of aggression into innocuous outlets, the second is the formation of a bond between two or more individuals.'

Thus, for many scientists, as Girard notes, 'chance has all the characteristics of the sacred'. Also striking is the fact that at the same time as profane things are sanctified, sacred things are de-sanctified. Festivals, even those which commemorate religious events, such as Christmas, Easter, and Whitsuntide, become secular holidays. When psychologists analyse religious experience objectively, they reduce it to a phenomenon, a profane object. Even theologians today are setting about demythologizing the gospel, reducing it to a profane subject of study.

In the ancient world, with its sacrifices and its Dionysiac festivals, as still today among primitive tribes, the social order rested upon a rigorous separation between sacred things and profane things, between the clean and the unclean. René Girard, Roger Caillois, Mircea Eliade and many other writers have abundantly demonstrated this. The sacred was immutable, respected by all, imposed by society, regulated by traditional rites which could not be changed in any particular. On the other hand, the profane was the domain of individual liberty. Thus there was established a system in which social cohesion was assured through the sacred, while a margin of personal independence was allowed for secular activities.

We find this same rigorous demand for separation between the sacred and the profane, raised to a frightening degree, in obsessional neurosis. I always remember a patient who had to wrap his Bible meticulously in a large number of boxes and wrappings, all in accordance with a more and more complicated and compulsive ritual. It is the same with the ritual washing of hands, which expresses a panic fear of mixing clean and unclean.

We can understand then the importance which Girard attributes to what he calls the 'loss of distinctions', of which he speaks with insistence. It is the removal of this watertight barrier between the sacred and the profane, the clean and the unclean. It is a sort of social cataclysm. If people are no longer unanimously sure of what is sacred and what is not, the cohesion of the community crumbles. Thereafter nothing is recognized by all as sacred, not even human life. 'Reciprocal violence' threatens, with the panic it arouses in its turn through its own vicious circle. The social order is in peril, and can no longer guarantee the lives of its individual members.

When Girard describes this fearful crisis as a crisis of civilization, one cannot help thinking of our present age. There are many who attribute the present crisis of civilization to the decay of religious belief, to the secularization of the modern world, to the loss of the sense of the sacred, of respect for the sacred, and to the disappearance of traditional values. I used to have an excellent friend who was always harping on this theme with the whole fervour of his Christian faith. I know of plenty of others like him. In the terms of the historical image we have already used, they are the Pompeys. They are the conservative spirits who look for a solution to the crisis in the restoration of the old order, while the Caesars seek it in the future, in a new order.

What are we to think of all this? It is true that there is nothing any longer that is universally recognized as sacred, that even a notion such as that of liberty has a quite different meaning in the East from its meaning in the West. It is true, as Girard says, that the loss of distinctions always brings in its train great disarray in society, because there is no longer any common sacred belief ensuring cohesion. Does that mean that the changes presently taking place in the world are to be regretted? I do not think so.

I thought as I read Girard's book that the person who had done most to break down the wall between the sacred and the profane was Jesus himself. This was the whole drama of the gospel. The Pompeys of his day crucified Jesus as a dangerous man who was threatening the system of sacred traditions. Read again the dramatic debates between Jesus and the religious leaders of his nation on the subject of the sabbath day (John 9). To the doctors of the law, the law of the sabbath was sacred. They denounce Jesus violently. 'This man cannot be from God: he does not keep the sabbath.' And Jesus says of himself: 'The Son of Man is master of the sabbath' (Matt. 12.8). Which means that he is not subject to the sacred law when it is contrary to the will of his Father, the God of love.

At this point Jesus is basing himself on a text from the prophet Hosea:

> What I want is love, not sacrifice;
> Knowledge of God, not holocausts.
> (Hos. 6.6)

We are back to sacrifices again, and with them to the whole line of the prophets who protested against the system of political and religious unification founded on sacrifices. They had already glimpsed what Jesus proclaimed. Re-read Isaiah:

> What are your endless sacrifices to me?
> says Yahweh . . .
> The blood of bulls and of goats revolts me . . .
> Your New Moons and your pilgrimages
> I hate with all my soul.
> (Isa. 1.11, 14)

It would not be possible to express more clearly the opposition between the religion of sacrifices and the sacred, and that of the inner call, of the personal encounter with God.

This contrast is basically the same as that which I have already referred to between the evangelistic preaching of Jesus, and the moralism of the Pharisees of his time and the puritans of our own day. The religion of the sacred was founded on the distinction between the sacred and the profane, between the clean and the unclean. The casuistical morality of the Pharisees, which Jesus challenged, was based upon a distinction between the righteous and the unrighteous. The righteous were those who scrupulously respected the sacred, and the arguments of the doctors of the law were all aimed at fixing its boundaries precisely. To these arguments Jesus brought a 'loss of distinctions': no distinction between righteous and unrighteous; all are sinners if one takes into account not the subtle quibblings of legalism, but the unlimited demands of God.

Jesus overturned the artificial, conventional barrier between the sacred and the profane. For him everything is sacred, and we are to seek God's will in profane things just as much as in sacred rites. The prophets had already denounced the violence of secular life; no ritual sacrifice washed clean the unjust man who used false measures and exploited the poor. The believer must act in every profane matter as if it were sacred. Jesus' adversaries were under no illusion: their whole religious system was being challenged, founded as it was upon the institution of a sacred domain and the good conscience one might have through adherence to its prescriptions.

Here again we may compare Socrates with Jesus. Four centuries earlier, he had been condemned to death on the same grounds. Socrates was accused by Anytos before his 502 judges of having violated a decree of Pericles – the Pompey of that time! And what was the decree? It forbade speculation upon divine matters. It is very clear, is it not? Socrates was accused of impiety in not respecting the interdict which protected the domain of the sacred. This was the vengeance of those conservative spirits whom Socrates had so annoyed by demonstrating that their traditional ideas did not stand up to his implacable dialectic. It was his claim to put man himself in question that was condemned.

Socrates was already appealing against a religion institutionalized upon the domain of the sacred, in favour of a religion of personal inspiration. He speaks too of his inner demon, who warns him when he goes astray. These two currents compete throughout Bible history and throughout the history of the church: the religion of the sacred, of laws, of prescribed ritual, and the religion of revelation, of the living Word of God. In the Old Testament they are represented respectively by the line of the priests and that of the prophets: the priests who preside over sacrifices and religious feats, and the prophets who proclaim: 'The word of Yahweh was addressed to me, saying . . .' (Jer. 1.4).

It is true that the two movements are not mutually exclusive. They are interdependent and complementary. They correspond to Bergson's 'two sources of morality and religion'. The law of Moses, with all its casuistry and ritual, had had its origin and its basis in the quite personal revelation when God spoke to Moses on Mount

Sinai. It was only later that there appeared the two opposing attitudes of the faithful to this law. The Pharisees' attitude is infantile, rigidly following the letter. That of Jesus is respectful, but mature, adult, thoughtful, and free. So all personal inspiration tends to ossify in commemorative rites which deny, as it were, free personal inspiration.

This sense of the sacred, which could unite the community when it adopted it in its entirety, can become a source of division when differing rites and interpretations come into conflict. When the Samaritan woman, for example, asks Jesus which is the holy place where one ought to worship God, Jerusalem or Mount Gerizim, Jesus answers her (John 4.23): 'The hour will come – in fact it is here already – when true worshippers will worship the Father in spirit and in truth': in the freedom of the Spirit and in true encounter with God – personal, not ritual.

Nevertheless Jesus did not forsake the religious practices of his people. He frequented the temple and the synagogue, and took part in sacred festivals. He took trouble to learn from the doctors of the law before he set himself up against them. He was not attacking the sacred, but the infantile attitude towards it which consists precisely in this division of life into two, the sacred and the profane. In the same way St Paul rejects any obligation upon the Greeks to submit to the sacred rite of circumcision, and speaks of 'the circumcision in the heart' (Rom. 2.29). The revolution that Jesus brought was not a denial of the sacred, but rather an assertion that everything is sacred, that religion does not reside only in certain ceremonies, but in a personal commitment to God which involves the whole of life.

This is what enables Henri Fresquet to say that 'the essence of Christianity contradicts the classic idea of religion, a collection of ritual acts based on the concept of a domain of the sacred which is distinct from the profane . . .' Christianity is the opposite of the 'ascending movement' by which man attempts to rise towards the divinity; it answers to the 'opposite movement . . . the irruption of God into history'.

This concept of two movements in opposite directions goes far beyond the framework of Judaeo-Christian tradition. It is universal. It is quite probable, as René Girard shows, that the idea of the sacred arose from an immense effort on the part of mankind in the face of the mortal danger of reciprocal violence, and that it is thus the source both of religions and of systems of law. But at the same time the other movement, from on high downwards, the concept of revelation, has developed every time that God, on his own initiative, has called men personally – Adam, Abraham, Moses, the prophets, the apostles, Paul on the Damascus road, but others also, attentive to the voice of God: Socrates, the Buddha, Mahomet.

There has been throughout history an oscillation between the two movements. In the bosom of the church itself, the tendency to ritualization is continually reappearing with the clericalism or the moralism of which I have spoken. Galileo was condemned in the name of respect for what was held to be sacred. Outside the church, modern secularism, for example, is strangely enough restoring the separation between the sacred and the profane. It tolerates churches provided that they concern themselves only with sacred matters, and do not interfere in secular matters such as politics, economics, medicine, and law. The churches for their part are trying to break out of this ghetto – the Roman Church with its promotion of the lay priesthood in secular work, the World Council of Churches allying itself with the revolutionaries in under-developed countries, at the risk – so often criticized – of seeing its grants used for buying guns.

So the time has gone, it seems to me, for dreaming of solving a problem such as that of violence by stepping back, by restoring the idea of the sacred, in a nostalgic longing to get back to the religions of yesterday. There is, alas, no longer any way in which all the individual violence in society can be assuaged by some sacrificial rite. If Christianity is to make a worthwhile contribution to the grave problems of our civilization, it will rather be by a host of inspired men and women, attached to Jesus Christ, being resolved to move forward under his inspiration to face the difficulties of personal obedience to God in secular life.

Oh yes, there are plenty of difficulties! We have seen how hard it is to distinguish between benign and malignant violence in our family, professional, and political life; how difficult it is clearly to see the violence that is required of us and that we must guard against; to see how to combat the scourge of violence, how to head it off by creating more justice and more personal fellowship between man and man. Perhaps a detour into another problem, the problem of power, may guide our search.

PART II

POWER

20 THE TWO HANDS OF GOD

It was three years ago. My wife was still living. One fine summer afternoon we were entertaining a friend from Vienna, Frau Isolde Emich, who devotes her life very successfully to the rehabilitation of children suffering from serious motor handicap. It was a real occasion to talk medicine of the person, since to help a child to express himself means helping him to become a person, not just a thing: a person entering into relationship with other persons. She has shown, too, the usefulness of the typewriter in the re-education of aphasics.

We were sitting under the pines, chatting. Frau Emich was talking to us about her work, and also about her own life and the personalities who had influenced her most. Among them was the priest and poet Heinrich Suso Waldeck, whose work she had greatly admired in her youth. She quoted for us the concluding lines of one of his poems, lines which she was in the habit of repeating to herself whenever her confidence was being put to the test:

> There can no serious hurt happen to me,
> For even though I slip from God's right hand,
> I can but fall into his left.

In fact the true text is a little different! Frau Emich looked it up, and was quite surprised not to find it as she remembered it. It is 'The Voice of the Creator':

> Do not leap out of my hand . . .
> You might escape me, had I not
> Another hand to catch you.

Such surprises happen to us all, often with familiar quotations which we think we know well. But the meaning is the same. In any case the important thing for us is not an author's exact words as he wrote them, but what we have understood and remembered of them, the thoughts that he has awakened in us.

That is what happened to me that day. The lines made an impression on me because they speak of the infinite greatness of God, which is a thing I have always felt most keenly – his sovereignty which none can escape. They recall Psalm 139, one of my favourites:

Yahweh, you examine me and know me,
you know if I am standing or sitting,
you read my thoughts from far away . . .
The word is not even on my tongue,
Yahweh, before you know all about it;
close behind and close in front you fence me round,
shielding me with your hand . . .
Where could I go to escape your spirit?
Where could I flee from your presence?
If I climb to the heavens, you are there,
there too, if I lie in Sheol.

It also made me think about the image of God's two hands, his right hand and his left. Of course it is only a poetic image, and has nothing to do with any anthropomorphic representation of God. God is always greater and more mysterious than we think. He goes beyond all the puny ideas we may have of his person. And just because he is so great he presents varying aspects which confound our rationalism because they seem to be contradictory.

The right hand of God obviously symbolizes his power. It fascinates mankind, for men are always seeking power because they feel they are weak, always under threat and exposed to failure. Man is always on the look-out for ways to increase his power. In many respects religion can be seen as an attempt to get possession of God's power, or at least to conciliate it. In the ancient world the Greeks tried to ensure the favour of the gods in order to succeed in their enterprises. They imagined that the gods quarrelled among themselves – violently! Men's fate depended upon the vagaries of these disputes among the gods. What one had to do was to put oneself under the protection of those who were most powerful.

The thinking of the Israelites is scarcely different at the beginning of the Bible. Yahweh is the God of Abraham, of Isaac, and of Jacob. He is a tribal God. Each tribe calls on its own god to grant it more power than other tribes. In Elijah's time the prophet still had to demonstrate that his God was more powerful than Baal, the enemy god. The whole history of the people of Israel is presented as a journey to the power that God might grant to the nation he has chosen as his own, in exchange for its submission.

Even the law, though it is a revelation due to God's initiative, is accepted as a sort of codification of the conditions for God's blessing. One must obey him in order to have many children, and 'have a long life' (Ex. 20.12); and above all in order to be powerful, to conquer the other nations and win the promised land. Thus the Old Testament is marked throughout by wars and violence, victories and defeats, all attributed to the obedience or disobedience of the nation.

Only the book of Job insinuates a doubt concerning the fate of the individual. But to the pathetic reproaches of the righteous and perfectly obedient Job, God's only response (discussed by Jung in his *Answer to Job*) is to proclaim his omnipotence (Job 38). This was indeed the picture of God that the ancient Israelites had.

Nevertheless, despite many vicissitudes, God grants his power to his people, and they invade the promised land and make it their own. It is 'a land rich and broad, a land where milk and honey flow' (Ex. 3.8). It is then not only military power that is involved, but economic power also. The great prosperity to which this adventure leads, in the reigns of David and above all of Solomon – the gold, silver, and ivory, the ships, and even the king's numerous wives and concubines – all are adduced as the sign of the divine power granted to the chosen people. God is proved by the success of those who serve him. Our modern Western world is no less proud of its prosperity than were the Israelites in the time of Solomon. And like them it looks upon it as justifying a clear conscience, despite all the violence and all the injustices that have contributed to it.

The idea of God's right hand often recurs in the Old Testament: 'Remember that you were a servant in the land of Egypt, and that Yahweh your God brought you out from there with mighty hand and outstretched arm,' says Moses (Deut. 5.15). And the psalmist: 'Your right hand upholds me' (Ps. 18.35). And Isaiah: 'I uphold you with my victorious right hand' (Isa. 41.10). In biblical thought all man's power derives from God; it is a gift from God. Not only his physical power (Samson!) but the intellectual power which enables him to dominate and exploit the natural world: 'Fill the earth and conquer it. Be masters of the fish of the sea, the birds of heaven and all living animals on the earth' (Gen. 1.28). Much more: by charging man to give every creature a name (Gen. 2.19), God institutes the basic principle of science, that of scientific and technological power.

God's power, however, is to be feared. Remember the formidable aggressiveness of the prophets! This God who can secure victory, can also bring defeat. 'It is a dreadful thing to fall into the hands of the living God,' cries the author of the Epistle to the Hebrews

(Heb. 10.31). The God who heals can also destroy. 'I am setting you over nations and over kingdoms,' he says to Jeremiah, 'to tear up and to knock down, to destroy and to overthrow, to build and to plant' (Jer. 1.10). And Moses, in his great hymn of praise at the end of his life, puts these words into the mouth of God: 'It is I who deal death and life; when I have struck it is I who heal (and none can deliver from my hand)' (Deut. 32.39). He smites the powerful and up holds the weak: 'Yahweh pulls down the house of the proud, but he keeps the widow's boundaries intact' (Prov. 15.25).

The New Testament also speaks of power. Right at the start, when the angel Gabriel comes to announce to the Virgin Mary that she will conceive and bear a son to whom she will give the name Jesus, he says to her: 'The Holy Spirit will come upon you, and the power of the Most High will cover you with its shadow. And so the child will be holy and will be called the Son of God' (Luke 1.35). And when John the Baptist (Matt. 11.2–6) sends to ask Jesus if he is indeed the Messiah, Jesus himself points to the miracles he performs through the power of God as evidence of his mission. All the gospel writers report his miracles in order to show that Jesus had divine power at his disposal.

Before leaving his disciples, Jesus says to them: 'You will receive power when the Holy Spirit comes on you' (Acts 1.8). Pentecost is an outstanding demonstration of the power which God gives to men through the Holy Spirit. Peter speaks boldly of it: 'God raised this man Jesus to life, and all of us are witnesses to that. Now raised to the heights by God's right hand, he has received from the Father the Holy Spirit, who was promised, and what you see and hear is the outpouring of that Spirit' (Acts 2.32f.). This power is what gives such dynamism to the primitive church, as well as to St Paul throughout the sore trials of his missionary life.

But let us return to the Old Testament. The glorious prosperity of the kingdom of David and Solomon did not last long! Civil war had already broken out between King Saul and David. It recurs with even more dire consequences under Solomon's successors. Soon comes the split into two hostile kingdoms. Next there are the foreign invasions, in accordance with the political vicissitudes of the great powers, Egypt and Assyria. Jeremiah finds himself accused of defeatism when he prophesies the disaster which threatens. Events, however, justify him. Jerusalem is taken and sacked in 587 BC. Solomon's temple, the pride of the nation and the sign of the presence of its God, is destroyed, the population is deported, captive, to Mesopotamia.

For a nation which has so totally identified its destiny with the power of Yahweh, it is much more than a military defeat, it is a religious calamity, the collapse of the very foundation of its faith. Having for so long proved God by the success of those who served him, they began to doubt him in the face of this complete catastrophe. Where is God's power? Why has he not even protected his own honour, the temple consecrated to him? Where is the right hand of God? Can it be that it is 'too short to redeem', that it has not 'strength to save' (Isa. 50.2)? They are conscience-stricken.

The prophets however actually proclaim that it is in fact the power of God which has raised up the conqueror against the Israelites. Jeremiah had already asserted that their conqueror, Nebuchadnezzar, was his 'servant' (Jer. 43.10), his instrument, and that he was going to deliver them into his hands. To Ezekiel God says: 'From the north, I am sending Nebuchadnezzar, king of Babylon' (Ezek. 26.7). Isaiah answers his own question:

> No, the hand of Yahweh is not too short to save,
> nor his ear too dull to hear.
> But your iniquities have made a gulf
> between you and your God.
>
> (Isa. 59.1f.)

It is not then a case of God's right hand being powerless to defend his people, but that that hand has smitten them. They may well pray, with Job:

> Take your hand away, which lies so heavy on me,
> no longer make me cower from your terror.
>
> (Job 13.21)

Unlike Job, however, the exiles in Babylon fall into despair. They feel themselves abandoned by God, even rejected by him, far from him. They feel, in the words of Frau Emich's poet, that they have fallen from the powerful hand of God, and he has let them fall. They have fallen, they believe, into a terrible void.

This is sometimes the way our patients or their families feel. 'God's letting go of me,' they exclaim. 'Almighty God, where are you? I trusted your promises. I've prayed and prayed! Where are you hiding? Do you even exist? Haven't you heard me? Why have you not answered my prayers?' That awful silence of God! And it is not just our patients: we ourselves, the doctors, we live this drama with them, and we do not know what answer to give them. We have received from God a power for healing. When we do heal, our joy is the joy of victory, the joy of power. Ours is a profession of power. I have no doubt that the fascination of power may well play an important part in the doctor's choice of his career. For my part I was no more than a child when I made up my mind to become a doctor. Afterwards I realized that what made me do so was the need to avenge the death of my parents, especially that of my mother.

This is what makes it so hard for the doctor to accept, and to admit, that he is powerless to heal. It is an extremely difficult experience for him to face. Often he avoids conversation with his patient when his science has no other power than to relieve. Faced with the invalid who is going to remain so all his life, the incurable who is going inexorably – on any human reckoning – to his death, the suicide of a patient who has become a close friend, the doctor does not only have a feeling of failure, but also one of guilt. In him too his patient had placed all his trust, now so cruelly disappointed.

Incidentally, it was in preparation for a conference on the medicine of the person, devoted to our attitude towards the incurable, that I began thinking about this impotence-complex in the doctor; and seeking in the Bible its message, apparently so contradictory, about the problem of power.

21 VIOLENCE AND POWER

The Bible describes the Israelites – defeated, humiliated, deported to Babylon, to that city which symbolizes human pride, to the city of which King Nebuchadnezzar said: 'Great Babylon! Imperial palace! Was it not built by me alone, by my own might and power to the glory of my majesty?' (Dan. 4.27). A great challenge to Israel! But the nation did not abjure its faith. Freud, in his book on Moses, speculated on why it did not abandon its God in such a desperate situation, and he attributed it to the prophets and their spirituality.

The Bible in fact shows that it was at this very time of the nation's most abject condition that those whom we call the prophets of the exile arose, to bring a new revelation of the mysteries of God, couched in a new and compelling style. What a contrast with the fearful thunderings of the God of Sinai, with the aggressive God who hurled the Israelites into a war of conquest, who spurred on Elijah to massacre the priests of Baal, or who faced Job with his insistence on his almighty power! This is the God of mercy and compassion, the God of forgiveness and love.

> 'Console my people, console them'
> says your God.
> 'Speak to the heart of Jerusalem
> and call to her
> that her time of service is ended,
> that her sin is atoned for.'
>   (Isa. 40.1)

These are the opening lines of the book of the second Isaiah. They are an evocation of another aspect of God, the one symbolized by his left hand, of which the poet spoke. The left hand which accepts, which picks up those wounded in the great battle for power; and, I may add, which will also gather in those who are now their conquerors, who will be just as much in need of grace, though as yet they do not realize it.

Such is also the meaning of the book of Jonah, who was sent to the proud and powerful city of Nineveh to announce its forth-coming destruction. Nineveh would repent and be spared, to the indignation of the prophet (Jonah 4), who was already rejoicing at the prospect of seeing the mighty wrath of Yahweh fall upon the city, particularly since it was greatly against his will that he had been constrained by Yahweh to undertake his irksome mission. 'What! Am I likely to take pleasure in the death of a wicked man,' God says to Ezekiel, 'and not prefer to see him renounce his wickedness and live?' (Ezek. 18.23).

God's forgiveness is offered to all. As the commentator of the Jerusalem Bible notes in regard to these texts, this 'teaching is quite close to that of the New Testament; the threats are but the expression of God's merciful will'. And in his vision of the dry bones, Ezekiel is shown this will to save, as yet hidden, and the resurrection of the people of Israel: ' "Son of man, can these bones live?" I said, "You know, Lord Yahweh" ' (Ezek. 37.3). But at the same time the vision brings to the prophet a more universal hope, that of a new humanity. 'I shall give you a new heart, and put a new spirit in you; I shall remove the heart of stone from your bodies and give you a heart of flesh instead' (Ezek. 36.26). The heart of flesh is gentleness and charity instead of the hardness and violence of stone.

The most striking feature of the message of the prophets of the exile is that God himself will change his ways. The miracle of salvation will not be wrought by constraint but by compassion. God will accomplish it, not by raising himself to the height of his terrifying power, but by coming down in humility – through the tenderness of which Hosea speaks (Hos. 2.21), the tenderness of a bridegroom towards his beloved, or a mother comforting her son, as Isaiah says (Isa. 66.13).

Four times does Isaiah utter his Song of the Servant of Yahweh, who will incarnate his love and self-sacrifice:

> He does not cry out or shout aloud,
> or make his voice heard in the streets.
> He does not break the crushed reed,
> nor quench the wavering flame.
> (Isa. 42.2f.)

These lines have rightly been seen as prophetic of Jesus Christ. But what a turn-about! The expected Messiah will not be a conqueror brutally crushing his enemies, but Jesus, who as St Paul says 'was humbler yet, even to accepting death, death on a cross' (Phil. 2.8).

We come back, then, to the non-resistance of Jesus in the garden of Gethsemane, when he says to Peter: 'Do you think that I cannot appeal to my Father who would promptly send more than twelve legions of angels to my defence?' (Matt. 26.53). I have already referred to the scene, in Part One, as an example of the renunciation of violence; but we can see it now in a new light, as a renunciation of power, and this gives us a deeper insight into its significance.

You remember, we were seeking the key to the problem of violence, where the line is to be drawn between legitimate and necessary violence, and the violence which is culpable and destructive. We saw that neither the biologists nor the psychologists had this key. That is what I am studying the Bible for. The unbeliever may think that I am misusing it. But like me as a believer, he too can recognize in Jesus a prime example of one who was able to be sometimes violent, sometimes non-violent.

This very fact, however, gives rise to a certain ambiguity: why was he now violent, now non-violent? I have answered in accordance with my belief: because his actions were not governed by any moral principle, but by the will of God. I believe that, but I should like to understand it. My desire to understand is no less than that of an unbeliever or an agnostic. The philosopher Jaspers, for example, clearly saw the ambiguity of Jesus' attitude to violence, his apparently contradictory behaviour, which I pointed out in the first part of this book. 'In the Gospels', he writes in his book *Great Philosophers* (vol. I, p.86), 'Jesus appears as an elemental power, by turns unbendingly aggressive and infinitely gentle.' He returns to the point later (p.89): in Jesus we find 'on the one hand struggle, hardness, the ruthless alternative; on the other infinite mildness, non-resistance, compassion with all the forlorn'.

What then does Jaspers mean by the term 'elemental power'? Doubtless an instinctive, spontaneous, unthinking drive. Indeed, as we have seen, aggressiveness and violence scarcely lend themselves to reflective thought. When a man is gripped by violent passion, it stifles in him all capacity for rational thought, and even his moral conscience: he hesitates no longer, but hurls himself into action. His reason no longer serves to provide him with good reasons to justify his conduct. The same can be said of love: as an 'elemental force', love is blind.

Does this mean that Jesus was unthinking, as Jaspers seems to imply? Ah! I do not believe it, and I do not think that anyone can seriously maintain it. Is not the Gethsemane scene which immediately precedes his arrest one that reveals the most intense reflection? Some pious reader may object that it is rather a prayer, a meditation, a seeking after God's will. Of course, but it is also an example of reflective thought, in the profoundest sense of the term.

Is not all true reflective thought, whether the thinker is aware of it or not, a search for God, since it is a search for truth? In Jesus the two are quite consciously the same. He reflects and invites us to reflect, in the presence and under the inspiration of God. The problem of power is an appropriate subject for reflection. Jesus did indeed renounce violence during his passion, and that was because he had resolved not to use the divine power for himself. This can be seen from the fact that these events on the eve of his death relate to the temptation in the desert, which had been a sort of prologue to his ministry: Jesus had from the very start reflected deeply upon the problem of power.

In the desert the question of violence did not arise (Matt. 4). Jesus had become conscious of his divine sonship, and was pondering upon his mission which followed from it. 'If you are the Son of God . . .,' Satan says to him. Clearly the true, the fundamental temptation does not concern the means to be employed, but the intention – the motivation, as the psychologists would say. What Satan proposes to Jesus is that he should make a show of his power, using it for himself, feeding himself miraculously from stones, or floating magnificently in the air, sustained by angels. Satan the tempter is even more explicit when he shows Jesus all the kingdoms of the world and says he will give him all their power and splendour.

We find the same refusal of political power when Jesus realizes that the enthusiastic crowds, having been fed on the miraculously multiplied loaves, want to 'make him king'. St John tells us that he 'escaped back to the hills by himself' (John 6.15).

Here again there is no question of violence, apart from the risk of the excesses that might accompany a popular mass movement. What we do have is withdrawal, solitude, and reflection upon the dangers of power. Clearly his life was marked by periods of reflection, and this enabled him at the moment of his supreme test to resist the temptation to turn to violence to defend himself, to establish his own power.

We see therefore that Jesus was thoroughly spontaneous, as Jaspers has pointed out, in his violent reactions, just as he was in his impulses of pity and tenderness. Faced with the scandals of the world, the injustices of society, the hypocrisy of the Pharisees, the domination of money and the commercialism of the temple traders, who exploited the credulity of the populace, he wielded a whip of cords, and the no less cutting lash of his tongue. He was not, therefore, a systematic follower of non-violence. He experienced holy indignation and holy anger.

On the other hand he maturely weighed the dangers of power. From the very first day of his ministry to the last hour of sacrifice, he refused to give in to the temptation of power – the temptation to use his power to procure personal triumph. This attitude of refusal of power, resolutely adopted after long meditation (forty days in the desert!) was what always held him back, even at moments when the natural instinct of passion might have led him into culpable violence.

One may ask whether it is right to analyse the behaviour of Jesus in this way, to draw psychological conclusions from it, as if he were a clinical case, or just a model, and not the Saviour of the world. Of course I know that the cross has a bearing quite different from the one I am referring to here; that it is God's great initiative, the accomplishment of his design for the redemption of the world, and that Jesus accepted it because he knew it was God's will, and not for any worldly consideration. But since Jesus is at once both true God and true man, I can leave it to the theologians to speak of him as God. I shall seek to understand him as man, from my own standpoint as a doctor.

That does not in the least signify that I believe in any sort of specifically Christian psychology, distinct from scientific or literary psychology. There is but one psychology, which seeks to understand the workings of the human mind, just as there is only one medicine, which seeks to heal the sick as best it can. In order to understand man let us attempt to bring together the teachings of all the various psychologies – experimental, clinical, social, and literary – from the great legends and myths of the poets to the realistic analyses of the novelists. Finally let us also recognize that there is nothing that can compare with the teaching of the Bible on this subject. Every doctor, whether or not he is a believer, can learn from it.

22 TWO CLOSELY RELATED PROBLEMS

Thinking thus about the way Jesus acted, it comes to me that the key to the problem of violence is to be found in that of power: that benign violence is that which is put at the service of others, protecting the weak, healing the sick, liberating the exploited, fighting the injustice of the powerful; and that improper violence is violence on one's own behalf, aimed at securing power for oneself, violence which is inspired by the fascination of power.

Doubtless the distinction between these two problems, violence and power, is a subtle one, but it seems to me to be important. This is why I am trying to compare and contrast them in this book. The two problems become confused in the heat of action. We dare to show our violence when we feel powerful enough, and we use violence in order to increase our power. But the two problems are distinguished most of all by the fact that only the problem of power is accessible to reflection. Violence, on the other hand, always rages with the heat of unleashed passion, and all reason is suspended. We have observed how difficult it is to see clearly whether the spontaneous impulse to violent action is legitimate or not at the moment when it grips us.

On power, on the other hand, one can reflect coolly, as Jesus did at length. Violence is a short-term, instinctive, immediate objective; whereas the thirst for power has a long-term objective in view, it works out a whole strategy, all the stages of a long progression. One can give oneself up to dreams of power without limits. But on the other hand, enlightened by thought and by revelation, one can weigh its dangers and voluntarily set oneself limits, renounce certain courses of action, and set one's face against any abuse of power. For the more powerful we are, the greater is the constraint, open or hidden, which we exercise upon others, and the more we thus provoke them to violent reactions.

Remember Pompey and Caesar, and the good reasons they had for fighting each other – Caesar to overthrow the unjust tyranny of Pompey, and Pompey to protect Rome against a seditious threat. But what really and inevitably brought them into conflict was that they were both powerful, and both thirsting for power. We can see clearly here the connection between our two problems, a connection which we tend to forget when we discuss only violence. Violence is therefore extremely difficult to arbitrate upon, whereas the abuse of power is accessible to objective judgment.

Though Pompey and Caesar were both actuated by a will to power, they were not both in the same situation. Pompey was in power. Consequently his violence was less visible, legitimized by his power, legalized by the Roman Senate which he controlled, camouflaged as the defence of this legality and of public order. But it was this very hidden violence, implacable and assured of its impunity, which drove Caesar to extremities and forced him to fight openly, to cross the Rubicon, and to act like a rebel.

We have seen that there is always this mutual and fatal interplay between the unseen violence of the powerful and the open violence of those who oppose them. The violence of the powerful triggers off that of the rebels. Violence against violence – one is incapable of judging between them, except in accordance with some irrational prejudice. But if the one aspires to power, the other possesses it, and obviously he is freer not to abuse it, to refrain from using his power with improper violence.

Oversimplifying a little, one might say that it is through violence that one passes from weakness to power, but that it is through power that one passes from proper to improper violence. What is especially important when we are considering our own period and the connection between the two problems of violence and power, is to realize that power confers impunity upon violence. If you are powerful, your violence may escape all retribution. Power is secured by violence, and violence is justified by power!

Read again Camus' book, *The Rebel*. In it he shows that man is never greater than when he is in revolt, when he commits himself totally to the struggle against an unjust power, ready to sacrifice his own life to liberate the oppressed. Jesus recognized this greatness, he was the incarnation of it, and he paid for it with his life. He was a revolutionary – the exemplary revolutionary, because he was totally disinterested. For Camus also shows us the sombre danger of rebellion: that every revolution ends with the advent of new masters, who are then themselves tempted to commit, with impunity because of their power, fresh injustices, provoking in their turn fresh rebellions.

Here indeed is the vicious circle of violence, but seen now in the perspective of that of power. In *The Rebel* Camus remained in perplexity, the same perplexity as that which gripped us in the first part of this book. Not all violence can be condemned, because it is in holy acts of violence that man reveals his noblest aspirations. Nevertheless, in his work as a whole Camus shows himself to be extremely sensitive also to the danger of power, of the established order covering a multitude of sins. Think of *The Outsider*, and especially of his play *Caligula*, in which the Roman emperor is led into the most frightful atrocities simply to prove to himself that he is really free and all-powerful. Camus portrays him as thirsting for power to the point of demanding of his most servile courtier that he bring him the moon, and so proud that he cannot bear not to be obeyed. Thus it is the impunity of power which provokes injustice. And so I here follow in the steps of Camus.

I have little to say about those who openly advocate violence – fascists, Communists, and other totalitarians, all of them in love with violence. I feel they have nothing important to bring to our thought, since while they are clever at justifying their own actions by their doctrines, they are only too ready to complain loudly as soon as it is their opponents who are acting violently.

On the other hand, there are various movements which campaign in favour of non-violence. They can point to great historical figures, not only Jesus and Socrates, but also political personalities such as William Penn and Gandhi. I admire them all the more because of the difficulty and delicacy of their crusade. Campaign is the right word – they have to fight, to demonstrate that non-violence is not cowardice or weakness in the face of evil, but a greater kind of courage. Gusdorf, in *La vertu de force*, quotes this remark by Gandhi: 'The prerequisite of non-violence is the power to strike.' What counts, then, is the renunciation of violence by the powerful. Maryse Choisy writes of non-violence that it is 'one of the subtlest forms of aggression'. I remember how in the first world war Gandhi's friend Romain Rolland tried to place himself 'above the battle', and was accused of defeatism, like Jeremiah.

They have in fact to struggle against passion in the heat of passion. When someone talks of using violence, he is in the heat of passion, in no fit condition for reflection; he even arouses violent passions. That is why I hope to help such people by going further back, to the source of all violence – the lust for power. The great merit of the personalities to whom I have just referred – and one could point to others – is precisely that they were exempt from all ambition for personal power in their struggle. They remained, even in victory, poor and meek, in the biblical sense.

I am not saying that the renunciation of violence solves everything, nor that it is easy to fight, even for the most worthy cause, without some personal ambition for power creeping in. Nevertheless these historical examples show that it is possible. And it seems to me that the matter becomes clearer if we shift the probe of our analysis away from the problem of violence on to that of power. That is why I have come to think that the key of the apparently insoluble problem of violence is to be found in the problem of power.

Yes, insoluble, remember. Not only insoluble in theory, since we cannot find any rational criterion for legitimate violence, but also in practice, since violence can be contained only by violence, and so the vicious circle is complete. Whereas the notion of power is unambiguous, easy to define: power is abused as soon as a man can with impunity impose his will upon another.

The equivocal character of violence is aptly described by Edgar Morin in an address on the subject given at the Fritz Ebert Foundation, in Germany: 'Faced with the idea of violence, I realized that it had never been a fundamental or an operative concept for me, and that finally I was no doubt right: the term violence lumps together a number of heterogeneous notions, without revealing what they have in common.'

Heterogeneous is right – violence can be legitimate or illegitimate, sometimes manifest, sometimes invisible, even to the violent man who does not feel himself violent so much as furious, outraged, called to strive for his idea of justice. Whereas power is always quite visible and quite conscious.

Finally, though the Bible is very ambiguous on the subject of violence, as we have seen, it is not at all so on the subject of power. The Bible strongly denounces the hidden violence of the powerful. For example, the violence of David who uses his power to engineer the death of Uriah, the husband of Bathsheba, the woman he covets. We have seen too that the great distress of the exile was more fruitful spiritually than was the prosperity of Solomon. There are innumerable passages in the prophets, the Psalms, and the book of Proverbs, stigmatizing the pride and iniquity of the powerful. This preaching of humility and poverty culminates in the gospel. Think of the Beatitudes. Jesus is violently opposed to the rich and powerful, especially those who wield spiritual power and abuse it.

We were left in perplexity so long as we tried to make a judgment in the light of reason or conscience upon an outburst of violence, as we are still invited constantly to do upon all the conflicts that are rending apart our modern world. Who is responsible? Who is to blame? Caesar, or Pompey? Caesar is, says Pompey! Pompey is, says Caesar! Each is sure he is in the right, convinced that his violence is legitimate and sacred.

But the Bible involves them both in the same responsibility, in a common guilt, not so much in respect of their violence, as in respect of their will to power, which they are unaware of, and which lies at the root of the conflict. The sin is the thirst for power, and it is universal, common to both camps. It impels the challengers into violence, but there is just as great violence in the decent folk they attack, the 'righteous' who invoke their legality in order to calm their consciences, and who claim to be defending themselves against the violence of the 'wicked'. A profound remark made by Paul Ricoeur in an article in *Esprit* has always helped me to see this clearly: he says that the sin which the Bible denounces is not so much the apparent sin of the wicked, as the hidden sin of the righteous.

In the same article he stresses that this sin of the righteous is unconscious, like that of David which I mentioned just now, and which King David only realizes on hearing the accusation of the prophet Nathan. Lastly he points out that this secret sin, less visible than overt wrongdoing, is covetousness. Now, covetousness is another way of saying thirst for power. It is the underlying source of all conflicts, and it is what makes it so hard to pronounce judgment upon them objectively and dispassionately.

23 HOW DANGEROUS IT IS FOR MAN TO BE POWERFUL!

We may say then that in the light of the Bible violence appears as a resultant problem, and power as a causative problem. If we wish to combat violence effectively, ought we not to attack it at its root? That is much more than a figure of speech; the wave of violence which is denounced today, is it not the fruit of a civilization which has exalted man more than any other has done, which has exacerbated the thirst for power and profit, which has proclaimed the omnipotence of man through the illimitable progress of science and technology, which has even claimed to set him free from God?

The wave of violence is really an alarm signal sounding because the world has gone astray in seeking power above everything else. Or, if you prefer medical language, may we not say that the flood of violent acts is a symptom, the symptom of a sickness in our civilization? And that the sickness is our headlong dash for power? Ever since the Renaissance the flames of human ambition and covetousness have been fanned. A lot of time is spent on the problem of violence and how it is to be contained; but very little thought is given to its underlying source, which is the orientation of the whole of our Western world to the fulfilment of the dream of ever greater power.

Power has become the supreme value, the only one that is universally recognized; all kinds of power: military, political, economic, industrial; the power of propaganda, of publicity, and of fashion; the power of technology, of organization, of standardization, of the concentration of big business and its trusts; the power of the masses; the power of sexual desire; the power of youth, of muscular strength and records counted in hundredths of a second; the power of money and wealth. Nations are classified in accordance with their Gross National Product, in block capitals: the GNP; and great firms according to their annual turnover, inscribed on honours boards; the GNP is the modern Golden Calf.

We have foolishly banked on the mirage of unlimited growth in production. Overall planning, the growth plans invented by the Communist countries, have been promptly adopted by the capitalist world. Our vainglorious programme is a race to see who will be the first to reach the commanding heights of power. As Albert Schweitzer wrote: 'We have crossed the threshold of the twentieth century with a conceited idea of ourselves.' And throughout the century until four or five years ago, the intoxicating process continued to accelerate, with brilliant successes which encouraged and gave colour to the belief in the omnipotence of man.

Do not be surprised, then, that violence is also being reinforced and spread. The present wave of violence is looked upon as an irritating and unforeseen accident, when it is in fact the logical outcome of our civilization. We talk of a technological civilization, of the consumer society. But what are we aiming at with our technology and growth? Comfort, certainly. But much more, power. Other civilizations set up different values for men's ambitions to aim at: wisdom, virtue, honour. Ours preaches only pride. For centuries man has been exalted, with his unlimited power, his conquests of nature, his right to take his destiny in his own hands, to shape history. Having for so long sown such high pretensions to power, we are reaping a whole harvest of violence.

There is one well-known fact which illustrates this connection of cause and effect between power and violence, namely the attitude of the motorist. A man needs only to be at the wheel of his car, with all the power of its engine beneath his foot, for his instincts of violence to be unleashed. He charges ahead, forces his way through, overtakes regardless of risks, and will fly into a rage at the slightest rebuke, even getting out of his car to rain blows on his accuser. Thus, the more powerful man is, the more violent does he become! It is paradoxical, is it not? It is quite the opposite to the animals – who has not seen the little terrier barking furiously at the big dog, while the latter, sure of his strength, remains placid and indifferent?

This brings us back once more to the views of the biologists. You remember Lorenz and the instinctive curb which he observes in wild animals, which prevents them from devouring each other.

Now, it is precisely among those animals endowed with powerful weapons that he observes this curb, and this, he believes, accounts for its absence in man. Man was not by nature a powerful animal, and this drove him to use his intelligence to invent tools and weapons. It would seem that when he thus felt more secure, he ought to have become less violent, like the big dog, but the opposite is the case.

Perhaps it is because he is not powerful by nature, but by artifice, endowed with a fragile power always under threat, which demands a constant effort towards greater power in order to consolidate itself. This fits in well with my daily observations as a doctor. It is the rich who feel themselves to be more seriously threatened by ruin. A paradox indeed: it is the powerful who are afraid, who are the hardest to deal with, who clam up as if they were too vulnerable, and who are impelled, despite themselves, towards a constant effort to increase their power still further.

So throughout the course of history man has not ceased to try to augment his power, and it has increased dramatically during the last few centuries. Violence necessarily follows the same ascending curve. One sees how dangerous it is for man to become powerful! Thus for example the pursuit of economic power has demanded out-and-out industrialization and urban expansion, but 'the large city means insecurity, crime, drugs, aggressive psychosis, and three bolts on every door', as Michel Albert and Jean Ferniot observe. Storr notes similarly the increase in aggressive impulses as a result of overpopulation and consequent stress.

We are very worried nowadays about the growth of violence, but hardly at all about the increase in power, which many people still look upon as a benefit. We have desired, we have sought, we have boasted of the growth of man's power due to science and technology: it is progress! And it is true: it has brought us great progress, with victories over poverty, disease, and death. But progress has its dark side. We have suddenly become aware of this. So many writers are talking of ecology, pollution, the lost harmony between man and his natural and social environment, the quality of life, that I do not need to dwell at length upon it here.

'Maximum profit, maximum pollution,' writes Edgar Morin in his 'California Journal'. Friedrich Engels had already written: 'Do not let us boast too much of our victories over Nature, she has her revenge for each one of them.' Yes, progress casts a shadow. The shadow – a typically Jungian idea: Jung might well have written that violence follows power like its shadow. Perhaps I may be permitted for a moment to dwell, albeit not in so learned a fashion as he, on this subject.

What are we to do? Follow the advice of the Irishman who suggested getting rid of the shadow by putting out the light? That would only make the shadow darker still. To stop technical progress, apart from being quite impractical, would merely take us back to the poverty and darkness of the Middle Ages. So what are we to do to eliminate the shadow? Well, during the war, while on military service, I constructed scialytic lamps for use in operating theatres, at first for the ambulance unit to which I belonged, and then for others which were soon asking for them. This is a special kind of lamp which illuminates the operating area without casting shadows, thanks to a large circular mirror which reflects the central light-source in all directions at once.

It seems to me that our civilization needs a scialytic lamp. That is to say that the area of our human activity should be illuminated from all sides at once, and not only by science and technology and the search for profit and power. It is one-sided lighting that casts the shadow! It is the 'one-dimensional man', as Marcuse says, who is impeded by his shadow. But I have never quite understood what other dimension Marcuse would like to give to man. It was on this point that Maurice Clavel commented: 'What would a second dimension be if the spiritual is excluded?'

In my view it is just this spiritual dimension that our civilization has left in the shadow, or at least in the twilight. It includes all that is irrational in man – his need for beauty, for poetry, for mystery and dreams, his need to find a meaning in his life, his need for love, for personal contact with others, with Nature and with God. All these things go for nothing so far as power is concerned. The hard, cold, objective light of intelligence accentuates the shadows, because it illuminates only one aspect of reality. We must rediscover the totality of man, the full circumference of the scialytic lamp which shines on all sides at once.

Another analogy occurs to me: that of stereoscopy. An ordinary photograph is flat, all on one plane. We need the double line of sight of the stereoscope to restore to landscape and figures their lost dimension of depth, the vibrant enchantment of life. If we look at man solely from the scientific and technological point of view, he appears to be no more than an automaton, a robot, a cold combination of physiological, psychological, and sociological mechanisms. He must be seen at the same time from the spiritual point of view if he is to be revivified, given back his warmth, so that the hidden meaning of all these phenomena will be revealed.

The great epic of objective rationalism, the triumphal march towards power and material prosperity which has been the mark of the last five centuries, has left its casualties by the wayside, those who could not follow, who could not stand the pace. The glorification of the powerful has gone along with the devaluation of the weak, the old, the sensitive, the shy, the scrupulous, the odd, the abandoned, and the dreamers. These are the ones who come flocking to us psychotherapists.

It seems obvious that this wave of mental depression is, in the same way as the wave of violence, a symptom of the malady of our times. It falls to all of us, to me and to my colleagues, to say to these casualties of life: 'Defend yourself, assert yourself, don't allow yourself to be used as a doormat! Life is a battle – if you don't fight you are mercilessly beaten.' Of course that is true. But does it not mean that we are bowing too easily to the law of the strongest which governs our society? Are we not ourselves reinforcing the universal suggestion which sets up power and success as the greatest aims in life?

Which of us has not very often asked himself these questions when faced with all these misfits who consult us? Which is the more humane task facing us – to render them capable of integrating themselves into a ferocious society, or to set about curing society of its ferocity? Society is depriving itself of incomparable riches of which it knows nothing, and which we discover in those whom it rejects. Riches of the heart, of sensibility, of creative imagination, of intuition and originality. Will they not lose them if they harden themselves in order to enter into the great competition for power?

Ours is a cruel age. Progress, as our age understands it, is the prize of a struggle without quarter. It proclaims that it is dangerous to be weak, whereas I think it is just as dangerous to be powerful. Listening to so many confidences from people crushed by life, I used in my younger days to judge too harshly those who had hurt them. I have become more indulgent as I have come to understand that we all hurt others without even knowing it, innocently, without malice, simply because of our power – we the privileged peoples of the West who play the game of this power-based society. For one is never powerful except at the expense of someone else, nor rich except at the expense of many who are poor. It is the system which is responsible, much more than the individual who is forced to harden himself.

A few examples will make my meaning clear. A girl who is pretty and clever may seriously humiliate her less well endowed sister if she chides her for her clumsiness, with the result that the sister will lack self-confidence all her life. This can happen without there being the slightest ill intention on the part of the more gifted sister. The latter may exclaim, with obvious sincerity: 'Me, despise my sister? Never! She just imagined it because she was jealous of me. I was the one who was hurt, because of her jealousy. But I was so fond of her, and she had so many good qualities which I appreciated. I always tried to encourage her, but it was no good.'

A man may harbour frightening memories of the terror his father inspired in him when he was little. He still shudders as he recalls his father's dictatorial voice, and he still finds himself paralysed with emotion in front of anyone in authority. Now that father may possibly have been a gentle, kindly, even a shy man. He could have had a mild little voice, which deceived no one when he tried to force it. He will protest vigorously if you hold him responsible for his son's difficulties, and rightly so. Few parents actually realize the impression they make on their children, because in their children's eyes they are all-powerful.

Again, everyone can see that a certain woman has lost all her own individual personality because of her marriage. You suspect her husband of being dictatorial, or lacking in respect and care for her? That is perhaps not the case at all. But he is a brilliant man, extraordinarily intelligent and active, admired by everyone. It is not easy to be the wife of such a husband. She is proud of him and feels so insignificant beside him. She talks about nothing but him, repeats everything he says, and follows all his advice.

It is said unkindly and unjustly that he has ridden roughshod over his wife. But what can he do? He loves her tenderly, but the more he shows his affection for her, the more does he subjugate her, so astonished is she to be loved by a man whom she considers so far above her. It is easier to break free from a selfish husband than from one who is full of love and care. Has he been too ambitious in his career? If he has gone from success to success, it is less from pride than from a sense of vocation. Ought he to give it up? That would not be easy; it does not concern him only, but also all those for whom he is responsible. And his wife in that case would blame herself for having been only an obstacle in his life.

24 POWER, SUCCESS AND DIALOGUE

I could give many more examples. I do not deny that there is wickedness in the world, but I believe there is less than is commonly thought. The tragic thing is that there are so many good people, full of good intentions, conscientious, even scrupulously so, and generous, who are trying sincerely to do what is best, and who do so much harm to others, without knowing it or wishing it, simply because of their success or their superiority. Does your chief at the office make life hard for you? You accuse him of being unfair to you and suspect that he dislikes you? But if you knew him as I do, if he told you all he has told me about himself, you would understand that he worries constantly over whether he is doing his job properly, because he doubts his own ability, and that is what makes him so fussy and difficult.

As soon as there is an excessive disparity in strength between two persons or two groups, a double risk arises: the weaker party will be crushed, or he will violently rebel. Of course the desire for success or superiority will never be eliminated from men's hearts. It is part of their very nature. Alfred Adler and his school have adequately demonstrated this. And Freud, in his work on psychoanalysis, despite the primary importance he attributes to the sexual libido, notes that it is quite simply our egotism and our desire for power which motivate our dreams and our fantasies, and which express themselves in them. Adults will always look like giants in children's eyes; there will always be some people more gifted than others; and there will be some who will succeed better than others, and they will not necessarily be the most gifted.

The emulation which results from this is an evolutionary factor favourable to life, as we saw at the beginning of this book, provided that the powerful are not too powerful. The danger lies in the inflation of these mechanisms. Life always involves oscillations, such as that in the temperature of an organism between evening and morning, but they are limited. Fever signifies disease. For this reason we have been constantly concerned with the question of limits, a question which applies equally to power and to aggressiveness. But there is a vital difference, namely that people who are quick to condemn explosions of violence find it easy to come to terms with a society which aims at unlimited power, and which knows no other criterion than effectiveness.

Is it not the effectiveness of violence which justifies it in the eyes of those who have recourse to it? This is the effectiveness which our modern world unreservedly advocates, which is the primary objective of education, throughout our schools right up to the institutes of scientific research, of the whole of our economic system, including our institutes of management studies, and of every national plan for economic growth. If we want to limit violence we must also set limits to our ambition for power. We feel the need for curbing violence, but we are less well aware of the need for curbs on the increase in man's resources and his power, having had it drummed into us that all progress depends on them.

What is the significance of this notion of limits and curbs – not for the experts who work out economic plans, but for us personally? It would require, would it not, some respite, some moderation in the race for success in which we all take part so eagerly. Is such a thing possible in modern society? Is it possible without betraying our responsibilities, without culpable cowardice? We have only one preoccupation – to be a success, in our examinations, our jobs, our sentimental and social lives, and even in our leisure occupations. A game of tennis with a partner who did not do his best to win would be uninteresting. Those who suffer from what the psycho-analysts call 'failure complexes' are looked upon as sick, needing to be cured.

However this question of limits is sometimes raised later, in the evening of life, when the exacting job-race is over. Then a man may reflect upon the frenzied life he has lived. He does not regret having put so much zeal into it. He is still proud of his success, of having done valiant service. Nevertheless he sees it in a different light. The trials which had to be faced one after another, which once seemed to him to be so vital, in which his whole life seemed to be at stake, now seem less important. Perhaps he sacrificed too much for those fleeting victories.

You are thinking perhaps that he is depressed? Not at all. He has more courage than others as he faces the true problems – the problems of the meaning and the quality of life. The problem of liberty, too. Once it seemed to him that it was he who was running the race, with laudable energy. Now it seems to him that it was the race and its demands that were running him. The ardour he put into it was genuine enough, but he could have devoted it to other tasks, and he begins to doubt whether success is the goal of life.

He is struck, perhaps, as I am today, by the fact that many of those who have given most to our world are in fact men who failed in their chosen goals: Socrates, Jesus, Confucius... Socrates, who had devoted his life to finding the answer to the injunction carved on the front of the temple of Delphi, 'Know thyself', and had the courage to admit to the end that he was getting no nearer to what he sought. In the case of Jesus you know what happened, after many successes – the cross. Confucius did in fact have one success. Jaspers, in his book *Great Philosophers* (vol. I, p.52), tells how Confucius had a vocation to become the counsellor of some prince on the conduct of public affairs. There was one who called on his services, but the great prosperity which his kingdom attained only caused him to sink rapidly into corruption and depravity. Confucius therefore resigned, and waited in vain for the rest of his life for another opportunity.

I am reminded of the story of Polycrates, which I referred to once in Germany at the time of the 'German miracle', when speaking to a group of industrialists who had invited me to address them on the dangers of prosperity. Polycrates reigned as tyrant on the Greek island of Samos, and was so prosperous that he became afraid of his success. Might not the gods become jealous of him? He therefore took a ring, the most precious jewel in his treasure, and cast it into the sea. But the next day he was served a fish, and in it found the ring. The gods had not accepted his expiatory offering. The following year Samos was invaded and Polycrates was slain.

These however, are exceptional destinies, outside our experience. I often think of a very ordinary fellow-countryman of mine, the educationalist Pestalozzi. At a time when the sole aim of schools was discipline, and the teacher was never without his cane, sometimes using it to point out something on the blackboard, and sometimes to rap his pupils' knuckles, Pestalozzi taught by love. Instead of teaching the children of the rich he took the poorest from the streets and opened schools for them. But all his schemes failed, one after another, and he died in poverty. Nevertheless he has had more influence on the evolution of educational methods than all the official teachers.

Have you not happened to meet some childhood comrade whom you remember as full of charm, sensitivity and poetry, and to find him sadly changed? He has had a brilliant career in business or politics. He has become curt, overbearing, self-assured and dogmatic. Have you not thought, 'His success has spoilt him'? What he has gained in power he has lost in humanity. It is a danger which threatens us all, though it does not make us give up the pursuit of success, however modest our own aims.

When my wife was struck down by the illness from which she was to die, one of my best friends said to me: 'Your wife is paying for your success.' It was kindly said, but it made me think, as you may imagine. I therefore talked about it, on the very day of her funeral, to some of my doctor friends. 'Yes, of course,' they said, 'there is some truth in the remark.' But they added, no doubt in order to reassure me: 'It wasn't you that made her do it. She took the job on herself; it was the thing she cared most about; she wanted to share your vocation to the utmost, even at the cost of her own health, and that is why she came with you on this lecture tour.'

Without doubt it was not I who asked her to do that, and yet did I not take advantage of her devotion? She knew how much I needed her, her presence, her support. Do not many wives pay for the successes of their husbands in all sorts of sacrifices, without their husbands always being properly aware that they are doing so?

In any case, though I am more and more conscious of the danger of success, the fact is that that does not stop me from seeking it in spite of everything. I must write this book as well as I can. This is in spite of the unease I experience when I receive from readers letters that are too fulsome in their praise. That they should tell me that a certain remark has helped them in their lives pleases me, naturally. On the other hand, I find praise very embarrassing. Was it not opposition and even persecution that Jesus promised to his disciples?

But the danger of power has a much more serious and general implication, in that it obstructs true dialogue between men. Everyone talks of dialogue nowadays, but true dialogue is extremely rare. What we get is more the exchange of threats and reciprocal aggressiveness, a dialogue of the deaf, confrontation by adversaries each of whom is sure his views are right and anxious only to impose them – not conversation between partners desirous of mutual understanding. There lies the whole difference between argument and dialogue. The latter is possible only between two persons or two groups whose power-relationship is more or less in balance. Otherwise there are obstacles on each side: in the case of the one in power, the more powerful he is, the less accessible is he to dialogue; sure of himself, he always hardens his attitude in confrontation. Not out of ill will, but because he always feels that if he makes concessions he is not forced to make, he is betraying himself. In the case of the weaker party, 'the losers become bad because they are losing', as Lorenz neatly expresses it. They are overcome by the anger of powerlessness.

One of my colleagues has written to me on this subject. He emphasizes, as I do, how difficult dialogue is in a situation of imbalance. But he says also that it is scarcely easier when both parties are powerful, because their very power predisposes them to rivalry. 'In order to be powerful and to feel powerful', he writes, 'one has to be more powerful than one's rival . . . and so power stands in the way of true dialogue, and at the same time isolates the person who possesses it.'

A French psychoanalyst, Mme Eliane Amado Lévy-Valensi, has made a subtle analysis of these relationships of balance and imbalance which facilitate or impede communication. In a letter on aggressiveness published in the periodical *Présences* she writes that aggressiveness is the result of a 'decay of dialogue'. Thus dialogue, the only hope of avoiding violence, may actually provoke it if it fails. And power is the greatest obstacle in the way of dialogue.

It is clear that in the climate of our world of today, which venerates power above wisdom, everything conspires to exacerbate these imbalances. There is a widening gulf between the rich and the poor nations, between the Establishment and those who challenge it and whom it harries and thus provokes to violence. No dialogue is possible with the powerful. But it is their misfortune: there is no worse solitude than that of the powerful. We pay dearly for our power; we live the drama of the lost dialogue.

All of this is closely bound up with the triumphant rationalism of our civilization. To be right, and to demonstrate logically that one is right, is to make certain of victory and of power. But it is a dangerous power, because it alienates the vanquished. In his book on 'The Challenge of Hope' Jacques Sarano has an excellent chapter headed: 'The wrongness of those who are always right.' 'The more you convince me, the more you put me on my guard,' he writes. Reason may indeed reign supreme in our technocratic world, but distrust lodges everywhere in its nooks and crannies, a seed ready to sprout into violence. What is being lost, wonders Sarano; is it 'the smile of a man'?

25 THE DOCTOR'S POWER

In order to throw light on the problem of power I am going to take a concrete example, that of my own discipline, medicine. Its evolution is a striking illustration of that of our modern world, with the prodigious advance in effectiveness that technical progress brings, and the serious dangers it gives rise to. Emmanuel Mounier, the 'philosopher of the person', was aware of this long before me, as is shown by the inquiry he opened in his review *Esprit*, under the title 'Medicine, the Fourth Power?' It was, in a way, Mounier's testament, since he died in that same month of March 1950, in which the magazine published his article.

I had known Mounier before he founded his Movement and his review *Esprit*. I had found myself very much in sympathy with him, but my outlook at that time was doubtless too traditional for me to understand the originality and importance of his thought. It was shortly after the first world war and the Russian Revolution. The idea of the person, as I had taken it from the work of that philosopher of liberty, Charles Secrétan, belonged to the liberal bourgeois ideology of my youth, whereas for Mounier the concept of the person was revolutionary; a challenge both to bourgeois society and to Communism, each of which exalts material progress at the expense of man.

Mounier's inquiry bore only on the techniques of 'psychological intervention', neuro-surgery, shock therapy, narco-analysis, and especially psychoanalysis. He asked whether these techniques amounted to improper manipulation, violation of the person and of his freedom. It is interesting, a quarter of a century later, to read the doctors' replies again. Some share his disquiet, but most are at pains to reassure him. Mme Boutonnier points out that Freud renounced the therapeutic use of hypnosis, which he had at first practised, precisely out of respect for the patient as a person, in order to preserve his 'responsibility for his actions'.

Dr Caruso also renders homage to Freud, for the aim of psychoanalysis is not to deprive a man of his freedom, but to restore it to him. Despite his 'naïve materialism', he writes, Freud revealed 'the fundamental importance of digging deep into the part of man that is determined by factors outside his control, in order to deliver him from some fatal power that is tyrannizing over him'. Nevertheless a certain ambiguity remains. Charles Baudouin writes that psychoanalysis 'may seem, according to the way one looks at it, to be either the height of indiscretion or the supreme refinement of discretion'. And he recalls that Jung preferred to use the term 'method' rather than 'technique' to characterize psychoanalysis, because the idea of a technique suggests that man is being treated 'as a thing'.

That is the problem, whatever the label: is there manipulation? Thus Drs Jean de Rougemont and Alphonse Maeder, who with me founded the sessions on the medicine of the person, put more emphasis in their replies on the danger of power: 'The patient under treatment', writes Maeder, 'is in a quite special state of suggestibility; an inflection of the voice, a gesture, can have an overwhelming effect.'

Since that time more and more has been written on the doctor-patient relationship, on transference and counter-transference, on the influence of the doctor on his patient. It was for this reason that Freud laid down that the doctor must be morally neutral. But even if the doctor professes no religious belief he necessarily has a personal outlook on life, and he communicates it to his patient even without saying anything; at the very least he has a tendency to interpret psychoanalytically all human relationships. I have never forgotten a remark made by one of my patients: 'One is always the prisoner of one's liberator.'

What is there that can restrain us from abusing the power we inevitably wield over our patients? The answer is to be aware of the danger of power. Thus Dr Maeder added: 'We cannot be too much on guard against the pride that degenerates into the instinct of domination and possession.' I myself wrote: 'It all depends on the spirit in which the doctor works.'

I do not go back today on what I said then. But there it is – you cannot teach spirit, but you can teach technique. The same is true of every other discipline as well as medicine, and that is the problem of our whole civilization, in which only techniques are taught, because the positive sciences have been divorced from the moral and spiritual disciplines. For the spirit, the spirit in which each of us practises the techniques he has learnt, we have to turn to our personal development, our independent convictions, our own concept of life. The pride of which Maeder spoke is only stimulated by the exaltation of the prodigious power of man.

In medicine we turn to the high moral traditions of our fraternity, though we know how fragile they are. We meditated upon this point in Germany, on the morrow of its collapse, in 1946. There were present some of the most eminent doctors of that country: Professor Richard Siebeck, Professor Viktor von Weizsäcker. Our discussion returned constantly to the terrible tragedy and distress from which they were emerging: the tragedy of the iniquitous laws of the Nazi régime, which put doctors at the service of death and imposed upon them the violation of the human person.

Senior doctors had resigned rather than act against their consciences. Others had remained at their posts, knowing that they would very soon be replaced by colleagues who were more compliant towards the régime. And they had been forced to manoeuvre and cheat in order to try to save lives, without always being successful. What could they do? It is not for the doctor to judge the law, only to submit to it! But our conversations went deeper: it was the very principle of our secular civilization which was called in question, with its proclamation of the autonomy of science, a science that was supposed to be neutral, knowing no other norm than that of reason. The Nazi horrors showed what that could lead to. Similar situations may arise again anywhere, so long as we do not renounce this claim of science to have nothing to do with the demands of the moral and spiritual conscience.

Nazism was the intoxication of power. But that intoxication may overcome doctors in a more subtle manner. Emmanuel Mounier's inquiry related as yet only to psychological intervention, but prophetically it raised a more general question – that of the 'increasing power' which technology is conferring 'on man over man himself', as Mounier wrote then. What would he have said today in face of the advances which we witness with bated breath – heart transplants, artificial kidneys, and especially the techniques of resuscitation which allow us to prolong life so long as the electric current which feeds these marvellous machines is not cut off by some sovereign hand on the switch?

It is this sovereign gesture, putting an end as it surely does to a man's life, which raises for the scientist a problem which science cannot resolve. Jean Ziegler, professor of sociology at the University of Geneva, in a profoundly disturbing book, calls such a doctor a 'thanatocrat', even a 'high priest'. 'Like the torero in the bullring, he stands in front of the wounded creature and decides the moment of death.' By means of ingenious techniques, to prolong life at will –

there is something to arouse the intoxication of power! But it also means assuming the awful responsibility of a master of death. 'Doctors', Jean Ziegler concludes, 'have plumbed the depths!'

It is not, however, only the resuscitation services and the notorious switch that are involved. There is also the more general question of what has been called 'therapeutic zeal', the limitless determination which drives the doctor to do everything possible to retard death. This is what some patients are afraid of. They feel they are lost, and beg to be allowed to die peacefully at home rather than to be sent to hospital.

In this connection there is a striking remark in Émile Ajar's novel, *La vie devant soi*, which won the Prix Goncourt in 1975. The author describes a little Muslim orphan in Belleville, a working-class district of Paris – Mohamed, called Momo. Momo's mother, a prostitute, had been killed by his father, who since then had been confined in a psychiatric hospital. The child has been put in the care of an old Jewish woman, Madame Rosa, poor, sick, and ugly, but tender-hearted, for whom Momo has formed such a strong attachment that he fights with indomitable energy to see that her last wish is respected – her refusal to allow herself to be taken to hospital. She makes him swear: 'Momo, I don't want to go on living just because the medical men say I must. I know I am losing my wits and I don't want to live for years in a coma just to glorify medical science.'

There is the striking phrase, 'the glory of medical science'. What does it mean? It means the proud power of medicine. A little further on Momo says, 'Medical science must have the last word, and do all it can to stop God's will being done.' We all feel we have the right to be left to die in peace when our time really comes. It is right to mobilize all the technical power of medicine to save a road-accident victim from dying. There is a chance that one day he may be restored to useful life. But that is quite different. Is it not clear that in one case the power of medicine is being used against the will of God – as Momo says – and that in the other it is being exercised as an act of God's mercy?

These, then, are not scientific and technical problems, but moral ones, whose solution it is often difficult to discern. Every doctor faces this increased power he has been given with mixed feelings: enthusiasm, disquiet, and perplexity. How many new and serious problems have been presented to us! But we are on our way to more distant horizons. Nothing will stop scientific and technical progress putting yet more power in doctors' hands. 'At least in imagination', writes Dr Guggenbühl-Craig, 'we can see the frontiers of medicine receding much further still. It will perhaps be possible for us one day to manipulate the genes, and influence heredity.' And Marcel Haedrich writes: 'The worst danger of atomic research is perhaps the manipulation of genes.'

I should like to return now, more modestly, to something that concerns us all personally as practitioners, and not only a few specialists and advanced researchers. I refer to our daily lives. When Emmanuel Mounier spoke of the danger of the increasing power of man over man, he was thinking of the threat to the patient, whereas I wish to underline the danger that this power involves for the doctor himself. The doctor is indeed powerful, too powerful, much more so than he realizes. But he gets used to it, he enjoys it, and that is dangerous for him, especially if he is not fully conscious of the power he has.

Always and everywhere it is he who gives the orders; and he is obeyed – at least, if he is disobeyed it is only in secret. To get his commands obeyed he has at his disposal a powerful argument: 'Your health, your life, is at stake.' We all know Jules Romains' amusing play, *Knock ou le triomphe de la médecine*. Doctors may laugh as they watch it, but there is something of Dr Knock in each one of us. The temptation is great: it is too easy to obtain blind submission. What we object to in Dr Knock is his commercialism. But we can enjoy something else that is more subtle – our authority. We are convinced, of course, that we are using it solely in the patient's interest, but our love of power does come into it.

We are so accustomed to being obeyed that it seems to us to be just as much part of the natural order as the rising and the setting of the sun. The slightest hesitation on the part of the patient to accept our advice strikes us as a serious lack of confidence on his part towards us. Many patients have told me of their astonishment in such circumstances at seeing their doctor's abrupt change of attitude. He had always been so kind and gentle, so easy, so long as they were completely submissive, and suddenly he flies into an unexpected and violent rage. In one of our conferences on the medicine of the person Dr Goust talked to us about this aggressiveness on the part of the doctor when he does not consider his patient is being sufficiently docile; or when a colleague lets him down. It is closely related to his claim to power.

Everything tends to bolster up his power. The most inflexible administration defers to a medical certificate. In hospital the medical superintendent enjoys the prestige of a monarch. He is followed about by a retinue of devoted assistants like a king with his courtiers. In vain does he adopt a more familiar or modest tone – no one dares to raise a voice in opposition to him. Nurses observe the most scrupulous deference towards the doctor. They may, among themselves, laugh at his eccentricities, call in question his pet theories, resent the way he treats them as servants; but to his face it is always, 'Yes, doctor . . . very well, doctor.' They would like more in the way of scientific explanation of the condition and its treatment, but the doctor cuts them short with his 'Just carry on, nurse!' – 'Very well, doctor.'

Even in his own family the doctor is king. Because his job is a vocation, his wife and children must share his dedication. He has enough worries with his patients without having others added. He looks upon it as quite natural that his relatives and associates should hide their own problems or their weariness. I have tended enough nurses and doctors' wives to realize that in their acute concern for their patients, doctors can blind themselves to the signs of exhaustion – often quite visible – in those who work alongside them.

26 UNCONSCIOUS MOTIVATIONS

It is not pure chance that the doctor enjoys such privileges. He has chosen a vocation of power. Goethe's Faust is a doctor, and it is because he is so learned that he is subject to the supreme temptation, that of omnipotence. Was it not because Goethe himself was such an exceptional and universal genius that he understood that temptation and turned his understanding of it into a masterpiece? Medicine is a vocation of power, just like that of the politician, the official, and the industrialist. The doctor is invested with the great respect which the modern world has for science, just as the primitive sorcerer had magical power. But it is not only social prestige that attracts him, nor even the power that money gives, as has been frankly admitted by medical students questioned in opinion polls. The choice of a medical career always involves, I believe, another less obvious factor, which I should like to bring out here.

I mean the wish to help others. It would seem to be the height of disinterestedness, but it is not entirely so. To succour those who are in distress is to play a gratifying and powerful role. It means tending those less fortunate than oneself, and that inevitably involves a certain domination. To be looked upon as a saviour leaves none of us indifferent. This aspect of our work plays a bigger part than we think. Observe how social workers rush to the help of the wretched, and notice the self-satisfaction with which they exercise their praiseworthy office. You will know many more such people who are fond of giving advice to all and sundry, and the flattering sense of superiority it gives them.

Do not imagine that I am engaging in carping and cynical criticism, or that I discount the value of effective dedication to those who need it. It is better to use one's urge to power in helping others than in exploiting them. It is after all the choice I myself made. But we must recognize that it is our power instinct that is involved, with all the dangers that that implies. The great joys of our profession – the healing of the sick, the rehabilitation of the disabled, the consolation of a person in despair, the liberation of a neurotic from the psychical inhibitions paralysing him, all these are victories, experiences of power.

The proof of this, as we have seen, lies in the heavy load of anxiety which weighs down upon the doctor in face of the patient for whom he can 'do nothing', as he says. Often he turns away, unable to bear his powerlessness; and he breaks off the dialogue at the very point where dialogue is most needed, as Dr Elisabeth Kubler-Ross has shown. The spectre of death reveals to us the fundamental fragility of our human condition which we may forget in the excitement of our power. The danger of power is just that – that we deceive ourselves and separate ourselves from others.

Remember what we were saying just now about true dialogue, that it is possible only between participants who are appreciably equal in power. This is far from being the case with the doctor and his patient. Dr Armand Vincent, in his book *Le jardinier des hommes*, has described this inevitable inferiority of the patient. He is sick and the doctor is well; he is uncertain what is wrong with him, while the doctor has his professional knowledge; he has been stopped in his activities, while the doctor is fulfilling his function and – as they both hope – is about to use his power in effecting a triumphant cure.

Neither can do anything about this situation, except to realize how superficial, formal, and artificial such attitudes are, when the truth is that as persons they are equal. Many of my colleagues have told me they agree with what I have written about the equality of persons in the doctor-patient relationship. They look for the intimate personal contact, reciprocal, trusting, transparent even, which characterizes the medicine of the person. It has a price which must be paid: it is that we must come down from the pedestal on which our technological superiority places us. To the extent to which advice, even orders, are necessary to the conduct of the scientific treatment which of course remains our first task, so they are harmful in the moral sphere, because they accentuate the dependence of the patient.

It is often, however, the patient himself who puts us on our pedestal. After many interviews one patient told me how he had viewed me at the start, and how the imposing image he had had of me prevented him from feeling at his ease. But which of us can free himself from worrying about the impression he is making on his patient? We have a good pretext. Naïvely we think that in order to keep up his morale we must appear to be all-powerful and all-knowing. A patient asks me what I think about a medicine I do not know but which has been praised in a newspaper article. Rather than simply admitting that I have never heard of it, I launch into a fine speech about the proliferation of medicaments.

A pearl of the art of safeguarding one's prestige is this piece of advice by Archimatheus of Salerno: 'Promise healing to the patient, but to his family stress the gravity of the sickness. If he does not recover, it will be said that you foresaw his death; and if he recovers, your fame will increase.' I borrow this Machiavellian quotation from Dr Guggenbühl-Craig's excellent book on the subject of the dangers of power in psychotherapy. In the title he uses the word *Helfer* – helper – suggesting that what he has to say applies not only to psychotherapists, but to all those who try to help others.

He addresses himself in fact to all kinds of 'helpers' – doctors, psychologists, churchmen, social workers, and even teachers – inviting them to carry out a rigorous self-examination in the light of depth psychology. 'No one can act only from manifest motives,' he writes. 'Even the most selfless acts proceed not only from manifest motives, but also from others that are hidden – some obvious, some obscure.' He refers to the phenomenon of the shadow which I have already mentioned. He recalls that C. G. Jung defines the shadow as 'the reverse side of the personal or collective ideal'. Now we all consciously profess the highest ideals of aid for others, disinterestedness, and scientific honesty. And at the same time we all carry about in our unconscious the opposite tendencies, which the author expresses in one word: the charlatan. The more the psychotherapist applies himself to the treatment of his patient in accordance with his ideal, the more developed does the shadow, the charlatan, become in his unconscious, 'working not for the patient but for himself'.

For himself! Remember: it was in precisely these terms that we defined, at the beginning of this second part, the temptation of power which Jesus was able to resist; not the impossible renunciation of all aggression, disinterested or not, but renunciation of the use of aggression for the increase of one's own power. There is therefore at this point complete harmony between psychology and what the Bible says. Dr Guggenbühl-Craig goes on to point out that this abuse of man's power over man is a deification of the self, for, he says, 'only God or the gods have the right to command men'. He adds that 'it is that power of which Jacob Burckhardt says that it is the essence of evil'.

These Jungian views are nearer those of Freud than is generally thought: the author recalls that for Jung every archetype is bipolar. If there is an individual shadow which is the dark side of the personal ideal, and a collective shadow which is the reverse of the common ideal, there is also an 'archteypal shadow', in which good and evil are in opposition. And for Jung this evil is not merely the absence of good, but 'an irreducible drive towards destruction' in the human mind. Is not this what Freud called Thanatos, the death instinct? You must not talk of archetypes to a Freudian! But it was none other than a bipolar archetype that Freud was describing in his famous contrast between Eros and Thanatos. Furthermore, the whole idea corresponds closely with what the Bible has to say about the struggle between God and Satan.

Let us then conclude that there is in us, especially in those whose intentions are of the purest, an excessive and destructive will to power which eludes even the most sincere and honest self-examination. It is disquieting, is it not? Especially when we have no chance at all of being able to measure it. How about me? Might I at least have some slight intuition of it?

27 'ORPHANS LEAD THE WORLD'

The question was raised in my mind quite recently. My colleague and fellow-citizen, Dr Pierre Rentchnick, the editor of the journal *Médecine et Hygiène*, published a sensational article entitled 'Orphans Lead the World'. He tells of a discovery he made on the subject, without actually seeking it. That reminds one of a profound remark by Picasso: 'I do not seek, I find.' What Dr Rentchnick was investigating was the political effect that the illness of a statesman might have. The idea had come to him because of the illness that had struck President Pompidou. It had led him to examine the biographies of a large number of historical figures. He had suddenly been struck by a remarkable fact: almost all of them had grown up in abnormal or frustrating family circumstances.

I have no room here to reproduce the impressive table he drew up. It contained almost all the great names of world history! Statesmen, generals, philosophers, founders of religions. There were only two well-known absentees from the list – Bismarck and General de Gaulle, both of whom had had the privilege of a normal home.

All had, for example, lost their fathers, before the age of eight like Cardinal Richelieu, Louis XIV, Peter the Great, Queen Victoria, and William the Conqueror; or before the age of fifteen like Lenin, Stalin, Attila the Hun, and George Washington; or before twenty, like Napoleon I, Marx, Hannibal, Roosevelt, Caesar, and Pompey (but I have had enough to say about these last two in this book!). Or else they were men who had lost their mothers in infancy, like Abraham Lincoln, the Buddha, Descartes, Pascal, and Rousseau; or were fatherless and motherless orphans like Mahomet and Hitler. Others had rejected their fathers, like Alexander the Great, Mao Tse-Tung, and Richard Nixon. Yet others were abandoned, like Robespierre, Winston Churchill, Indira Gandhi. Lastly there were others who were illegitimate, like Fidel Castro, Juan and Evita Perón, Joan of Arc . . . In short, a list of 280 great names.

One cannot help thinking that this is something more than coincidence. Dr Rentchnick had no difficulty in deducing 'a new theory of the genesis of the will to political power'. The point is inescapable.

The author quotes the confidences of Hitler in *Mein Kampf*, and of Sartre in *Les mots*, the painful sensation of 'nothingness' against which the orphan or the forsaken child must fight. 'We see them,' writes Dr Rentchnick, 'in so far as they are of the requisite intellectual and personal calibre, revealing themselves as aggressive and dominating . . . these men cheated by life . . . they emerge from their existential nothingness to end up as political, religious, revolutionary, or spiritual leaders.'

Naturally all this concerns me personally, since I was an orphan. Suddenly I find myself among a numerous company, and that makes me more frightened than proud. I wrote to my colleague. He at once invited me to go and see him. In the event I felt like a 'case' in his presence: 'How old were you when your father died?' 'Three months.' 'And your mother?' 'Six years.' 'What were your feelings at that time?' 'Mostly that I didn't matter to anybody.' We talked at length about my personal life. He had been a student when he read my first book. Talking of books, it was he who drew my attention to the novel by Émile Ajar which I mentioned earlier – you remember, the story of Momo, the indomitable little orphan.

So there it is. I must clearly suspect that in the obscure depths of my mind, without knowing it, I am possessed by a will to power greater than that of the majority of people, greater than I had ever thought. I have always thought of myself as gentle, kindly, tolerant, and liberal, but this is probably only an overcompensation for a dangerous tendency towards domination. I questioned my children, friends, former patients. Their replies were soothing. Perhaps they were trying to allay my fears. I recall a remark by one of my colleagues to whom I had been talking about my hesitant character, always lacking self-confidence. 'Yes,' he told me, 'there is that in you, but when you *are* convinced, nobody can possibly stop you. That's what makes you a leader.'

Where does that feeling of unease come from that I mentioned earlier, the acute disquiet that I feel when someone congratulates me on a success? Could it be that there is in me an over-powerful desire for success? Whence comes the sympathy I feel for all revolutionaries, even when I in no way approve of their ideas? And my fellow-citizen Jean-Jacques Rousseau, an orphan like me – why did he have a constant need to justify himself? Might it not be that he had a vague intuition of the dangerous forces boiling within himself, which in the end brought down the *ancien régime* and helped to bring about the French Revolution?

I have often spoken of the considerable part played in my life, as I believe, by the death of my mother, of the feeling of black solitude into which I was plunged at that time, of my shy, aloof and unsociable character. Then how I slowly emerged from it, helped by my studies, and by a teacher who took an interest in me and who, by talking with me, made me aware of my personal existence, and helped me by means of my intellectual activity to take my place in society.

But the importance of my father's death had largely escaped me until now, and the realization of it I owe to Dr Rentchnick. The father symbolizes power, the power on which we depend at first in infancy, and against which we measure ourselves in adolescence. Its absence means first insecurity, and then the lack of the opportunity of asserting oneself against it, and finally the need for a will to power. That, I imagine, is why this will to power has remained more unconscious in my case. It is not surprising that I chose in medicine a vocation of power.

Nor is it surprising that it presented itself to me in the mild and inoffensive light I spoke of just now – the desire to help others, which seems the complete opposite of the will to power, but which may act as a cover for it. It seems to me that that has been a merciful opportunity granted to me – to work it off to some extent in a career as a doctor, and then as a writer. For after all this dangerous will to power, which we have to master, is also what saves us! This is true of all the statesmen mentioned by Dr Rentchnick. They too were convinced – in their conscious minds – that they were dedicating themselves to their country, that their careers had no other motive than that of service, but in reality they were saving themselves from the feeling of non-existence into which the frustration of their childhood had plunged them.

We come back here to the same problem which occupied us from the earliest pages of this book in relation to aggressiveness: we need it in order to live. If it remains bottled up in the unconscious, if it cannot get out, we are left disabled, in a sort of living death. Dr Rentchnick knows very well that there are millions of orphans who have never been able to break out of the state of inhibition, of blockage, in which an abnormal childhood has left them. His article clearly demonstrates it. These millions elude his researches simply because history throws up only the exceptions, the ones that have discovered a means of sublimating their will to power, unfortunately with the danger of abuse that that involves.

It would seem, then, that the frustrating family circumstances enumerated by Dr Rentchnick always represent a redoubtable test, which like all tests may produce two opposite reactions – one weak, the other strong, both of them dangerous. Deprived in childhood of natural support and normal developmental factors, the subject may be left psychologically disabled for the rest of his life if no one comes to his aid. He is endowed, it would seem, with a rare will to power, but if it remains unconscious, it also remains uncontrolled.

It may then, in many cases, turn inwards as a self-destructive force and cause further damage. But in other cases, the exceptions, it can explode outwards. In the absence of family support such individuals rely only on themselves, become intransigent, authoritarian, domineering, even tyrannical. Yet others may rely on God, and find in him the support they have missed.

Naturally I talked with my colleague about my religious vocation. He said at once that that did not surprise him, and that while his list contained nearly all the political leaders in the history of the world, it also included (without exception in this case!) religious leaders, from Moses, abandoned as a baby in his basket on the waters of the Nile, and Mahomet, whose father and mother both died before he was one year old, and the Buddha, left motherless, to Luther and Calvin who rejected their fathers – and many others.

We spoke too of Jesus himself, and of his father St Joseph, whose history is very mysterious, since the last mention made of him dates from the time when Jesus was twelve, and who in any case was not really his father. In his book *Les années obscures de Jésus*, Robert Aron imagines him initiating Jesus into the religious rites of his people and into his carpenter's craft, but he recognizes that he has no proof of this. In any case, during Jesus' ministry it is interesting to see that no further reference is made to St Joseph, notably for instance when Mary, in company with other relatives, makes an urgent approach to Jesus (Matt. 12.46).

Let us return to the subject of my vocation. It was God who called me to become a doctor. Concretely that means that I have always thought that it was he who was entrusting each one of my patients to me. It was also God who called me to faith, to be his witness, more or less faithful, to all those whom he made me meet or who read my books. But these certitudes of faith do not stop me studying as a psychologist the motivations of my choices, because it is by means of such psychical mechanisms that God leads us where he wills.

Throughout the entire universe, God's will is accomplished through the phenomena of nature which science investigates. These physical, chemical, biological, psychical, or sociological mechanisms are not our invention; all we do is discover them. It was God who invented them long before we discovered them, and they are much more numerous and complex than we shall ever discover. Moreover it was he who invented and endowed us with the intelligence which allows us to discover and understand them, to sing the wonders of creation, or if we like, to deny the existence of the Creator!

I have already recognized in myself several of the motivations of my choice of a medical career, and Dr Rentchnick showed me one more, which is valid also for my religious vocation. If medicine is a vocation to power, the ministry, whether clerical or lay, is much more so! Think of it: to be the bearer of a divine mission, charged not only with contributing to men's health, but also to their salvation, to be the trustee of a religious message! Dr Rentchnick makes the point: 'Politics and religion, to these great personalities whom life has cheated, seem to be the ideal means of creating, of recreating an order that is more in conformity with the view of the world that is taken by a human being intent on vengeance.'

28   SPIRITUAL POWER

'Politics and religion', says Dr Rentchnick. The worst danger of all is that there should be collusion between these two, when religion is used to win power, and political power is used for religious ends. This is true not only of those religions that one might call theological, but also of modern Communism, for example, which from the psychological point of view has all the characteristics of a religion, with its orthodoxies, its heresies, its schisms, its missionary ardour, and its claim to a monopoly of the truth. The Christians had already shown the way.

Near Hämeenlinna, in Finland, I was shown a lake called the Lake of Purification. I concluded at once that this must be where the first Christians were baptized. Quite the contrary, I was told. When the Swedes came to conquer the country, they consciously looked upon themselves as the soldiers of Christ, and they forcibly baptized the inhabitants: 'I baptize you or kill you!' In order to preserve their lives, the Finns submitted to baptism, but they would at once make their way to this lake and plunge into it in order to purify themselves of their Christian baptism.

The anecdote suffices to illustrate the point. I could point to innumerable similar campaigns – the conquest of the land of Canaan by the Israelites, the Holy War of the Arabs in which they advanced as far as Spain, the Crusades in the opposite direction, and all the wars of religion and colonial expansion. Or again, persecution of all kinds; the Inquisition; the extermination of the Jews by the Nazis. All this is too well known for me to need to dwell upon it. Too well known, and universally condemned.

Condemned by all? Yes, of course, all except those who committed all these atrocities. That is something to make us think. Which of us has never asked himself whether it is really religion which makes men so fierce? All these combatants acted in good faith; we should be lacking in good faith ourselves not to recognize it. They threw themselves into their battles, ready to sacrifice their lives, not just thinking it was permitted, but that it was their sacred duty.

Their conviction – in both the opposing camps – was sincere, unanimous, and compelling. They were fighting for the noblest of causes, the least selfish, the most generous, for the triumph of the purest values recognizable by man. How then is such a thing possible?

It seems to me that it is incomprehensible unless one recognizes the enormous part played by the power instinct in the way all human beings behave, generally without being aware of it. They need to love, but they also need to fight. They love peace, but they enjoy victory even more. They are never so enthusiastic or fulfilled as when they are engaged, with all good conscience, in some great struggle into which they have thrown their whole strength to win.

They need an adversary to confront, in order to demonstrate their power, in order to feel themselves fully alive. They need a target, for without a target one cannot shoot. Basically they seek conflict, without knowing it, the conflict of ideas if not armed conflict. I imagine that many of my readers are inwardly protesting as they read these lines. They think that man is not as bad as all that; that it is only injustice and frustration that brings to life in him a combative ardour that is not pre-existent, already threatening to burst forth. Perhaps they have already suspected me of masochism when I wondered on reading Dr Rentchnick's article whether my apparent mildness and my idealism did not conceal a tremendous will to power. But how then do they explain wars of religion?

The need to fight which I am talking about does not seem to me to be 'wickedness', but much more a manifestation of life, which is power, explosive power. When the fighting leads to atrocities those who have committed them always say that they did not mean it to come to that. What they desired was something good, and they wanted to sweep aside the obstacles in the way of its achievement. There are plenty of obstacles, of course, to the explosive life-force: the whole of education, social pressure, the police, the moral conscience, the need to be accepted and approved of, esteemed and loved, by others. All these things prevent this wild force from showing itself. But it goes on living underneath, like smouldering embers ready to burst out and start a mighty conflagration.

It seems then that this force is always there, on the watch, in the back of the human mind, awaiting the moment to spring. I was about to write, 'awaiting a good excuse'. But it is the wrong phrase because it suggests cunning, deception, whereas we have seen that the combatant in a religious war is sincere. His conviction of his innocence is total; it is equalled only by his conviction of the culpability of the enemy, to whom he attributes Machiavellian trickery and an evil lust for power, at least in the case of their leaders, who have deceived their people. The participant in a religious war needs no pretext, since his cause is completely valid in his eyes, fully justifying his actions.

What more valid reason could there ever be than a divine vocation, a mandate from God, a holy mission to defend that which is most sacred? Then conscience gives the go-ahead, and the forces of nature are unleashed like a pack of impatient motorists when the red lights turn to green. From the psychological point of view there is scarcely any difference in this respect between religious people and atheists. It applies to every kind of messianic belief, from the secular idealism which I knew in my childhood, and which believed in human progress through universal education, to modern Marxism, as well as the formal religions. Perhaps one day the present conflict will look like a war of religion analogous to those of past centuries.

There have indeed been as many wars of religion between the adherents of different confessions as there are conflicts today between believers and unbelievers – and even between members of the same church! Think of all the controversies which have torn Christendon as well as Islam. They break out as soon as one man or one community claims to be the sole possessor of truth. Nothing gives such a feeling of power as the certainty of possessing the truth. We need to repeat that it is dangerous not so much for a man to be right, as to be sure he is right. The tragedy is that nothing does more to awaken this certainty than an illumination of the spirit, a religious experience.

I always remember a worthy pastor, apparently humble and shy, who had brought his sick wife to see me. As I was beginning to question his wife, asking her what the trouble was and how it had begun, the husband interrupted me impatiently: 'It's quite simple, doctor. I have the Holy Spirit and my wife has not.' My first, rather wicked, reaction was to think that it was no wonder the wife was ill if her husband could say a thing like that. But I at once checked myself – I was doing just what the husband had done, jumping to a false conclusion about the origin of the illness. The true cause we never discovered.

But I was astonished. It really is terrible for a sick woman to hear her husband pass such a wounding and unjust judgment upon her. I felt as much pity for the husband as for the patient. Poor man! He was certainly sincere. No doubt he had had a genuine experience of the gift of the Holy Spirit; and it had so intoxicated him that, modest though he was by nature, it had given him a sense of superiority and power that had quite blinded him. He had no notion of the harm that he was doing to his wife.

That story reminds me of another quite personal one, which it is much more unpleasant for me to recount here, but I cannot escape it. In 1932, intrigued by the surprising progress towards recovery of one of my patients, I made contact with a religious movement which had visibly transformed her, and which was called the Oxford Group, because it had begun among the students at Oxford. The testimony I heard from its members overwhelmed me. They laid stress on concrete obedience to the inspiration of God. I realized all at once that up to then my faith had been too intellectual and theological, and very poor in personal experiences; that I had been preoccupied with the need to have the right ideas about God, and very little with the ideas that God might have about me.

God had thrown out a challenge to me, but in the face of it I hesitated for several weeks. I discussed it excitedly with my wife, with friends, and especially with one of my colleagues who had been more prompt than I was in coming to a decision. One morning I was in the bathroom, and my wife asked me through the open door from the bedroom: 'At heart, do you consider yourself committed to this Oxford Group?' I hesitated for a second or two, and then I replied firmly, 'Yes.' 'And me?' she asked. 'Oh, no.' When I went through to her I found her in tears.

Without my realizing it, a thoughtless and certainly vainglorious remark on my part had brought us close to a spiritual separation the possibility of which my wife had foreseen and feared. At the very moment when I was still so hesitant about committing myself, when I still harboured so much inner resistance, when I was so unsure that I would overcome it, I had given the impression to my wife that I was shooting ahead on my own without bothering about her, the impression that I was leaving her behind.

A religious experience or decision can often in this way have as it were a double face: on the one hand a humbling of the self, self-abandonment, a difficult abdication of one's personal will before the authority of God; and on the other a subtle and gratifying feeling of victory, as yet almost unconscious, the feeling of having taken a decisive step, of having discovered a great truth ignored by other men – in brief, a feeling of superiority. But though the person concerned often does not realize this, those around him are aware of it, and are frequently irritated by the triumphant tone of voice in which he tells them how humble it has made him. On the one hand a narrow gate through which one cannot pass without getting scratched, and on the other such a dazzling sense of wonder that one feels one can embrace the whole world and its problems; in brief, an exciting feeling of power.

Mention of a narrow gate reminds me of a conversation I had with a well-known psychoanalyst whom I hold in high esteem. We were lunching together at the Bossey Oecumenical Institute, which prompted him to make a comparison between psychoanalytical experience and the gospel: 'My didactic analysis has really been for me what Jesus calls the narrow gate' (Matt. 7.13), he said; 'a humiliating test! The favourable image of myself that I had built up was crumbled away session by session. Everything of which I had been proudest was pitilessly unmasked.'

Yes, I do think that for many people analysis is more than a scientific technique. It is a spiritual experience, having the characteristic double face that I have just described, one narrowing, the other broadening; or in biblical terms, of dying to oneself and of resurrection. So that we find psychoanalysts reacting with the same triumphant tone of voice which strikes us in believers talking about their conversion, as if their experience were exemplary and definitive, as if it had solved all life's problems at a stroke. I have experienced this kind of exaltation, but with hindsight I must now recognize it as an exaltation of power.

I committed myself wholeheartedly and militantly to the Oxford Group over a period of fifteen years. Yes, I was a militant, for one can be a militant in the church just as much as in a political party. It is clear that in a party the militant is aiming openly at winning power. But if we use the word of a religious movement, it is because there has slipped into it a certain temptation of power to which it is less easy to admit. Are not even anti-militarists militants?

Of course I am not disowning this stage in my life – quite the contrary. It was a wonderful school of the Christian life for me. In it I had some marvellous and tremendous experiences of meeting God, as also of meeting fraternally with others. It was there that I learnt that what makes a man a person, infinitely to be respected, is just this relationship with God and one's neighbour. It was a great and beautiful adventure, and also my initiation into that other adventure, my career thereafter as a psychotherapist.

During those years my wife and I took part in countless gatherings which were called 'house-parties', or simply sharing groups. Great was our joy to see more and more new friends joining us to undergo in their turn decisive religious experiences and to become reconciled with themselves, with other people, and with God. It was a legitimate joy, of course, but it was mingled with the joy of conquest! Five years later we called a national rally in Lausanne. There was an enormous crowd present when I opened the proceedings.

29　THE CHURCH AND POWER

But when my wife saw my photograph on the cover of an illustrated magazine she felt a certain unease, and she told me of it. At first I did not understand her, and tried to justify myself. Was it not for God that I was undertaking the whole thing? When we did not agree I was always inclined to think that I was right and she wrong. Nevertheless, from that day on doubt began to enter my mind, a growing repugnance for mass movements and collective enthusiasms. Shortly afterwards the terrible adventure under Hitler just across our frontiers in Germany was to open my eyes and to reinforce my dislike of propaganda. I had not yet reached that point, but I was beginning to feel that though we were doing good to others, it was doing harm to me. The intoxication of success is a perfidious snare even in the best causes – especially in the best causes.

I was trying hard to remain modest and simple, at least to seem so. But I was not. Was it not a lack of modesty even to try? We often talked naïvely of transforming the whole world. We had a song, the French version of which I had written, along with the poet René-Louis Piachaud, and which I used to sing with all my heart:

> D'un nouveau monde,
> Qui sur Dieu se fonde,
> Compagnons,
> Nous jetons
> Les assises profondes.
> Voici que nos chantiers
> Vont couvrir le monde entier . . .

('Friends, we are laying deep the foundations of a new world built on God. See how our building-sites are going to spread the whole world over . . .')

It was more a song of triumph than of humility. In fact it took me a long time to realize it: my will to power was only too happy to turn it to advantage as soon as the adventure, begun in tears, began to prove a success.

I have become increasingly aware of the danger of spiritual power. It is not only a matter of public success, but also of our personal relationships with others and the spiritual authority that is attributed to us. They look upon us as experts, God's mouthpieces, the interpreters of his will – to begin with for ourselves, but very soon, before we realize it, for other people too, especially since they insist on requiring it of us. Very soon too we find ourselves thinking that when they follow our advice they are obeying God, and that when they resist us they are really resisting God.

Throughout history there have been religious movements like

the one that attracted me then. It has happened whenever the wind of the Spirit has begun to blow. They have all brought in a like harvest of worth-while spiritual experiences. They have all borne good fruit. They have renewed traditional churches locked in their citadels of secular power. They have raised great hopes, as well as painful controversies; they have drawn great crowds. But when one thinks about it, one sees that their very success is what has exhausted them, that they have become ensnared by power.

It is a most delicate problem. The church is a missionary church, not by its own choice, but because God has called it to its mission in face of the distress of the world. I have a missionary soul, and I believe that it was God who gave me it. But mission means conquest! Where is the frontier between missionary zeal and the will to power? Not in the aim, but in the spirit in which we act – the spirit of our unconscious motivations much more than our conscious ones.

We come back to the grave warning given by Dr Guggenbühl-Craig, of which I spoke in connection with the power of the doctor: the higher the conscious ideal, the more does there develop in the shadows of the unconscious that other self which he calls the charlatan, 'the one who works for himself'. Here we are once again, in relation to the church this time, confronted with the essential distinction which the example of Jesus led us to make between power used in the service of others, and power used for oneself.

Added to these thoughts are those aroused in me by my work as a psychotherapist and a healer of souls over the last forty years. I find this even more difficult to speak of. I have seen a great number of souls suffering from traumas caused by well-intentioned religious influences. They have often been weak people, unsure of themselves, immature or neurotic, lacking the intellectual equipment that would enable them to tackle theological controversies, and torn between contradictory doctrines powerfully asserted by eminent preachers. Or else they are people full of scruples, brought up in a pious and puritan atmosphere that was valid enough for their parents, because it was freely chosen by them, but it was imposed on the children with all the authority of God, before they were mature enough to make a personal choice of their own. Sometimes they have been emotional, impressionable people, so sensitive to enthusiasm that they have become utterly dependent upon some strong spiritual personality.

Faced with psychological disasters like these I often say to myself,

'How dangerous it is to be powerful, to have so much influence and spiritual authority!' One cannot blame the authors of these disasters, for that would be to blame them for what is best and most generous in them, their talent, their missionary zeal. And may I not have unwittingly provoked such disasters myself?

This touches also the problem of the sectarianism which is so unconscious that those who are most impregnated with it will protest if they are accused of it, and assure us in good faith that they are quite free of it, that their only concern is for the truth and its defence. Actually I admire many sects for their exemplary consecration to God, and their emphasis on aspects of the Christian faith too often neglected by the traditional churches. And sectarianism is by no means unknown among the members of these churches as well.

Remember the pastor who told me that he had the Holy Spirit, but his wife had not. I sympathized with him rather than blaming him, for he had spoken with so much candour. I felt he was the victim of a sort of blindness resulting from the very intensity of the experience he had had, and which, to do him justice, he would have been glad to bring his wife to have as well. We are all in the same danger, because of the thirst for power that we have hidden in our hearts, and which drives us to make the most of ourselves. The tragic thing is that even missionary zeal can be used for this purpose.

Mission always aims at mastery. Missions to heathen lands, as they were conceived when I was young, were permeated throughout with a preconception of the superiority of the white race. Missionary committees followed their progress with the satisfaction of a General Staff following the advance of their victorious troops on a headquarters map. Happily all that has changed.

Military imagery, however, dies hard in the churches, symbolic of the thirst for power that besets them. It was St Paul himself, wonderful missionary as he was, who began it when he enumerated in his letter to the Ephesians the armoury of the Christian (Eph. 6.14–17). He has at least the merit of frankness. The Salvation Army, too, has its military vocabulary, its command structure and its discipline. I was talking about this only recently with one of its most famous leaders, and particularly about their journal which has the audacity to call itself the *War Cry*.

But notice that it is this very Salvation Army which has dedicated itself with more charity than any other body to the succour of the most wretched outcasts of society, and which demonstrates the greatest theological tolerance in imposing no dogmas upon its members. It is as if by freely admitting its warlike intentions, which other churches carefully conceal, it is able to liberate charity because it has brought its aggressiveness out into the light of day. This just goes to show how true it is that we never rid ourselves of our instinct of power, and that it is better to face it squarely in order to control it. But what a lot of harm it has done in the history of the church!

Jaspers, in his book on the great philosophers, remarks (vol. I, p.49) that 'Buddhism is the one world religion that has known no violence, no persecution of heretics, no inquisitions, no witch trials, no crusades.' This is possibly because it has more faithfully preached poverty, self-denial and renunciation. These were also preached by primitive Christianity, when Christians were grouped in tiny, poor communities, dispersed, lacking all power, and very soon the object of persecution. A decisive turning-point came in the fourth century when the Emperor Constantine made Christianity a state religion.

Note that he did so chiefly for political reasons. This means that the church had already become powerful enough for Constantine to need its support in consolidating his authority. But at the same time he was giving the church an enormous access of power in the support it received from the political Establishment. Thus though powers sometimes fight each other, they may also become allies in order to augment their power. This was a historical disaster for the church from which it is scarcely beginning to recover even now. Ever since then the church has been a pawn in the power-game of the world. It has been compromised, manipulated, in all the wars and injustices of political power.

Until quite recently it has appeared as a conservative, if not a reactionary force throughout its history, which is truly paradoxical in view of the radically revolutionary character of the gospel. Constantine presented it with a poisoned gift. He set it on the inexorable road to power. Its worst errors, as we all recognize today, were committed at moments when it was at the height of its power. It had become not only a military power, but also exerted the strictest constraint upon men's minds, strong enough to obstruct the development of science and of liberty of thought.

It has used and abused its spiritual power by exploiting the fear of death and of the Beyond. True, we owe to this masterpieces of art, and in literature the *Divine Comedy*; but all this domination of men's minds by fear, when the gospel message was of the love and grace of God, has severely compromised the cause of faith. Think of the famous formula, 'No salvation outside the church.' The schism of the Reformation, which the Roman Church deplores today, came about because the church believed itself to be powerful enough to stifle the voice of Luther. And the Protestants in their turn at once made the great mistake of making pacts with the political powers, which then exploited the religious movement to increase their own power.

I realize that I am skimming too quickly over all this. It is so painful! I am oversimplifying it because I want above all to get across what seems to me obvious: that all the errors and misfortunes of the church are closely bound up with the curse of its power. I am aware that at the same time there has been an explosion of charity of a kind unknown in the ancient world; there have been innumerable instances of humble devotion, admirable thinkers, great saints and mystics. It is on the level of the church that all is spoilt, precisely because it has become powerful, and because anyone who has power inevitably makes use of his power.

The same pattern then always emerges: consciously, the single aim of serving God and mankind; unconsciously the satisfaction of the need for power which is embedded in the human mind, and which seeks its justification in the nobility of the conscious aim. In my little city of Geneva, that is perhaps what makes it possible for us to understand the figure of Calvin, and the contradiction between his dictatorial authoritarianism and his extreme tenderness towards the souls of men.

So let us be glad that today the church has lost some of its power. For the first time since the Emperor Constantine it finds itself in a minority, an almost negligible quantity in the eyes of the powers of this world. This, it seems to me, is what Pope John XXIII understood. His influence over the whole of Christendom derived from the very fact that he did not have the soul of a powerful prelate, but that of a poor country priest. In the same category is the recent speech by the Rev. Philip Potter, Secretary of the World Council of Churches, in which he said how salutary it is for all our churches to find themselves weak, cast off, and scorned; how much nearer they are then to their leader Jesus Christ!

But how difficult it is to overcome the yearning for power! How many Christians continue to deplore what they call the de-Christianization of the modern world! They bitterly compile their statistics of 'practising members', as if the number of them were what mattered. The number has indeed gone down, a sign of loss of power by the church. But at the same time there is an increasing number of thinkers, doctors, even economists, or again, just ordinary folk, who are asking themselves anxious and essential questions about the meaning of life, of society, and of civilization.

They feel acutely what our civilization lacks – its sterility, and the fact that technical efficiency and economic power are not sufficient for man. They sense that he needs something absolute, something that touches his heart and not just his rational intelligence, and that he must recover the sense of community. All this is an obscure search for God, whom they had thought they had been able to throw out, and who is not to be found in the excitement of power. How comes it that this passionate quest for a real meaning to life is taking place very largely on the fringe of the official churches?

An illustration occurs to me – the child who has just been given an ingenious toy. His father wants to show him how to make it work, and the child protests: 'No, I want to do it on my own!' He rejects the paternal power on which he relied when he was younger, because he wants to be free of it now. The father is put out. He liked it when his child looked to him for everything. In the same way the church has been so long a teacher, conducting a monologue, formulating doctrines, teaching catechisms. The age of her omnipotence is over. But if she accepts the fact, she can enter into dialogue and help her children still further in their search, but in a different way, more humbly, more disinterestedly, not aiming at conquering souls, but serving them.

30   THE ABUSE OF POWER

We must therefore beware of our reaction of resentment when people turn away from our influence. It is because it has been too oppressive, too possessive, since it has been poisoned by our unconscious will to power. The thirst for power enters without our being aware of it into all our conflicts. I could say of any marital dispute what I was writing just now about wars of religion: husbands and wives with high moral standards, cultivated, even well versed in psychology, devoutly religious, can find themselves treating each other with astonishing harshness and brutality, while at the same time each believes that he or she is acting from the most virtuous motives, and defending justice, honour, and truth.

Each of them may spend hours explaining to you how right he is, how genuine his complaints are, and how outrageous the partner's conduct is; he is certain he is right, and calls on you to witness to the fact. As I was saying of the wars of religion, one would have to be dishonest and prejudiced against him not to recognize that he is speaking in good faith. How is it possible? Marriage counsellors, whose numbers continue to grow, take endless trouble, preoccupied particularly as they are with the conditions for successful sex, shorn now of all its mystery. But while we are making subtle analyses and constructing ingenious theories, true and important though they may be, we run the risk of overlooking something that is quite simple.

This simple fact is that we are all moved without knowing it by an imperious will to power which brooks no obstacle. The obstacle, of course, is our nearest neighbour, if he does not submit. I remember a friend who prefaced his remarks to me once by saying: 'I have never come into conflict with the Empress of Japan, but I have frequently done so with my wife.' The will to power is sometimes openly encouraged in the name of psychology, in the way that reconciliation and love used to be enjoined by the church: 'Assert yourself,' we are told, 'be yourself, defend yourself!' To make concessions, to try to see one's own errors, to ask for forgiveness – all this is put down nowadays as weakness, a castration complex, deriving from a slave morality now happily out of date. Do not be surprised, then, that there are conflicts of will and that sexual harmony is compromised.

What has often greatly astonished me when I have been questioning couples after a serious dispute, asking them what had actually sparked it off, is the fact that neither of them could remember. They recalled clearly enough the culmination of the conflict, the wounding words or the harsh gestures that had inflamed them, but however they searched they could not remember how it all began. Just occasionally one of them may eventually remember, and he will laugh rather ruefully, saying, 'Oh, it's silly! It was so pointless!'

There could be no better confirmation of what I am saying, that the true cause is generally unconscious, the power drive in quest of a target, like a missile with a homing head. Once our passions have been set alight our minds are flooded with grievances, often ancient ones which we have promised never to mention again. Each sees the aggressiveness of the other and is blind to his own. All he is doing is to give as good as he gets, and, as Lorenz says, to look upon his own behaviour as being an attitude of defence.

Let us now go further. We all know that we can be blinded by passion, a fact that has been abundantly illustrated by dramatic literature. What we must also see is that power too blinds the conscience. And that is much more tragic; for our passions are explosive, which means that they are quickly over, however violent they may be. They subside, exhausted by their own vehemence. It is well known that an outburst of anger makes it possible for the subject a moment later to be calm and reasonable, and even to laugh at his own anger. The passions blind us only momentarily.

Power, on the other hand, is lasting. It even bears within itself an inevitability of growth The rich always become richer. The powerful always find it harder and harder to put up with resistance to their power; they become more and more capable of crushing all resistance, and so become more and more powerful. Is this not why it has been necessary to make anti-trust laws? This is true not only of individuals and commercial firms, but also of humanity as a whole, which has for several centuries been committed because of its technological progress to an escalation of power, spiralling inexorably upward. Will the whole adventure end in catastrophe? This is what a growing number of thinkers are asking.

Power blinds the conscience. This is what I should like to impress upon my readers as urgently as I felt it myself as I read Dr Hacker's book to which I referred at the beginning. Of course one can point to notable historical examples: Caligula, Nero, Attila, Robespierre, Hitler. But they were exceptional personalities to whom neither you nor I feel inclined to compare ourselves. One might in any case wonder whether they became powerful because they were inhuman, insensitive, and unscrupulous, or whether they became pitiless tyrants because they were powerful. The question is whether it could happen to ordinary people such as you and me.

Well, what may open our eyes is the impressive frequency of cases of children being ill-treated by parents or teachers. It is shocking. I pick up an ordinary press-cutting with a statistic from the United Kingdom: in that country seven hundred battered children die every year from violent injuries! But let us listen to what Dr Hacker says:

Because children have kept on crying, they have had boiling water poured over them, they have been sat on hot stoves, they have been strangled to death, they have been thrashed until the blood flowed and their flesh was in ribbons... All this has happened ... in the most important modern educational institutions, in the two great cities of the USA, New York and Los Angeles. In Los Angeles, for every million inhabitants about 120 cases of serious ill-treatment of children have been reported, 20% of these ending with the death of the victim. In New York City, 700 cases were reported in 1967, and 2,500 in 1970.

Wherever statistics are available they reveal a frightening increase in the number of cases reported to the authorities of physical and moral torture inflicted upon defenceless children, in America as well as England and in central Europe. The statistics, it is true, have little significance. All the experts agree in putting the number of children in cities subjected to cruelty at a figure ten to fifteen times greater than that shown in the statistics. In country districts the underestimation of the facts amounts to between 100% and 200%. No statistic admits of such an enormous margin of error.

So, while we indignantly read the accounts of a few political or criminal acts of violence, given with full details in the newspapers, there are millions of children in the world of whose sufferings we know nothing. Neighbours hear the cries, the howls of pain, but only rarely do they dare report the matter to the authorities, partly because they are not sure what is going on in the secrecy of another family, partly too because they do not want to be dragged into all the trouble of a police enquiry. Furthermore, in all our countries, legislation is so respectful of the rights of parents that they have to be guilty of the most serious brutality before they can have their children taken from them. All the agencies for the protection of children are aware of this, and their greatest fear is of being accused themselves of unwarranted meddling in the private lives of the families concerned.

Dr Hacker has called attention to these facts about the ever-increasing violence of our modern world. My readers will understand, I am sure, why I pointed them out with the same insistence. They will realize that I do so in this Part Two, devoted as it is to the problem of power, and not in my Part One, because my aim is not so much to describe the escalation of violence as to discover its root cause. This cause is, I believe, to be found in the modern idolatry of power. 'Be powerful'; such is the first commandment, as much in our so-called Christian West as in Islam and in the Communist world – except perhaps in China; I do not know.

In the tragedy of battered children the power factor is obvious: the disproportion between the strength of the parents and that of the children is complete. It is just because the child is physically incapable of defending himself, because he cannot hit back, that parents in their nervous exasperation can allow themselves to commit such brutal and unjust acts of violence. And also because the child can make no official complaint, because he dare not, and does not even know to whom to complain. 'In fact,' writes Dr Hacker, 'children are devoid of rights.'

When later on they do enter into continual conflict with their parents, it is when they have reached adolescence, and are physically strong enough to return the blows they receive, and even to win. Even if there are no blows, it is clear that it is this relationship of their respective strengths which underlies the conflict. The adolescent is at last free from the handicap of weakness under which he has laboured since infancy. Or else he has cast off that other handicap of economic dependence, since he can leave home and manage on his own, even if it means poverty for him.

More serious and thought-provoking still, however, is that none of the parents who batter their children shows any sign of remorse or repentance. Dr Hacker is categorical on this point, and he certainly ought to know! Torturers and even murderers, when interrogated they all claim to have a clear conscience, and protest their innocence. The child needed to be chastised! The parents beat him only for his own good! This is the same complete denial of guilt that we used to hear from the mass-torturers and executioners of the concentration-camps. They were only doing their duty. A moving detail pointed out by Dr Hacker is that the battered child is often the favourite child, the one who was most vehemently longed for, and in whom the parents are all the more disappointed because they had pictured to themselves the little angel he was going to be. They find it all the more difficult to put up with his tears and his continual crying.

There is such an enormous number of these unworthy parents that we cannot look upon them as exceptionally wicked people.

Rather must we consider them as bearing witness to human nature as it is, always ready to abuse its power the moment it can do so with impunity. If you are revolted by such a person, remember the words of Jesus: 'If there is one of you who has not sinned, let him be the first to throw a stone at her' (John 8.7). Which of us parents can boast that he has never used his superior physical strength in order to impose his will upon a recalcitrant child? Which of us is proof against Dr Hacker's pertinent remark: 'We use violence on children in order to teach them not to be violent.'

To be fair, did we not say, like all those others, that it was for their own good? Did you seriously think about it? It was so easy to turn to the use of force. Not even actual blows, perhaps, but merely the forcible grasp of the child's hand to stop him escaping from us. Did we ever ask his forgiveness, we who were so strict about making him say he was sorry for his smallest fault? And if anyone criticized us would we not have promptly excused ourselves by saying, 'What do you expect? My nerves are all on edge?'

We often invoke our nerves as an excuse. Others, more clear-sighted, feel it as an unavoidable fate, an irresistible force that suddenly grips us, submerging all our sincerest moral resolutions. Psychology can throw some light on the problem, showing why it is that we get more irritated by one child than another. But that does not take us very far. It is a real torment for many parents, who feel themselves to be at the mercy of their moods. One day my wife asked me to pray with her, to ask God to restrain her because she could not do it on her own. Some time later she said to me, with a happy smile, 'It's better now, since I prayed.'

Do we even remember these incidents clearly, whether they have been exceptional or frequent? It is easy to repress one's bad conscience when one is powerful. I had the idea once that when a child attains his majority his parents could have a session with him to ask his forgiveness for all the mistakes they had made in bringing him up. But I am afraid that the parents would not have much idea what to say. Vague allusions to their authority, or to not being loving enough. But as for precise facts, they would no doubt have difficulty in finding any. And they would perhaps be readier to excuse than accuse themselves. When one thinks of the innumerable mistakes, some of them serious, which every parent makes, this is truly surprising.

And teachers, who wield enormous power over their pupils, because they can compromise their careers, their progress in life, and who make so many mistakes without realizing it! In their classes also there is cruelty to children – scapegoats who are laughed at, in order to cement the solidarity of the class. There is a whole literature, of which Jules Renard's *Poil de carotte* is an example, bearing witness to the extreme sensitivity of public opinion to the sufferings of children victimized by heartless adults. And this sensitivity is in contrast with the insensitivity and the absence of remorse on the part of those who make them suffer. Here we see how violence is condemned only by others, not by those who practise it.

31 REALIZATION

The whole subject of battered children, discussed by Dr Hacker, seems to me eloquently to confirm this sombre truth: that a man's moral conscience is in inverse proportion to his power. The more powerful he is, the more is he proof, not only against criticism from others, but also when it comes from his own conscience. And when he is very powerful and guilty of the worst abuses of power, when his conscience ought to be crying out aloud – then, it is silent.

The fact is, then, that the moral conscience has not the imperious character that Kant accorded to it. Just as Descartes was under an illusion when he thought that commonsense was the most widespread virtue among all men, so Kant was under an illusion when he thought similarly about his categorical imperative. This, I think, is why secular morality fails. It is before God, not by oneself, that one is able to discover oneself more truly, especially when one is powerful. Modern man, who claims to be all-powerful, who believes that thanks to the progress of science he is at last liberated from God, who has held him in painful subjection for so long – this modern man is most severe where others are concerned, most indulgent towards himself.

Let us be realistic: the powerful man is hard of hearing when his conscience speaks, very hard, extremely hard of hearing, harder still the more powerful he is. Consider the argument at present going on between poor nations and rich nations, the Nairobi conference which is in progress as I write these lines. A heart-rending cry goes up from the greater part of humanity, subjected to poverty, distress, and famine, while the other part boasts of its prosperity; but it is a cry that goes unheard. Of course the problem is an exceedingly complex one. But it seems clear that the rich are not prepared to pay more for the raw materials held by the poor, and are using their power to oppose it. When it was a matter of oil, they bowed to more powerful countries.

The same has happened with all the most revolting injustices of history. It has needed apostles to rise, to cry out loud and long, to struggle with violence to put an end to them, and even then only with partial success: apostles of the slaves who were sold in the market-place, apostles of the exploited working-classes, of the despised blacks, of child labourers, of those who are still dying of starvation in their millions, of the lepers, of massacred animals, and of many another innocent victim, of all the victims of all-powerful dictators. Apostles! It is a biblical term, but the Bible calls them prophets, those who cause the voice of God to be heard. Any man who denounces injustices is a prophet, the spokesman of God.

Ah! You think that the Bible is an old out-of-date story, and that I am very old-fashioned because I talk about it? I tell you that it is burningly up-to-date. Look again at the books of the prophets. Point by point they condemn our modern society. Read how Amos was taken by God from following his flock in order to go and denounce the iniquity of his time (Amos 7.15), how Elijah denounces the powerful Queen Jezebel and King Ahab (I Kings 18), Isaiah the rich merchants, and Nathan King David (II Sam. 12.7). We find the same accents today in Simone Weil, in Charles Péguy, in Albert Camus, to mention but a few of the French authors who have most moved me.

Now remember Pompey and Caesar, who symbolized for us all the conflicts which break out between men: face to face, two violences, provoking and exacerbating one another in fateful escalation. The violence of the rebel is easy to see, to denounce and to stigmatize. But it is not the only violence involved. That of Pompey is just as responsible, though it wears a cloak of legality. It can with impunity have Caesar recalled from his command in Gaul by a vote in the Senate. I have called that invisible violence. I can define it better now. What distinguishes Pompey from Caesar is that he is in power. Invisible violence is the abuse of power.

There is abuse of power whenever a man or a group, because of their power, can exercise an unjust constraint over another, whether or not their power is legal. Such abuse of power is to be found everywhere: in every undertaking, in every office, every workshop, every school, every society, every party, and every church. Fortunately it is often minimal, and you are going to accuse me of being over-scrupulous in attaching so much importance to it. But little streams make great rivers. Revolutions spring from an accumulation of petty bullying and insults. Revolt against the abuse of power is always legitimate.

Hidden abuse of power provokes open violence. 'Woe especially,' said the Rev. Fr Pire in an address on the subject of violence given at the Peace University, Hué, Belgium, on 8 June 1968, 'woe especially to him who provokes violence by his injustices!' It is the 'manipulation of man in our society', much more widespread than is generally thought, from the cradle through school and working life, as Professor Adolf Portmann writes in a remarkable article. The abuse of power is the unsophisticated violence of the privileged, including us, the 'decent folk' of the prosperous civilized West.

The most serious aspect of this, as we have seen, is that the abuse of power is almost always unconscious. The weak are conscious enough of their weakness, but not the strong of their strength, of the pressures they put on those who depend on them. You may imagine how often I have listened with sympathy as an employee has told me of how he has had to bear insults, keeping, as we say, his clenched fist in his pocket, biting his tongue to keep back his indignation, because his career is at stake. And I am not talking only of junior clerks; it is often right at the top of the hierarchy that the worst examples of dirty tricks, favouritism, or blackmail are to be found.

I have written a book about secrets. A bookseller wrote to me pointing out that I had omitted the innumerable instances of dishonesty that are involved in the keeping of state or trade secrets. On this subject I have listened to many a confidence from junior employees who have found themselves unwilling accomplices in some irregular manoeuvre, and yet could say nothing.

Of course that is not to say that managers should not manage. Failure to provide firm management is often the criticism levelled at top executives by their subordinates. What is involved there is the tendency of some seniors to permit themselves what they would not be permitted were they not so highly placed. A chief is always respected when he demands of himself as much as he expects from his staff, and when he shows them the same consideration and loyalty as he expects from them.

But he is despised if he makes use of his power for his personal advantage, or in order to protect himself from adverse circumstances. Now, while such conduct will not escape the notice of his subordinates, he is only rarely conscious of it himself. He would protest if he were criticized for it. However, no one would criticize him to his face – his power protects him; but it also protects him from his own conscience. 'They're just jealous,' he thinks. Is it not by his own merit that he has been able to climb the rungs of the ladder of promotion, and is it not right that he should now enjoy the benefits? As you will see, we find here exactly the same criterion as we saw was involved when we analysed Jesus' actions: what Jesus would not do was to use his power for his own benefit.

I do not claim that it is easy, in the complexities of everyday life, to distinguish clearly between the two lines of conduct which this criterion sets out one against the other: the use of our power for the benefit of others, and its use for ourselves. In business, for example, is it not the duty of each participant to put himself, as we say, in a position of strength so as to obtain an advantage which he would not obtain if he were less powerful? And when a job advertisement states that what is looked for is a 'dynamic' character, does that not mean that he must not be too scrupulous? But where lies the frontier between scruples on one's own behalf and those one may have on behalf of the enterprise in which one works, between the advantages one seeks for it, and those one seeks for oneself?

No, it is not easy to see what is right. That is why one must step back, away from the frantic whirl of life, and keep certain times for reflection. It always takes a long time to become aware of oneself. Even for Jesus it was a long and difficult process: he had been in the desert for forty days; when they wanted to drag him into politics he withdrew and spent a whole night meditating in solitude. As the Passion approached he took his disciples with him into retreat near Caesaraea Philippi.

Reflection, however, is not enough. We have seen how the conscience is stifled by power, how readily it finds good reasons to justify itself in the race to power into which our instinct impels us. It is face to face with God, in the presence of his sovereign greatness, that we feel the vanity of our pretension to power. Meditation is reflection in God's presence, turned towards God, waiting on God,

as Simone Weil said. Then we can realize how much of our behaviour has been vainglorious will to power even when it seemed to
us to be prompted by the purest idealism.

I have so often experienced this. I have so often listened to
others telling me of it. In the marital dispute which I took just now
as an example, everything happened, of course, as I described it. In
the heat of the conflict each of the two partners becomes more and
more sure of being in the right, and more outraged at the aggressiveness of the other. But later on, while meditating prayerfully, one of
them may become aware of his own aggressiveness, his own wrong
acts, and ask for forgiveness. It is a second movement.

The first – natural – movement is always to make use of all the
power at one's disposal in an attempt to win. And the more power
one has, the less one realizes the harm one is doing to others. I saw
in a newspaper the following amusing remark by a humorist: 'Now,
my dear, do stop pulling the cat's tail!' – 'But mummy, it's not me
that's pulling, it's the cat!' So much for the little power that the
child already has over the cat. And then there is the pertinent
comment by Lorenz: 'The first murderer realized at once the
enormity of his act, whereas one does not perceive it when all one
has to do is to press a button in order to massacre at a distance of
thousands of miles enemies whom one will never see.'

32 ECONOMIC POWER

In reality, as soon as a man is powerful, or thinks himself to be so,
he abuses his power without realizing it. He is never short of
reasons to justify his conduct, as La Fontaine aptly remarked:

> La raison du plus fort est toujours la meilleure.
> (The stronger man's argument is always the best.)

And long before him a humble Greek slave, Æsop, had said it.
Yes – I could give many, many quotations from every age. What
we are concerned with here is our present-day world, and the fate of
our power-based civilization. Never has man's power been so

celebrated as in the course of the last few centuries; and in no other domain has it been more desired, organized, recommended – I might even say required – than in the economic sector.

I have already spoken of this whole aspect: the obsession with the Gross National Product, the triumph of the Manager. I return to the point now, not only because it has been the most eloquent expression of the unlimited ambition for power, but also because it has been the occasion for one of the most extraordinary turn-abouts in history. It is a quite recent volte-face. In my book on old age I quoted Denis de Rougemont, who, half in jest, half in earnest, referred in his book *Man's Western Quest* to the fine predictions of expert economists that there was a golden age just around the corner. Thanks to the continuing increase in production, the whole of humanity would be living in opulence, supported by one quarter of their number working only three or four days a week. Management would be compelled to organize leisure on industrial lines, for fear of people becoming bored as a result of having nothing to do.

Denis de Rougemont confessed that he was no expert in economics (nor, I admit, am I). But he suspected that behind these exciting anticipations lay a philosophy that glorified man's genius, and that they answered only too well to the old dream of power, still present in the human heart. A philosophy, did I say? Rather an absence of philosophy, perhaps, or a counter-philosophy, which went something like this: was it not because man was so weak and poor that he constantly gave way, and saw his destiny only in terms of insoluble problems? Let him be granted prosperity, and he would be freed from his morbid prognostications! While philosophers spend their time splitting hairs, the industrialist is way ahead. Movement cannot be demonstrated by stopping to think, but only by walking, and from now on it will be demonstrated by running.

So, belief in the unlimited growth of production through technological progress had for many people taken the place of the old beliefs, in the West as well as in the Communist world. There might be arguments about the means of achieving prosperity, either through free competition or through a statist economy, but not about the goal. Remember Khrushchev and his challenge to the Americans that he would catch up on their standard of living. Arguments about doctrines paled into insignificance before the great game of economic power-politics.

And then with incredible suddenness, almost from one year to another, we witnessed a radical turn-around in the thinking of our economists. Their fairy-tale predictions collapsed like a house of cards. Economists found themselves suddenly having to think again, so that, for example, in their book *Les vaches maigres* ('The Lean Cows'), Michel Albert and Jean Ferniot were actually able to entitle one of their chapters 'About turn!'. I could quote other works, for there is a whole crop of indictments against the policy of intensive economic growth, blossoming before our astonished eyes, with the abundance of snowdrops in spring.

The particularly interesting thing about this book *Les vaches maigres* is that one of the authors, Michel Albert, does not conceal the fact that he had collaborated some years previously with Jean-Jacques Servan-Schreiber when the latter was preparing his book *The American Challenge*, which appeared in 1967 and which had enormous success. It was in fact this book which presented to Europe – and especially to France – the 'American model' for them to follow, on pain of being finally eliminated from the race for power. The argument was reinforced with a mass of statistics on economic growth, GNP, numbers of major firms, of computers, and of students in the universities.

Amusing, is it not? The very same economists who only a short while ago were lauding accelerated growth suddenly became its severest critics. Particularly since we are dealing with eminent and learned men, who are fond of invoking the scientific rigour of their discipline. But we have often observed how prone science is in every sphere to turn-abouts of this sort, which form a singular contrast with the age-old permanence of moral and spiritual doctrines. So then, those very prophets who were quite recently promising us a golden age through prosperity, are turning into Cassandras. All honour to them! I am always surprised that such severe criticism is made of a person when it can be shown that he has contradicted himself, and that we are all so afraid of being caught doing so ourselves. We should have to have become fossilized, never to contradict ourselves, for our hearts and our entire lives are contradictory.

And here we have our authors writing: 'Our good old rose-coloured futures are done for!' Thereupon there flow from their pens, often full of biting, sparkling wit, criticisms of our advanced industrial society which only recently has been looked upon with such pride. For example, this remark about the way those who work in our society have been divided into two levels:

The upper level is that of the leaders who take part in the great economic game. They live the life of big business as the patricians in Rome lived the life of politics. They lay down the scale of values. They get bored when they are not working. . . The rest, proud and aloof, live resolutely in a different universe and hold strictly to the contract of hire of their arms or brains. They are bored when they are working.

The authors add that 'to the great banquet of economic development a certain number of "unexpected guests" ' – the expression comes from Jean Fourastié – 'have come and spat in the soup: the women of Women's Lib, students smashing windows, prisoners wrecking their prisons, immigrant squatters, merchants burning their stocks, peasants sending the dung of their devalued animals to government officials. . . To all of these the apostles of growth have paid no heed, even if they knew of their existence.'

I have quoted enough to show that it is the whole of our so-called advanced industrial system which is on trial. What should be noted is that the point at issue is the basic principle of that system, namely the worship of power. The 'model' of *The American Challenge*, our authors hasten to point out, was 'the law of the strongest' – might is right. It was claimed in justification for it that 'the selfishness of each guaranteed the prosperity of all'. Ambition for power was looked upon as the motive force of industrial progress, from which all would profit: 'Private vices, public benefits', as Mendeville puts it. And now the USA has become 'the country where the American Model is under greatest challenge'.

Our authors quote the title of Dr E. F. Schumacher's book, *Small is Beautiful*. They flatter my little country by heading one of their chapters 'Switzerland Preferred'. They quote an opinion poll in France which asked the question, 'In your opinion, in which of the following countries are people happiest?' Of those who replied, 12 per cent named the USA, 2 per cent the USSR, and 43 per cent Switzerland. I am not taken in by this praise: the smallness of Switzerland had nothing to do with its own merit – at any rate not with that of its present-day citizens. Yet even Switzerland has not escaped the lure of the GNP. When the sudden fall in the exchange rate of the dollar promoted us speciously to the top of the list in this respect, many of my fellow-citizens were proud. For my own part I felt a keen sense of disquiet, for there is something outrageous about being too rich in a world that is too poor.

I think that my country is very fortunate in being so small, and in being broken up by its federal structure into twenty-six tiny states, in having no gigantic city within its borders, no huge commercial organization, no great proletarian concentration, and that it is still more or less on a scale in which the citizen remains close to those who rule him. This good fortune we owe to a saintly man, a politician who became a hermit, Nicolas de Flue. He meditated deeply on the danger of power, and was able to head off the Swiss in their zeal for conquest.

That was just half a millennium ago, since we are at present celebrating the five hundredth anniversary of the Battle of Morat, in which the Swiss defeated Charles the Bold, Duke of Burgundy, smashing his dream of uniting Europe under his domination. You see how it is always victories we celebrate! Morat however was one of the last of the Confederates' victories, and Nicolas de Flue, seeing the corruption and the internal squabbles that war brought, issued his command: 'Do not meddle in the quarrels of the great!'

It seems to me that history has come to a similar turning-point today, with this crisis of conscience on the part of the economists, who feel, as Albert and Ferniot say, that 'we are beginning to pay the price of our excessive growth', and that we are coming to 'the end of the megas, the hypers, and the maxis'. Some philosophers have already spoken out, like Bergson, who demanded a 'soul supplement' as a counter-weight to our material enrichment; like Emmanuel Mounier, in his book *Be Not Afraid*, contrasting the 'universe of people' with the 'universe of technology'; like Karl Jaspers, with his concern, in *The Future of Mankind*, about the atomic bomb; or writers like Duhamel, and theologians such as Jacques Ellul with his critique of technology. They were not economists, however, and that made it possible to dismiss their views as the nostalgia of belated romantic idealists.

Now it is the specialists in economic and social sciences, with all their authority, who are sounding the alarm. There have been precursors: Rachel Carson's *Silent Spring*, with the light it shed on the problems of ecology, the environment, and pollution; David Riesman, also in the United States, who put the question, *Abundance, for what?*; Bertrand de Jouvenel, in France, with his book *Arcadie*, in which he asked whether the GNP was really a measure of progress. But he was as yet scarcely listened to. Similarly, many people gave a sceptical reception to the famous Report of the Club of Rome in 1972, 'the alarm signal for technological determinism'.

It was soon proved right by events. The oil crisis came, and behind it stalked the spectre of the exhaustion of the world's natural reserves, while the injustice of the gulf between rich and poor nations was revealed. None of this was talked about six or seven years ago, yet it has now become a major preoccupation of everyone. This is indeed a turning-point in history. We are now seeing a succession of books by economists denouncing what Galbraith has called 'the collective hypnosis' which makes increasing the volume of production a predominant objective of society.

33 'THE RESOURCES WE NEED'

There is now appearing, then, an abundant literature subjecting our technological civilization to severe criticism. A book that has particularly struck me is one by Georges Friedmann on 'Power and Wisdom'. As you see, this examination of the conscience to which the economic scientists are submitting themselves is taking on a profoundly personal tone.

Friedmann tells the reader about his own intellectual journey. He has always had a basic concern for the human person. A long time ago he noticed how in the modern industrial system the workers suffered from depersonalization. He dedicated himself therefore to the study of the sociology of work, not only in Europe, but also in the United States, Russia, Latin America, and Israel. He then turned to the study of the consequences of mechanization and urbanization. He sided resolutely with technical progress against its systematic detractors who foolishly ignored its incontestable benefits. But he turned his attention to all possible means of 'humanizing technology', and to this end he suggested reforms in the organization of work.

Nevertheless, he now has to admit that 'these external remedies are useful, certainly, and even necessary, but not sufficient'. They require to be supplemented, he considers, by a spiritual revolution, an inner transformation of man himself, an inner change of life, and the discovery of a new meaning to existence. For the sickness is too deep-seated. The technological adventure has altered man himself; it has produced a *homo technicus*. He explains: 'I mean a man who is mad with technology, extremely powerful but at the same time in utter distress.' It is the 'distance between the progress of the machine and the backwardness of man' that obsesses him now.

He meditates upon the 'risks of power'. 'Every technique can, in some measure, be turned dangerously against man,' he writes. Here he rejoins Dr Hacker, whose book I considered at length in Part One, and who said: 'It remains to be seen whether the sudden increase in his power and responsibility is going to be a benefit or a scourge for man.' So then the victims of power are not only the weak, those crushed by life, whose misfortunes are only too evident, but also the powerful themselves!

I have been considering for many years the writing of a book on the theme of how dangerous it is for man to be powerful – I have made that the title of one of my chapters, but really it is what my whole book is about. The idea came first only from the individual experience of my own consulting-room. Of course what I received there was mainly the confidences of the weak, the victims of the powerful, who turn to the psychotherapist in great numbers. But beyond these everyday confessions I could see how dangerous power was for the powerful themselves, how their conscience, their sensitivity and their humanity was smothered. Added to that were the cases, less rare than one might think, of people who had made a brilliant success of their lives, only to be suddenly overtaken at the height of their success by a strange and crippling distress.

And here I see the same problem arising in the minds of eminent sociologists and economists, only now it is in regard to society as a whole rather than on the individual level. Thereupon my project was broadened. I could see also that the question was raised by the present wave of aggression and violence, which seemed to be the price to be paid for a too powerful social constraint: 'Industrialization and its offspring urbanization', write the authors of *Les vaches maigres*, 'have manufactured zones of criminality.' I set to work then to write this book in order to bring together all these thoughts.

The whole of our technological civilization bears a singular resemblance to those people who have consulted me, who, having been successful in life, are gripped nevertheless by a mysterious anxiety. They seem in some way to be the victims of their very success, of everything they have had to sacrifice in order to attain their power. What has been sacrificed to power? Perhaps what is most human in man: his soul, his affectivity, his need to find a meaning in his personal life, to be a person and not a thing, a mere instrument of production.

Georges Friedmann's thought, however, goes still further, more deeply, to the sources of the malaise of our civilization. What have we sacrificed? What have we forgotten as we travelled along the road on this great epic adventure of objective rationalism, of science and technology? 'What we have lost on the way', replies Friedmann, 'is wisdom.' We have lost the wisdom which ought to guide us in the right use of the power which technology puts into our hands, which ought to teach us how to regulate its use, and avoid its abuse, for fear that it might turn against man.

You understand the importance of this word 'wisdom' coming from the pen of a scientist. At any rate the author himself is well aware of its importance, since he uses it in the title of his book: 'Power and Wisdom.' For a scientist to talk about wisdom is almost like violating a taboo; because for scientists the vocabulary of morality and spirituality is taboo. Like Moliere's Tartuffe, who could not bear the sight of Dorine's breast, they dare not let their gaze fall upon that territory forbidden to science. It has long been the same.

Since the time of the Renaissance a rigorous frontier has been drawn between the objective and the subjective disciplines, between science and morality, physics and metaphysics. On both sides eminent men have worked, written, pondered, but without crossing the frontier, because they were afraid of 'confusion' between the two domains.

That is the thing I am most often accused of – confusing the two domains, mixing the data of science and those of religion. It is true that I naïvely walk on both sides of the frontier. In my book *The Whole Person in a Broken World* I have denounced this frontier as the great schism of our day, and I seek to put together what has been separated. The dogma of this separation has culminated in the positivism which is still, as Georges Gusdorf has shown in his book about them, the philosophy of most doctors. Morality and faith have nothing to do with science and technology, which know nothing other than what can be counted, weighed, and measured.

Wisdom is a virtue, and virtues are not counted, weighed, or measured. I have emphasized its role on the individual level in health, both physical and mental. And now here is an economist acknowledging its role in the health of society – both its economic and its moral health. But what is this wisdom, unrecognized and forgotten by the technologists, after having been a central pre-occupation of Greek civilization?

Georges Friedmann puts the question: 'Where shall we find the resources we need?' Where shall we look for lost wisdom? Is it not the prerogative of the great religions, the great revelations, to which science has tried to forbid itself all reference? It did not deny them, of course; it simply thrust them aside – to the other side of the frontier. There lay a domain into which the scientist must not venture, which he must leave to others, to poets, dreamers, believers.

Now we have an economist crossing the frontier in search of lost wisdom. It is moving to see this honest man, this man of good faith, freeing himself from rationalist prejudice and feeling his way humbly forward on unfamiliar territory. Goodness gracious! An economist is not a theologian! How can they possibly even begin to communicate or understand each other? Nevertheless here he is, looking for enlightenment and support. He finds very little, and so it is the more precious to him: Emmanuel Mounier, the prophet of Christian personalism, and Karl Jaspers, the prophet of spiritual evolution. Then he questions the great religions – Christianity, Judaism, Hindu spirituality. He seems to have missed the importance of Islam, but he does question Marxism and a certain scientific messianism, for they are also religions.

It is not a religious quest. That of course could come – who knows? God might one day personally call Georges Friedmann, but that would be something different. His present approach is a pragmatic one: have the religions some answer to give to the problems raised by the present crisis of technological civilization? And just because he does not take personal religious experience into account, he seeks an answer in the religions rather than in faith, he listens to the voice of the churches rather than that of the Bible.

He does not hide the fact that he is rather disappointed. As for Judaism – he is a Jew – he sees it on the defensive, turned in upon its spiritual integrity, having given up any idea of conveying a 'Jewish message of universal validity'. In regard to Christianity also, he is understandably struck by the caution and timidity of its rep-resentatives, who are most careful not to offer advice to the secular world, over which science reigns alone.

Is not this because the sealed frontier of which I was speaking has also cut communication in the other direction? To each his own job: the theologian must confine himself to his spiritual domain, and he does not feel himself competent from the scientific point of view to dare to discuss economic problems. Calvin was still concerned to decide interest rates on loans in the light of the Bible (see the study by Pastor André Bieler). But very soon afterwards the frontier between the spiritual and the secular was being barred and bolted.

For several centuries to begin with the sciences were applied to the study of nature. Then they tackled the phenomenon of human society. New faculties of economic and social sciences were set up in all the universities. I remember how in my own student days we looked with a certain disdain upon this upstart faculty whose credentials in the scientific field we took leave to doubt. But it soon established itself as a nursery for specialists, breeding economists and sociologists of real stature, whose qualifications in these subjects were unique. Then came the foundation of illustrious institutes charged with the training of a new class of experts, skilled in management, who opened the way to prodigious development in the economy, to unlimited growth in production and profits. Man was henceforth endowed with a new power – economic power.

From then on it was the moralists who were looked down upon. They were mere dreamers, idealists attached to bygone values; they lacked realism and objectivity. Religion was a private matter about which those who cared might argue in their chapels. But such people had nothing to say about the conduct of business affairs, which belonged to the realm of technology and science. And so the whole of the West was secularized.

And now all of a sudden, by a most curious turn-round of history, we have experts, specialists, sociologists and economists taking note of the importance of the 'human factor', the moral factor in business quite as much as in medicine. They are beginning to see that it is not without cost, even in economic terms, that a dividing wall has been built between the domain of science and that of morality, between the world of things and the world of persons. And it is they who are picking up an old and quite unscientific word such as wisdom! But what is wisdom? We no longer know; it is so long since we thought about it! Will believers be able to take the ball in flight, and answer this anxious appeal? I wonder.

It seems to me that it is Islam especially which has retained the sense of the sovereignty of God over the whole of human life, over social and economic life as well as the life of the individual. This is what gave their special flavour to the discussions I had with Islam in Teheran, both with the Faculty of Theology and with the high dignitaries among the clergy and the psychiatric fraternity. I had in my hands a paper by a Mohammedan colleague, Dr Shah, who maintained that obedience to God is the most important factor in health. We found ourselves in full agreement on that point, my Islamic partners and I. Obedience to God – could that be the wisdom sought by Georges Friedmann? Wisdom for economic health, as well as for physical and mental health.

34 DISENCHANTMENT

And now we have many economists admitting that the super-inflated public economy is sick, and that they are very perplexed as to what remedy to choose. They recognize all the benefits of a prosperity the world has never known before, thanks to which great social progress has been possible: the reduction of working hours, the setting up of social security, holidays for all, security in retirement, a rising standard of living in industrial countries. However, although industrialization has brought to humanity unbelievable material power, it has scarcely favoured the development and the welfare of the human person.

The younger generation is particularly aware of this and often reacts with unthinking violence. In this connection a psychologist writing in *La Suisse* (15 June 1975) has said that industrialized societies 'frustrate the individual in his fundamental needs: contact with nature, human relationships, relaxation, and silence'. Adults too, however, even those with greatest power and those who are proudest of the technological miracles they have achieved, are not proof against the malaise which Paul Ricoeur in his book *Histoire et vérité* has called 'the ennui of industrialized societies'. Friedmann dwells at length on this 'psychological distress in a technological environment', and, like Viktor Frankl in his work on psychotherapy, attributes it to 'the absence of values in technological civilization'.

Then along comes Ivan Illich with his radical criticism, asserting that the poor are frustrated and the rich are dissatisfied. What is missing, he says, is 'conviviality', true community on the personal level, person-to-person contact, as well as contact of the person with his personal tool. Michel Albert and Jean Ferniot also write: 'The degree of satisfaction is inversely proportional to the size of the country.' Raymond Aron speaks of 'the disillusionments of progress'. And Max Weber says of the modern world that it is 'disenchanted'.

Thus, at the end of a great epic adventure of power – the fabulous growth of science, technology, and industrialization – our Western world is showing signs of disappointment. Of course this is due in part to the economic and monetary crisis, to inflation and recession. But the doubt is more profound: it derives from the disturbing realization that the economists – the masters of our modern age – are wrong. Not long ago they were forecasting an age of prodigious prosperity based upon ever-increasing production. Our misfortunes arise from the very system they boasted of: 'Inflation', write Albert and Ferniot, 'is the consequence of a situation in which the strong are super-powerful.' They quote the historian Henri Pirenne: 'Great monetary mutations are always the precursory sign of the collapse of civilization.' Many people feel that what we are witnessing is not just an economic crisis, but a crisis of civilization.

A few years ago the BBC came to interview me in my study, by my own fireside, for a television film. The Rev. Vernon Sproxton put to me the following question: 'Why do you say that we live in an age of disappointment?' We are disappointed, I think, because we embraced exaggerated hopes. We are disappointed with politics, with the UNO, with the churches, and most of all with science. Think of the enthusiasm with which Ernest Renan wrote *The Future of Science* in the last century.

Science has more than kept its promises. I do not understand my colleagues, or Illich, in their severe criticism of official scientific medicine. We meet people every day who would be dead without it, and that is sufficient justification for it. But other diseases are spreading – the neuroses, which are so symptomatic of the disorganization of our age. The mistake has been to expect of science and technology something that they are unable to provide.

Furthermore, for many of the intellectuals whom I have quoted in this book, many of the French men and women who fought in the wartime Resistance and experienced the tremendous hope that it engendered, allied to a greater or less degree with that of Marxism, there is the enormous disappointment at what has happened to

Communism in practice, and at the fact that nowhere have we seen the appearance of the 'new man' prophesied by Marx, as Georges Friedmann points out.

On the other side of the Atlantic, am I mistaken? I seem to feel that the United States are just a little disenchanted with their power. I know well what we owe them, and that it seems to be too often forgotten in Europe; without their generous intervention we should still no doubt have been under the tyranny of Hitler, forced into line or driven underground. But into what misfortunes has their power drawn the United States since then! The joy of victory is short-lived. One can tire, even of power. Are we anything better than spoilt children whom nothing will ever be able to satisfy?

Spoilt children is indeed what we are. There is only a small minority of them in the world, but we are part of that minority, I and doubtless most of those who will read these lines. Nevertheless there is a real, genuine, concrete problem which I should like to bring out here, and which arises from the fact that man is naturally possessed of such an overweening ambition for power that the more he acquires, the more he is obsessed by it. In this respect technical civilization is providing just what he wants, at least in those countries that have embraced it even to its atomic bombs which it stockpiles underground by the thousand megatons.

I am not decrying power. Throughout this Part Two we have noted that the Bible asserts that all power comes as a gift from God, granted to man so that he can gain the mastery over nature, tend it and preserve it. What God has forbidden man to do, in order to protect him from great evils, is to judge on his own between good and evil, what is the boundary between good and bad violence, between useful and dangerous power. It is a temptation to universal power which is contained in the notorious promise of the serpent: 'You will be like gods' (Gen. 3.5). There is no question of a return to primitive times, to their misery and distress; what I am advocating is the harmonious organization of society in the service of the human person.

What the Bible condemns is not power itself, which God gives generously to man, but man's claim to all power, the arrogance of power and wealth. 'God opposes the proud', writes St James (James 4.6). That is why the Bible comes down so severely, for example, against the practice of magic and all kinds of sorcery. The scriptures warn us against the vicious circle of power, the seduction of power intensified by power, the madness of power.

The wisdom of the nations accords fully with the scriptures. 'Power tends to corrupt, and absolute power corrupts absolutely,' said Lord Acton. Power seems like a sort of drug, and like all drugs it brings with it the dangers of excess and unconscious addiction. Montesquieu says: 'Every man who has power tends to misuse it; he goes on until he finds limits.' And the biologist Lorenz says somewhere: 'The race for money at present indulged in by the big industrialists is a veritable disaster.' Each technical advance further excites human ambition. The most recent is in the field of cybernetics and computers. In reference to them Georges Friedmann quotes this revealing remark by one of those who triumphantly sing their praises: 'From now on nothing is impossible for man.'

The thirst for unlimited power is not of course of recent date. It has always occupied the human mind, impelling the great conquerors of history into the most disastrous adventures: Alexander the Great, Pompey, Caesar, Napoleon, and many more. My own generation saw in consternation the latest attempt, by Adolf Hitler. One is still astonished at the wild enthusiasm with which the crowds acclaimed Hitler in Germany, and Mussolini in Italy. The explanation is that the dictators brought to the surface in the masses a passion for power that had long been repressed, but which remained there ready to break out. After the war C. G. Jung asserted (in the article I have already quoted on p. 47) that no nation could ever be sure that it would not be overcome by a similar madness.

While the war was still in progress, in July 1942, my friend Eric de Montmollin published in a Swiss newspaper an article which was sufficiently striking for me to preserve the cutting in my files. I shall refer here to some passages from it, which I think will still serve to direct our thoughts.

In truth, it took courage to publish such an article at that time, when our little country had already been completely encircled for two years by the German and Italian armies. I myself recall that day in 1940, after the fall of France, when I listened, along with all the comrades of the unit into which I had been mobilized, to an order of the day by our general, Henri Guisan, saying that from then on we could count only on our own army and God's protection, an order of the day which concluded with a call to prayer.

Two years later, in July 1942, Hitler was at the height of his power. He was master of the greater part of Europe, and had won victory after victory in Russia – Stalingrad was still six months away. It was only a few months, too, after Pearl Harbor and the entry of the United States into the war – they were as yet too involved in the Pacific to think of coming to the aid of Europe. And so Eric de Montmollin wrote: 'The Germany army . . . is at this moment capable of conquering and imposing the price of conquest on almost any country it wishes. . . I do not know any more than anyone else does what the outcome of all this is going to be.'

Nevertheless our journalist predicted with fine audacity 'the victory which will be won one day on the plains of Russia' – a Russian victory he meant, of course! The thing that interests us is that he appeals to philosophical rather than to political or military considerations, which were still quite uncertain at that time. Furthermore he entitled his article 'The Philosophy of Events'. He suggested that there was a mysterious law of destiny which imposed limits upon human power, of whatever kind. This limitation 'is the moment when another, inner voice makes itself heard, saying: you will not always succeed; and with it there creeps into the heart the fear that the tables are about to be turned'.

Eric de Montmollin recalls how surprising it was that Hitler suddenly gave up the idea of invading England after the defeat of France and the bombing raids over the Channel which seemed to be in preparation for it. He recalls also the lightning campaign of Rommel in North Africa, miraculously halted at El Alamein by Montgomery, and he wonders whether this was 'a temporary exhaustion on the part of a conqueror, a hesitation before the unknown which must follow such a long series of successes? It is very difficult to say.'

However, he does say that it seems to him that 'beyond a certain point of success the army which is exploiting its victories sees the final consequences eluding it, without this failure necessarily being attributable to any mistake it has made or to any particular manoeuvre on the part of the defeated enemy'. He continues:

It is as if the conduct of the war (and of the world) were in fact in other hands than those we observe . . . almost what the ancient Greeks called Athena, Phoebus, or Zeus, whose interventions are recorded all through the Trojan War, whenever the warriors thought that victory was within their grasp. . . It seems as if there is a power that is bent upon teaching men gradually to see themselves as they are, puppets in his hands, being used one against another to achieve some end which we do not know.

And here is the conclusion of the article: without expressly mentioning divine authority, Eric de Montmollin speaks of a sort of full stop which the conqueror 'does not at the moment wish to hear about, since he thinks himself strong enough to avoid it. But he can already hear a voice saying to him, "My child, you will not always fly from me".'

35 THE SUPPRESSION OF GOD

'My child, you will not always fly from me.' It is quite clear that in his mad rush towards total power, it is God that stands in his way, and God whom he tries to elude. Call him what you will – the Creator, Yahweh, Allah, or simply the Father, as Jesus did. I have never hidden my own personal convictions, but this is not a matter of religious controversy. I should like to go back to the fundamental dilemma of anthropology: is man an autonomous or a dependent being? Is he only the fruit of the spontaneous evolution of nature, 'chance and necessity', as Jacques Monod says? Or is he a creature willed by the Creator?

In the first case, he is responsible only to himself and to the institutions he makes for himself, either by a 'social contract' or in accordance with the principle that 'might is right'. He has no limitations apart from those he himself sets up, in accordance with his own judgment or reason, and the obstacles in his way can only stimulate his powerful drive to overcome them or cleverly to avoid them.

But if he is the fruit of a special creative act of God he is responsible before God, and remains dependent. He may use the gifts which God grants him – liberty, power, reason – but only within the limitations of the will of his Creator, limitations which he can know only to the extent that God reveals himself. At that price he will find harmony in his person, in society, and in his relationship with nature.

Faced with this fundamental dilemma, all believers find themselves in the same camp, despite the diversity of their beliefs. They may make many mistakes and blame each other for them, but they meet at one point: they recognize the sovereignty of God over the world, and they listen to God in order to correct their mistakes and rediscover harmony. I hope that in present circumstances they will become more aware of their unity and of their common responsibility to bring to the conduct of society that wisdom which scientists feel to be so cruelly lacking.

Emmanuel Mounier has spoken of 'remaking the Renaissance', not this time in the sense of the complete emancipation of man, but in the 'sense of the person'; that is to say in seeking a social order that would permit the full development of man as willed by God. In fact the history of the West since the Renaissance is not unlike a brilliant series of victories won by a conqueror, which may run out of steam one day, reach its limit, and falter, because there is a wise divine order which cannot be disregarded with impunity.

The whole of the history of the last few centuries has been a matter of power. Man has become intoxicated with his growing power. Yes, great victories: the development of science, of technology, of economics; and in the realm of thought, the triumph of rationalism, and of the dialectic which sweeps away every contradiction. Science in itself has been neutral. All it has done is to produce in accordance with its own methods its crop of knowledge. But rationalism has used its success as an argument to deny every transcendental reference. On such a glorious road the concept of the power of God was singularly embarrassing, and therefore it was challenged. We even hear now of the death of God.

Naturally I am not unaware that there are other causes of the atheism of our day, notably the errors of the churches, which have identified themselves with the powerful and not with their victims. And psychological causes; is it not the case that a certain kind of vulgarization of psychoanalysis has propagated the idea that one cannot become fully oneself without killing one's father, at least symbolically? But there is also the serious and infinitely respectable work of sincere thinkers, who turned to doubting God in face of the mystery of evil, without seeing that the negation of God opened the door to every kind of violence. 'If God does not exist,' said Dostoyevsky, 'everything is permissible.'

But with all due reservations being made, there has still been a sort of power game: the power of man against the power of God. Man first freed himself by means of reason – God's gift to him! – from the dogmatism and scholasticism of the Middle Ages, as well as from the abuse of its power by the church. Finally, however, man claims to be freeing himself from God himself and his wisdom. This is the epic adventure of objective rationalism. It in its turn has become dogmatic, as Bernard Morel points out. The existentialists have protested in vain in the name of subjective experience, and the psychologists have shown in vain that man is governed more than anything else by irrational drives – rationalization has still triumphed in industrial society, which is now beginning to have second thoughts.

A strange reversal of history! The upheaval is not coming so much in the form of a counter-offensive on the part of believers, as from a hesitation, a feeling of unease, on the part of the victors, from the scientists themselves, from rationalists, technologists, and economists. It closely resembles the faltering in the full flood of triumph of which Eric de Montmollin spoke in connection with the fortunes of war.

Let us therefore look at this period of history, from the Renaissance down to our own day, in the light of Maurice Clavel's excellent book, *Ce que je crois*. He describes it as the 'God-man drama', the drama of 'the elimination of God by man'. He divides the period into three stages: 'the Renaissance, the classical age, the modern era . . . each of which lasted about a century and a half'. And in the epigrammatical fashion he is so good at, he sums it all up: 'The Renaissance eliminates sin. Classical order eliminates revelation. The modern era eliminates at a blow, and almost with ease, what remains: faith.'

Maurice Clavel is to me a surprising and fascinating figure. A doctor of philosophy who is not afraid of wielding his pen with the racy vigour of a pamphleteer. A virtuoso of dialectic who uses his virtuosity to condemn dialectic. A man who is intelligent enough never to be short of arguments, yet who avoids all argument with atheists, saying, 'I have nothing to say to an unbeliever except that I am too stupid.' An erudite philosopher who manipulates ideas with the dexterity of a juggler with his balls and rings, for the purpose, as he puts it, 'of giving the *coup de grâce* to all possible philosophy'. 'If I had had faith,' he says, 'I should never have been a philosopher. If I had remained a philosopher, I should never have had faith.'

He describes himself as 'the most unbelieving of believers . . . I have not even got faith. Faith has got me.' The fact is that when he least expected it conversion came to him like a thunderbolt, in the manner of St Paul, who was also a philosopher. 'Ought I to call it a thunderbolt,' he asks, 'since I heard nothing?' What did he feel? – 'Two states of mind coexisted in me, neither destroying or even affecting the other; I recognized them as beatitude and terror.' He asserts vehemently that what happened was an initiative on the part of God. 'I fiercely deny having done everything I could to believe. I did everything I could not to believe.'

He was called by God. Then at last he discovered his own identity. Our absolute individuality, our ineffable singularity is affirmed when God speaks to us by name, saying 'You'. Is not this precisely what I call the person, which comes into being through personal relationship? He repeats several times that 'no one seeks God, but God seeks us all'. Faith is an act of grace, but 'grace is not a gift. No one receives it any more or less than anyone else. Since we are free, it solicits us.' And faith is accepting this solicitation.

What strikes me about Maurice Clavel is his moderation as regards the content of faith: 'What I believe is contained in the Creed,' he writes. But he goes no further than that summary declaration. When one thinks of all the arguments of theologians and philosophers about the contents of the Creed, one is surprised at this reticence in a man who is elsewhere so ready to throw himself into controversy. It is as if the prodigious intellectual outpouring which fills so many other pages were suddenly silenced, out of respect for the great mysteries of God. Dogmas manifestly do not interest him, and he says jestingly that 'obviously there are no dogmas in Paradise'.

That is not all: what clearly counts for him in faith is not beliefs, but the personal encounter with God: 'I do not believe that God exists, for I do not believe *that*, I believe *in* . . .' There is therefore in him a certain contrast between faith as trust in God, and what is called religion: 'Faith has at last delivered me from religious sentiment.' Hence there is a certain antipathy for organized religion, the churches: 'God can therefore make contact only by breaking religious societies.'

On the other hand he is passionately interested in the anthropological problem which I mentioned just now. What is man? He underlines two strange paradoxes: the first is that by seeking power, man has discovered his own finiteness, and is obsessed by it. The second is that the whole movement of thought since the Renaissance, which is called humanism, which has glorified man, which has attempted to make him the measure of all things, leads in the end to a crisis of man, to the 'existential question, new and from now on primary: no longer "Why do I exist?" but "Do I exist?"'.

Whence comes this great doubt which so preoccupies modern philosophy? Well, says Clavel, it comes from the fact that to the question 'Do I exist?' there are two contradictory answers: 'All knowledge says no. Only faith says yes.' Knowledge: indeed, as far as science is concerned there is no personal existence. Science knows only an endless process of physico-chemical phenomena which succeed and determine one another in a chain of cause and effect. In biology, it is cells which are organized and disorganized, which join together or die. Even in psychology a succession of conscious or unconscious mechanisms determines our feelings and our apparently free and willing choices. It is only through faith, through personal encounter with God and real encounters with other persons, that man becomes aware that he exists.

Finally, it was from reading Maurice Clavel's book that I learnt that Kierkegaard had spoken of the suppression of God. I knew Plato's remark, which I have already quoted (pp.63f.), which shows that the fact of psychological suppression was known to him, even if the actual word for it was not. Kierkegaard, however, actually uses the word. Yes, my dear psychoanalyst colleagues, that does not detract one whit from the merit of your master, but it is remarkable that the term suppression was used by Kierkegaard half a century before Freud.

Nevertheless as Kierkegaard used it, it referred not to the suppression of the libido, but to that of God. I am sure, however, that you will allow that once the existence of the phenomenon is admitted, it must also be admitted that it may be valid in both senses. And my psychoanalyst readers are not likely to be surprised that militant atheism may be a conscious over-compensation following upon the suppression of God into the unconscious. Do you not say yourselves that we suppress what we fear or find embarrassing? How could the power of God not be embarrassing to men with a passion for power, as we have seen. Might we not say that the atheists in denying God are aspiring to possess themselves of his power? As Camus says in *Caligula*: 'For someone who loves power, the rivalry of the gods is rather irksome.' One can no more destroy God than one can destroy the libido; we can only suppress either.

It seems to me, in fact, that this expression of Kierkegaard's sums up admirably the evolution of our modern Western civilization, so in love with power, as Maurice Clavel has helped me to describe it. It enables us to make a diagnosis, which a doctor is always trying to do: the technological society suffers from the suppression of God. We can suppress God in the way sex used to be suppressed. 'Today', Viktor Frankl writes in his book on psycho-therapy, 'we no longer blush at sex, but at religion.' And he writes a book on 'the unconscious God'.

Is it permissible to talk of suppression not by an individual but by the whole of society? I readily grant that this is a metaphor, just as it is a metaphor to talk of the mind of a people. The mind, as the object of psychology, is individual. Suppression, as Freud described it with his constant concern to remain scientific and not to be poetic, is an individual phenomenon. I do not think that even Jung, with his 'collective unconscious', ever employed the term 'collective suppression'.

One metaphor always leads to another, and there comes into my mind an image which I should like to use here in order to introduce a note of poetry into the discussion, to make my learned and serious colleagues smile – as well as my readers, after all this sombre talk of violence. Imagine a beach; on the one hand there is the dry land, and on the other the vast and fascinating sea. But between the two there is this zone where one is already in the sea, without having left the land, since one still has a foothold on it.

Our organicist colleagues stand on the land without getting wet, deaf to the song of the sirens. They stay in safety on the solid terrain of the body and its physiology. Freud ventured into the sea, but he was very careful not to go too far out, where one is out of one's depth. He kept contact with the land. Jung, on the other hand, is like the swimmer who goes out freely into the deep sea, carried on waves of poetry, images, and metaphors. Perhaps it is only a matter of temperament.

36 GOD'S POOR

What then are we to do? De-suppress God? Yes, it is perhaps with this barbarous scientific neologism that we may translate for our modern scientific world a very old message – the message of the prophets: 'Come back, disloyal children – it is Yahweh who speaks –

for I alone am your Master' (Jer. 3.14). All the biblical prophets compare the bond between God and man with the oath of fidelity exchanged between a husband and his wife. An eternal covenant had been made, and men ceaselessly betrayed it. Then God sent them his prophets, who spoke to them as to an unfaithful wife: 'Come back to me with all your heart' (Joel 2.12).

The prophet is the chosen means whereby God intervenes in the affairs of men. The whole of history demonstrates this, not only that of the people of Israel. And not only in religious matters but also in politics, economy, law, and social organization. Our hope today in this crisis of our civilization is that God will send us prophets, speaking clearly and without any taint of compromise with power.

The covenant was renewed in Jesus Christ, broadened now to include the whole of mankind, and sealed by God in his own blood. And now once again modern man has broken the covenant. Intoxicated with the power that has been procured for him by science, technology, rational thought, and his peaceful and military inventions, he has proclaimed his own freedom as sole master and author of his destiny. He has suppressed God by shutting him away in the gloom of cathedrals and chapels, where his followers may continue to worship him, but well away from real, political, economic, and cultural life.

The modern West is like the Israelites exiled in Mesopotamia. It is cut off from its sources. Not only its Christian sources, but also its sources in Greek civilization with its piety, its devotion to moderation and harmony, its awareness of man's limitations and of his dependence on God. Then Georges Friedmann, the economist, asks: 'Where shall we find the resources we need?' He questions the great religions – Judaism, the Christian churches, the spirituality of the East – and he is disappointed. They are rich and powerful, they possess spiritual treasures, but our author does not find in them what he seeks, the master-word that will resolve the crisis of our civilization; rightly perhaps, because for four centuries they have been thrust aside from its development.

The resources we need are not to be found among the rich, the learned, and the powerful, but among the poor; among 'God's poor'. This expression came to the lips of the prophets of the exile of whom I wrote at the beginning of this Part Two. It found an echo in the hearts of that poor nation in exile. In a remarkable essay entitled 'The Poor Man and the Prophet', the French Jesuit Father

Pierre Ganne makes the point clear, using as his starting-point that historical context, which is so close to our own.

Israel had been caught in the maelstrom of the rivalry between the two super-powers of the day, Egypt and Assyria. The temptation was great to enter into the ruses of politics, to make alliances with the great powers and so to take advantage of their power. 'Well, the poor of Yahweh', writes Father Ganne, 'refused categorically to entertain such propositions. They said "No!" – a conscious and resolute no to the pretensions of the powerful.' 'The rich man is the man of property . . . of power and authority.' The poor man can make use 'of all the good things in the world', but without allowing himself to become their slave.

The author warns us not to confuse poverty with destitution. We do not have to turn our backs on the economic progress which has driven back the borders of destitution. God has always been with those who fight to liberate men from destitution. The poverty he is talking about 'is not principally concerned with possessions, but (to use the language of the gospel) with the heart, the conscience, and freedom'. He makes clear what is to be understood by 'the heart': 'it is the centre of the person, the seat of responsibility'. It is then quite precisely what I call the person. The poor man of Yahweh is the man who is free in regard to power and its fascination, who does not rely on power, that is to say on himself, but on God alone – so that as one reads Fr Ganne's essay one realizes that in the last analysis the poor man is quite simply the prophet.

Then from the 'poor of Yahweh' he passes to the 'poor of Jesus', whose message culminates in the Beatitudes, for 'Christ is poverty in person'. This is very much what we have been feeling here, that what characterizes the conduct of Jesus is not the renunciation of all violence, but the renunciation of the quest for personal power. Fr Ganne also speaks of 'the poor church', and he notes that the worst danger lies not in the material wealth of the church, but in a spirit of domination: 'Spiritual imperialism can always parasitize the most generous intentions and actions.'

A poor church? Humble prophets for our time? You are thinking perhaps that the idea is utopian? Open your eyes, then. I see them appearing on all sides, without fanfares and organization, without learned and well-formulated doctrines. So that one may – as the gospel says – have eyes and not see them. Alongside that wave of violence which is sweeping over modern youth, and which obsesses you, there is another wave, huge and world-wide, of innumerable tiny evangelistic communities of young people. They pay no heed to the distinctions between Catholics, Protestants, Jews, or Communists. They are built only on the personal experience of encounter with Jesus and of fraternal fellowship.

This is all happening rather on the fringes of our great and powerful churches, which perhaps do not so much despise them as majestically ignore them. Perhaps these young Christians could not pass an examination in the catechism, but they are in the reality of life. They seek out drug addicts, and have more success with them than the psychologists do. They do not issue any propaganda; they even have a horror of propaganda, which alienates the masses of today. They want most of all to be genuine. They are bringing something quite new into our modern world, something which bids fair to transform it more rapidly than all your committees of experts.

It is one of the most striking features of modern youth, this intense need to rediscover the community spirit which is too often lacking, even in the churches. It is a spirit which can flourish only among small groups, in which personal bonds may be forged, in which individuals may get to know one another intimately, on a personal level, and open their hearts to each other about their personal problems. It is very much that which is missing in our modern world, with all its power, prosperity, and organization, so that it is turned into an inhuman world, an enormous collection of desperate, lonely people. The young feel this intensely, and rightly blame us for bequeathing to them a world empty of love.

I believe in small groups. With Jesus there were twelve, and they lived together. The number is an indication. Not far from here are my friends of the community of Taizé, under their Prior, Roger Schutz. Success there has already raised the problem of numbers. It has been necessary to divide up, in order to safeguard the intimacy of the working units. The enormous rush to join their Youth Council has raised a further problem which can be resolved only by preserving among the mass of members the spirit of liberty that was born in the small group. Then there is Marcel Légaut, who has spread all over France his countless tiny groups. He was a senior university professor, and he left the university – another seat of power – in order to become a shepherd in the mountains. From the mountains, in his shepherd's dress, he travels everywhere, and everywhere he goes small groups spring up. He maintains that the future of Christianity is in small groups.[1]

I am with him in that, and I think it is in that way that he will bring a valid solution to the crisis of our modern world. In our traditional churches the liveliest activity is to be found in little groups of men and women, Protestant and Catholic Study Centres. Then there are the Focollarini, the Little Brothers and Little Sisters of Jesus, started by Charles de Foucault, the eucharistic groups, those of Lanza del Vasto, Jean Vanier's *Arche*, Mlle Claire-Lise de Benoît's League for Bible-Reading, the University Bible Groups, Dr Philippe Gold-Aubert's Association of Christian University and Business Men, Dr Pierre Bernard's Medical and Paramedical Evangelical Union, and so many more that they would take too long to list. A young man rings my doorbell. He hands me a leaflet, 'And if it were true', in which I read with emotion the exciting story of his little community of which I knew nothing, though it is quite near where I live. It is a very special emotion that I feel: it is Jesus touching me personally through the story of those he has touched.

In the United States this movement of small intimate groups is taking on impressive proportions. There is nothing surprising in that, since the USA is in the forefront of technological development, where the problems of our soulless civilization are most acute. Where the disease is, there the organism produces its health-giving reaction. Keith Miller's books show clearly that it is from the heart of tiny intimate groups that there arise the concrete experiences which change the lives of the participants.

The question is whether these experiences can go beyond the framework of personal and family problems, and penetrate the life of the world outside. The remarkable thing about Keith Miller is that he worked in an oil company, and he realized one day as he was on his way to the office that he was leaving Jesus in the car-park with his car. How could he bring him in? Once again he turned to the small group – a small group in the company itself, and soon the climate was changing.

Has this something to say in answer to Georges Friedmann's question about resources? Might some other factor than that of intensive production modify the course of economic development? Does not Friedmann himself talk of a 'change of life', without yet being able to say exactly what form it might take? Was not this our

[1] Addresses and other details of some of the groups mentioned in the following paragraphs will be found on p.202.

own experience in our own little group of 'doctors of the whole person' – a tiny group indeed, compared with the vast numbers of the rest of the profession? Its very intimacy, however, was the factor that wrought a profound change for each one of us in our daily medical practice.

Small personal sharing groups are proliferating spectacularly in the United States. There are already those of Pastor Sam Shoemaker, and Pastor Norman Peale. And now there are those of Pastors Elton Trueblood and Cecil Osborne; there are the many small groups started by Pastor Bruce Larson, and those of Bill Scott. If only they manage to resist the siren-song of propaganda! It is quite impossible to keep count of the many spontaneous groups which are formed and reformed among the young as the Spirit blows, especially in California, that huge state with its criss-cross of the best and the worst in life. If you would like to gain some insight into what is happening there, read the book *Journal de Californie*, by the French sociologist and philosopher Edgar Morin.

Morin appeals to me throughout his writings as one of the most lucid minds at present tackling the problems of our civilization. He is sympathetic and incisive because he does not talk in theoretical abstractions, but writes in the first person of his own experiences and about the questions he is asking himself, with extreme intellectual integrity. He went to California in 1969 at the invitation of the Salk Institute, founded by John Hunt – one more orphan for my colleague Rentchnick, since John Hunt was seven when his father died!

It is only in the United States that one can find an organization like the Salk Institute, which will install you in an ideal situation with no other task than that of reflecting upon the great problems which preoccupy you. Edgar Morin was there for several months, asking himself these questions: 'What is life? What is society? What is man?' Apparently – to judge at least from the *Journal*, his harvest of ideas on these vast questions was somewhat meagre!

The remarkable thing, however, in a philosopher of his stature, is that he did not confine himself within the bounds of intellectual dialectic, but observed with increasing interest what was taking place among the youth of California, in all those little spontaneous communities, unorganized, poor but keen, in the 'Crisis centers' which are entirely devoted to the assistance of the down-and-out and the drop-out, harried by the police because they harbour drug-addicts, but performing miracles, and so very happy! 'The privilege of these sons of the rich', Morin remarks, 'is that they are able to be happy to be poor.'

Edgar Morin was seduced – there is no other word for it. All through his book one sees the great bio-sociological problems becoming blurred, and the author becoming more and more captivated by this singular spectacle. He even forgets his own *Journal*! After his return to Paris he writes: 'I should like to try and say what happened from mid-December to mid-February. Only now, because it is in the past, do I dare to call it by the name that I did not then dare to utter: happiness.'

Ah! It is not often that a philosopher talks of happiness, not as an intellectual concept but as a living experience of his own! It moves us profoundly when it happens to a Pascal, for example. That it should happen to a simple person such as myself carries little weight – but to a philosopher! As for Morin, he himself explains that to the great impression made on him by the young Californians had been added, to awaken in him this feeling of happiness, a personal event which is extremely interesting to a psychologist.

At the end of his stay he was awaiting the arrival of his aged and ailing father. He was not in conflict with his father, but felt a stranger to him without knowing why, and this had been the case since the death of his mother. Now, during the night before his father was due to arrive, he had a terrifying dream – a real psycho-analytical experience – which made him see that he had never accepted his mother's death. The matter had a certain piquancy since a few years previously Morin had written a book entitled 'Man and Death', which had been highly praised. Nevertheless he had not realized, nor been freed from, his own refusal to accept his mother's death.

And so when the father arrived their meeting was a series of moving rediscoveries, in easy, happy intimacy. Edgar Morin is well aware that his recent experiences among the little communities of young Californians had prepared the way for this happy relationship. He had found among them the resource that we all need, the contagious spirit of reconciliation and love. He concludes his book with the following words: 'In that dream-like land I received in the kiss of life the resurgent message of the ancient gospel – Love, Peace.'

Happily, of course, the 'poor church' has never ceased to exist in the bosom of the powerful official churches themselves: those millions of humble believers whom their faith has impelled to help all the victims of fate and of our cruel institutions, like those young Californians who impressed Morin, the Franciscans, and all those monks and nuns and Salvationists who have embraced poverty. These at least have their labels – but apart from them there is the great cloud of the unknown faithful of all generations who have followed in secret the path of true charity. Nevertheless, though they devoted themselves tirelessly to society's victims, they scarcely ever questioned the structure of society itself, in which the church with all its power had a vested interest.

What is new today is that all over the world countless young people, outside all the established hierarchies and bearing no label, are throwing down a challenge to society itself and to its scale of values. For the first time they are sowing a seed of doubt about its very structure, a doubt which bites deep into the doctrine of the primacy of power, which for four centuries has governed all our societies, both liberal and Communist.

What a fascinating age it is we live in! So many young people who are determined to break with our power-based society. It is not just the power of money that is involved, but that of expert qualifications as well. In this connection I may mention one factor which helped to make Georges Friedmann so attractive to me. It was the fact that he is prepared to commit himself personally in his critique of our society. He tells of how he turned down posts at the Sorbonne and at the Collège de France, and also declined to accept appointment to the great committees of the state, preferring to keep his freedom. In that he is one with all these young people of whom I am speaking, and with their cultural revolution.

Who could have told me, when I was their age before the first world war, that I should live to see the rise of new generations who would radically question the too rational, too materialist, and too well-organized society in which I had been brought up, and which despite its faults seemed to me to be the only one possible? It seems to me that we are coming to the end of a tremendous drive which has carried humanity since the Renaissance on a mad race for power. And this is happening at the very point where its course has taken it beyond its wildest dreams with the fantastic power of nuclear energy, which is now encumbering us with its poisonous and indestructible waste.

This epic adventure has brought us undeniable benefits, but at what a price! An inhuman world, in which man feels he is treated as a thing, caught in a great machine which is geared inexorably to the production of things. We were dazzled by the lights of this process. The young are showing us its shadows, everything that has been suppressed along with God, all that has been thrust into the shadow: all that is irrational in man, his affectivity, his need for fantasy, for liberty, for time to wander at will, for poetry, even for the chance to be idle, and above all for fellowship. The relation between this lack in the modern world and the problem of violence is obvious. The reaction of the young is a symptom which must be taken seriously.

Above all, it is personal relationship which is tragically lacking in a world of power in which men are entirely preoccupied with fulfilling their function, with playing their part in the great economic machine which has tamed them so thoroughly. For personal relationship belongs to the realm of affectivity and irrationality, not that of function and logic. This is indeed what the psychologists have discovered.

Nowadays we have to take refuge in their consulting-rooms if we want to be accepted as persons, become our genuine selves again with our masks off, not play-acting any more. I often think about it: that exceptional and wonderful relationship in the consulting-room, that genuine person-to-person encounter, ought really to be the normal relationship between us as human beings, but it is so rare in everyday life. It seems to me that that is what the young are seeking so ardently when they come together in their small groups, often without saying anything, without doing anything, down in a cellar, listening to a pop record: a tremendous need for human fellowship. How I count on the young to cure our world of its frenzy for power! And Lorenz also, the scientist, who suddenly changes the tone of his book, up to then full of science, to conclude with a declaration of hope in youth!

This does not mean that we should turn our backs on science and technology. In our consulting-rooms too they must be used in the service of the person. What we need is some way of harmonizing power and love, and that is what I am trying to discover. I began this Part Two with the allegory of the two hands of God. We doctors also have two hands. Our right hand is the power that objective science gives us. I have already described, in my chapter on the power of the doctor, our joy in being able to hold death at bay.

Sooner or later, however, our power reaches its limit, our patient slips between our fingers – the expression is not inappropriate, as Mme Emich's poet spoke of slipping from God's right hand – when he slips towards death, or towards the death in miniature of anxiety and depression. Then the doctor is often discouraged and tempted to give up because he thinks there is nothing more that he can do. We cannot expect him to be taught at medical school, devoted to science as it is, to use his left hand – his heart.

How embarrassed we Westerners are when it comes to showing our feelings, to entering into a personal relationship! In suppressing God we have suppressed one whole side of man's nature: his need for fellowship, his aptitude to commit himself personally to another person, without reserve. That is why we moderns find our emotions an encumbrance. We do not know what to do with them; we are ashamed of them; we are reduced to going and releasing them in the darkness of a cinema hall. We are like men who have had their left hand amputated.

The medicine of the person is a two-handed medicine. It makes use of science as competently as possible, but it also uses that mysterious personal communication which our patients stand in need of to the very end. But it is not enough to have two hands. They must be joined. To put the hands together is to adopt the universal, age-old attitude of prayer, the sign that one is waiting upon God and his presence, recognizing his sovereignty, and asking for his grace. That is why the medicine of the person leads us straight to prayer. I have taken my own profession of medicine as an example, but the same problem arises in every other. We must not cut off our right hand either, turning our backs on technology and economic growth; we must use them as our hearts dictate: to feed the poor rather than to enrich the rich. That is what Roger Schutz, the Prior of Taizé, calls the sharing society – sharing of goods, and sharing of feelings as well. What is needed is to replace the veneration of power, which still reigns, with the ideal of harmony which inspired the Greeks, as Sophocles says in his *Ajax*: 'The gods love moderation.'

Why quote 'the gods' when there is but one God? As Paul Diel

rightly maintains in his book on biblical symbolism, our mono-
theism is nearer than is generally thought to the polytheism of the
Greeks, whose divinities symbolized the various aspects of our God.
I know that my universalism arouses objections among some
Christians, despite their brotherly feelings towards me, Christians
whom I love for their zeal. Like them, I believe that Jesus came to
reconcile men with God – all men, not just those who say 'Lord!
Lord!' to him, as he himself said (Matt. 7.21).

This attitude of the joined hands which I was talking about just
now, the attitude of prayer, has been common to countless worshippers of all ages, whether they know the gospel or not, because it
expresses one and the same attitude of respect and devotion to a
superior Power and Love, an attitude incompatible with man's
pretension to omnipotence and autonomy. And I believe that
God loves them as much as he does me, those who claim independence of him. And I am carried away, just as they are, by the
human instinct for power. Where better could I realize it, recognize
its folly and overcome it to some extent, than where I am face to face
with my Creator?

Remember René Girard and his book *La violence et le sacré*, of
which I spoke at length in Part One: 'without religion there is no
brake on violence', he writes. Here is the comment of a young
psychoanalyst, Roland Jaccard, about him: 'If you take religion in
its etymological sense, i.e., that which binds, which unites men
with each other . . . it is not wrong to say that our society is sick
because it has lost the sense of the religious, of the sacred.' He goes
on to quote Delacampagne and his book *Antipsychiatrie*: 'Feudal
society, Delacampagne observes, had a guarantor which justified
its order and made it loving and alive; that guarantor was God. . .
Our society is sick because it has thought it possible to substitute
money for worship, and to replace the voice of God with . . . television, as ideological guarantor of the system.'

We have been measuring the difficulty of the problems: power
begets injustice, injustice begets violence, and violence begets power.
So violence is the offspring of injustice, injustice the offspring of
power, and power the offspring of violence. How can such a chain
of cause and effect be broken without the grace of God? I am certainly not one of those who think that faith solves all problems. I
have shown clearly enough how believers themselves find it difficult
to realize their own violence, their own will to power and their own
injustice. At least it is the duty of all of us to set going a process of

détente, of healing, of 'de-escalation', by submitting ourselves more
faithfully to the will of God.

Then a man as timid as Jeremiah may become more violent (Jer
4.19), and a man of violence like St Paul assert the primacy of love
(I Cor. 13). The opposite of power is not weakness but self-denial
The opposite of wealth is not material poverty, but the poverty of
'the poor in spirit'. Our instincts are a gift from God which we have
to manage in accordance with his commands. It is not easy, I know
One can grope for a long time in thick darkness. But sometimes
suddenly, as if the heavens were opening, a light can shine out
bringing a solution which one had never imagined.

Such, for example, is forgiveness. I have read a large number of
learned books in preparation for writing this one, and I have been
struck by the fact that I did not find one line about forgiveness.
which is the solution *par excellence* to every conflict and all violence.
I gave a talk once about my own experience of forgiveness at a
meeting of doctors. As we were leaving a young colleague came up
to me and said: 'For years I harboured a terrible feeling of bitterness
towards my father. And suddenly one day, without my knowing
how or why, my bitterness disappeared. Was that the forgiveness
you were talking about?' – 'Good heavens!' I exclaimed, 'I wish
you had said that at the meeting!'

Yes, forgiveness is an act of grace which resolves in a moment
what long efforts at reconciliation fail to resolve. But true forgiveness
is very rare. Christians try to forgive, because the church tells them
they must. But to try to forgive is like trying to lift oneself up by
one's own bootstraps; it is completely ineffective. Because it leaves
out of account the grace of God. At best one manages to pretend
one has forgiven, and that only adds hypocrisy to hostility. The
person whom we have wronged is never taken in by the smiling
facade. Repressed bitterness of this kind poisons parish life. It is
better to tell the truth to each other, even violently. The pretence of
forgiveness is an obstacle to forgiveness, just as the pretence of love
is an obstacle to love.

At the last International Conference on the Medicine of the
Person in Geneva, whose theme was 'Solitude and communication',
one speaker made a profound impression, Professor André Siniavski
of Paris. Having spent seven years in Soviet concentration-camps,
he spoke of the awful solitude and destitution in the camps, where
in spite of everything the irrepressible need to communicate invents
new modes of language. At the end he told of how one day he had

ollowed two Pentecostalists into some dark corner of the camp
vhere they were going to pray.

Respectfully he stood at a distance. He saw them kneel down,
hen he heard them 'speaking with tongues'. He could not under-
tand any of this 'language of the angels', as he called it. But it
:onveyed to him a message clearer than any intelligible words. He
inderstood well enough that these two 'little ones', these two who
vere 'poor' in the gospel sense, were truly free under the worst
oossible oppression. Later on, when questions were coming from
he floor, he answered one questioner with these fine words: 'Only
wo languages can reconcile men: the language of poetry and the
anguage of prayer.'

LIST OF WORKS QUOTED

Adler, Dr Kurt, 'La violence, une façon de se prouver qu'on existe' interview in *Gazette de Lausanne*, 8 April 1975.

Ajar, Émile, *La vie devant soi*, Mercure de France, Paris 1975.

Ajuriaguerra, Professor J. de, interview in *La Suisse*, Geneva, April 1975.

Albert, Michel, and Ferniot, Jean, *Les vaches maigres*, Gallimard Paris 1975.

Aron, Raymond, *Les désillusions du progrès*, Calmann-Lévy, Par 1969.

Aron, Robert, *Les années obscures de Jésus*, Grasset, Paris 1961.

Badiche, Dr André, 'L'aggressivité à l'hôpital psychiatrique' *Présences*, Draveil 91210, France, no. 111, 1970.

Baruk, Dr Henri, *Psychiatrie morale expérimentale, individuelle e sociale*, Presses Universitaires de France, Paris 1945.

Bergson, Henri, *The Two Sources of Morality and Religion*, trs. R. A Audra and C. Brereton, Macmillan, London and New York 193

Bieler, Pastor André, *La pensée économique et sociale de Calvi* Georg, Geneva 1960.

Caillois, Roger, *L'homme et le sacré*, Gallimard, Paris 1950.

Camus, Albert, *The Rebel*, trs. A. Bower, Hamish Hamilton, Londo 1953, Knopf, New York 1954.

—*The Outsider*, trs. S. Gilbert, Penguin Books, Harmondswort 1969.

—*Caligula*, in *Collected Plays*, Hamish Hamilton, London 1965.

Carson, Rachel L., *Silent Spring*, Houghton Mifflin, Boston 196 Hamish Hamilton, London 1963.

Choisy, Maryse, *Potala est dans le ciel*, Buchet-Castel, Paris 197

Clavel, Maurice, *Ce que je crois*, Grasset, Paris 1975.

Delacampagne, Christian, *Antipsychiatrie, les voies du sacré*, Grasse Paris 1974.

Diel, Paul, *Le symbolisme dans la Bible*, Payot, Paris 1975.

—*Le symbolisme dans la mythologie grecque*, Payot, Paris 1952.

Durkheim, Émile, *Elementary Forms of the Religious Life*, trs. J. W Swain, Allen & Unwin, London 1915, reissued 1976.

Eliade, Mircea, *Myth and Reality*, trs. W. R. Trask, Harper & Row New York 1963, Allen & Unwin, London 1964.

Ellul, Jacques, *The Technological Society*, trs. J. Wilkinson, Knopf, New York 1964, Jonathan Cape, London 1965.

Emich, Isolde, 'Totale Rehabilitation – eine Frage religiöser Bereitschaft', *Soteria*, May 1966.

—'Aphasiker brauchen Schreibmaschinen', *Zeitschrift für Therapie*, Berlin, July 1973.

Fourastié, Jean, *Les 40,000 heures*, Laffont-Gonthier, Paris 1965.

Frankl, Viktor, *La psychothérapie et son image de l'homme*, Resma, Paris 1970.

—*Le vide existentiel*, Service bibliographique Roche, no. 7, 1972.

Fresquet, Henri, *La foi toute nue*, Grasset, Paris 1972.

Freud, Sigmund, *The Psychopathology of Everyday Life*, trs. A. Tyson, Standard ed. vol. VI, Hogarth Press, London, and Macmillan, New York 1960.

—*Totem and Taboo*, trs. J. Strachey, Standard ed. vol. XIII, 1955.

—*Civilization and its Discontents*, trs. J. Riviere, Standard ed. vol. XXI, 1961.

—*Moses and Monotheism*, trs. K. Jones, Standard ed. vol. XXIII, 1964.

—*An Outline of Psychoanalysis*, trs. J. Strachey, Standard ed. vol. XXIII, 1964.

—*The Complete Introductory Lectures on Psychoanalysis*, Allen & Unwin, London 1971 (= Standard ed. vols XV, XVI and XXII).

Friedmann, Georges, *La puissance et la sagesse*, Gallimard, Paris 1970.

Fromm, Erich, *The Anatomy of Human Destructiveness*, Holt, Rinehart & Winston, New York 1973, Jonathan Cape, London 1974.

Ganne, Pierre, SJ, 'Le pauvre et le prophète', *Cultures et Foi*, summer 1973.

Girard, René, *La violence et le sacré*, Grasset, Paris 1972.

Glidden, Harold W., MD, 'The Arab World', *American Journal of Psychiatry* 128, 1972.

Goust, Dr François, 'L'agressivité du médecin practicien', *Présences*, Draveil, no. 111, 1970.

Guggenbühl-Craig, Dr Adolf, *Macht als Gefahr beim Helfer* (Psychologische Praxis, no. 45), S. Karger, Basel.

Gusdorf, Georges, *Dialogue avec le médecin*, Labor & Fides, Geneva 1962.

—*La vertu de force*, Presses universitaires de France, Paris 1957.

Hacker, Friedrich, MD, *Agression, Violence dans le monde moderne*, Calmann-Lévy, Paris 1972.
Haedrich, Marcel, 'Le secret de Dieu', *La Suisse*, Geneva 23 May 1975.
Illich, Ivan D., *Tools for Conviviality*, Open Forum, Calder & Boyar, London 1973.
—*Medical Nemesis*, Open Forum, Calder & Boyar, London 1975.
Jaccard, Roland, *L'exil intérieur, Schizoïdie et civilisation*, Presses universitaires de France, Paris 1975.
Jaspers, Karl, *Great Philosophers*, trs. R. Manheim, vol. I, Rupert Hart-Davis, London, and Harcourt Brace, New York 1962.
—*The Future of Mankind*, trs. E. B. Ashton, University of Chicago Press, 1961.
de Jouvenel, Bertrand, *Arcadie, essai sur le mieux vivre*, SEDEIS Paris 1968.
Jung, C. G., *Answer to Job* in *Psychology and Religion*, trs. R. F. C. Hull, Collected Works vol. 11, Routledge and Kegan Paul, London, and Pantheon Books, New York 1958.
—'After the Catastrophe' in *Civilization in Transition*, trs. R. F. C. Hull, Collected Works vol. 10, 1964.
Klein, Dr Melanie, *The Psychoanalysis of Children*, Hogarth Press, London 1959, Grove Press, New York 1960.
Kubler-Ross, Dr Elisabeth, *On Death and Dying*, Macmillan, New York 1969, Tavistock Publications, London 1970.
Legaut, Marcel, *Introduction à l'intelligence du passé et de l'avenir du christianisme*, Aubier, Paris 1970.
Levy-Valensi, Eliane Amado, *La Communication*, Presses universitaires de France, Paris 1967.
—'Lettre sur l'agressivité', *Présences*, Draveil, no. 111, 1970.
Lorenz, Konrad, *On Aggression*, trs. M. Latzke, Methuen, London, and Harcourt Brace, New York 1966.
Maeder, Alphonse, *Ways to Psychic Health*, trs. T. Lit, Scribner's, New York 1953, Hodder & Stoughton, London 1954.
Marcuse, Herber, *One-Dimensional Man*, Routledge & Kegan Paul, London, and Beacon Press, New York 1964.
Mieville, Dr C., *Bulletin des Médecins suisses*, no. 11, 19 March 1975.
Miller, Keith, *The Taste of New Wine*, Word Books, Waco, Texas 1965, Hemel Hempstead 1970.
Monod, Jacques, *Chance and Necessity*, trs. A. Wainhouse, Knopf, New York, 1971, Collins, London 1972.

de Montmollin, Eric, 'Directions de la guerre – La philosophie des événements', *La Suisse*, Geneva July 1942.

Morel, Bernard, *Cybernétique et transcendance*, La Colombe, Paris 1964

Morin, Edgar, *Journal de Californie*, Le Seuil, Paris 1970.

—*L'homme et la mort*, Le Seuil, Paris 1951.

Mounier, Emmanuel, *Be Not Afraid*, trs. C. Rowland, Rockliff, London 1951.

—'Refaire la Renaissance', *Esprit*, no. 1, Paris.

—'Médecine, quatrième Pouvoir?', *Esprit*, 18th year, no. 165, March 1950.

Nodet, Charles H., 'Psychanalyse et culpabilité', *Pastorale et péché*, Desclée de Brower, Paris, Tournai and Rome 1962.

Portmann, Adolf, 'Manipulation des Menschen', *Pharmazeutische Zeitung*, Hamburg, 113th year, 1968, no. 35.

Renan, Ernest, *The Future of Science*, trs. A. D. Vandam and C. B. Pitman, Chapman & Hall, London 1891.

Renard, Jules, *Carrots*, trs. G. W. Stonier, Grey Walls Press, London 1916.

Rentchnick, Dr Pierre, 'Les orphelins mènent le monde', *Médecine et Hygiène*, Geneva, 26 November 1975.

Ricoeur, Paul, *Histoire et vérité*, Aubier, Paris 1955.

—'Morale sans péché', *Esprit*, Paris, 22nd year, nos. 217–18, August-September 1954.

Riesman, David, *Abundance, for what? and Other Essays*, Chatto & Windus, London, and Doubleday, New York 1964.

Rogers, Carl R., *On Becoming a Person*, Houghton Mifflin, Boston, and Constable, London 1961.

Rolland, Romain, *Above the Battle*, trs. C. K. Ogden, Allen & Unwin, London 1916.

Rollin, Charles, *Roman History*, 2nd English edition, London 1754, vol. XIII.

Romains, Jules, *Knock ou le triomphe de la médecine*, Gallimard, Paris 1968.

de Rougemont, Denis, *Lettres sur la bombe atomique*, Gallimard, Paris 1946.

—*Man's Western Quest*, trs. M. Belgion, Harper Bros, New York 1957, Allen & Unwin, London 1958.

de Rougemont, Dr Jean, 'La responsabilité de malade', *Dynamique de la guérison*, Delachaux & Niestlé, Neuchâtel 1967.

Sarano, Jacques, *Le défi de l'espérance*, le Centurion, Paris 1973.

Sarano, Jacques, 'La fin du péché – Déculpabiliser – De l'excuse à l'aveu – La force du pardon', *Christus* 1974.

Shaull, Richard, in H. Gollwitzer, J. M. Lochman, R. Shaull and C. C. West, *Une théologie de la révolution?*, Labor & Fides, Geneva 1967. (Cf. *Christians in the Technological and Social Revolution of our Time*, the Report on the World Conference on Church and Society, Geneva 1966, World Council of Churches, Geneva 1967, sections 80–85.)

Schumacher, Dr E. F., *Small is Beautiful*, Blond & Briggs, London, and Harper & Row, New York 1973, Abacus Books, London 1974.

Schutz, Prior Roger, *Introduction à la vie communautaire*, Labor & Fides, Geneva, and Je sers, Paris 1944.

—*Violent for Peace*, trs. C. J. Moore, Darton, Longman & Todd, London 1970, Westminster Press, Philadelphia 1971.

Servan-Schreiber, Jean-Jacques, *The American Challenge*, trs. R. Steel, Penguin Books, Harmondsworth 1969.

Shah, Dr Mazhar H., 'Mental Health and Islam', Fédération mondiale pour la santé mentale, Berne 1964.

Siniavski, Professor André, *Solitude et communication: 'Moi' et 'eux'*, Rencontres internationales de Genève, La Baconnière, Neuchâtel 1975.

Storr, Anthony, *Human Aggression*, Allen Lane, Harmondsworth, and Athenaeum Publications, New York 1968.

Tournier, Paul, *Guilt and Grace*, trs. A. W. Heathcote and others, Hodder & Stoughton, London, and Harper & Row, New York 1962.

—*Learning to Grow Old*, trs. Edwin Hudson, SCM Press, London, and Harper & Row, New York 1972.

—*Secrets*, trs. J. Embry, SCM Press, London, and John Knox Press, Richmond, Va 1965.

—*The Strong and the Weak*, trs. Edwin Hudson, SCM Press, London and Westminster Press, Philadelphia 1963.

—*The Whole Person in a Broken World*, trs. J. and H. Doberstein, Harper & Row, New York 1964, Collins, London 1965.

—contributor to *Medicine of the Whole Person*, Word Books, Waco, Texas 1973.

Vanier, Jean, *Ouvre mes bras*, Éditions Fleurus, Paris 1973.

Vincent, Dr Armand, *Le jardinier des hommes*, Le Seuil, Paris 1945.

—'La violence', *Somme mondialiste*, Club humaniste, no. 3, Box 97, Paris XVe.

Waldeck, Heinrich Suso, *Gesammelte Werke*, Tyrolia Verlag, Innsbruck 1948.

Weber, Max, *Economy and Society*, ed. G. Roth and C. Wittich, trs. E. Fischoff and others, 3 vols, Bedminster Press, New York 1968.

Weil, Simone, *Waiting on God*, trs. Emma Craufurd, Fontana Books, London 1959 (= *Waiting for God*, Putnam, New York 1959).

Ziegler, Jean, *Les vivants et la mort*, Le Seuil, Paris 1975.

Biblical quotations are normally from the
Jerusalem Bible.

Some of the Small Groups mentioned
in Chapter 36 (pp.187-9)

Association d'Universitaires et d'Hommes d'affaires chrétiens, Box 49, 1211 Geneva 2, Switzerland (Dr Philippe Gold-Aubert); magazine: *Acte*.

Centre Protestant d'Études, 7 rue Tabazan, 1204 Geneva, Switzerland; publishes a Bulletin.

Et si c'était vrai?, Éditions Maranatha, 1033 Cheseaux, Switzerland (Jean-Michel Cravanzola).

Group Research and Individual Learning Project, 1525 San Carlos Bay Drive, Sanibel, Florida 33957, USA (Bruce Larson).

Guideposts, Carmel, New York 10512, USA (Pastor Norman Peale).

Ligue pour la lecture de la Bible, route de Berne 90, 1010 Lausanne, Switzerland (Mlle Claire-Lise de Benoît).

Union évangélique médicale et para-médicale, Petite-Synthe 59640, France (Dr Pierre Bernard); magazine: *Aimer et Servir*.

Union internationale des groupes bibliques universitaires, 31 rue de L'Ale, 1003 Lausanne, Switzerland.

Yokefellows Inc., 19 Park Road, Burlingame, California 94010, USA (Pastors Elton Trueblood and Cecil Osborne).

See also Marcel Légaut, Keith Miller, Roger Schutz and Jean Vanier in the List of Works Quoted.